GORE VIDAL:

sexually speaking

COLLECTED SEX WRITINGS

GORE VIDAL:

sexually speaking

COLLECTED SEX WRITINGS

Donald Weise, editor

CLEIS
PRESS

Published in the United States by Cleis Press Inc., P.O. Box 14684, San Francisco, California 94114.

Printed in the United States.
Cover & text design: Scott Idleman / Blink
Cover photograph: Clifford Coffin © British Vogue/The Condé Nast Publications Ltd
Logo art: Juana Alicia
First Edition.
10 9 8 7 6 5 4 3 2 1

Grateful acknowledgment is made for permission to reprint the following:
Preface by Gore Vidal Copyright © 1999 by Gore Vidal. Sex and the Law/The Sexus of Henry Miller/Pornography/Doc Reuben/Women's Liberation: Feminism and its Discontents/Eleanor Roosevelt/Sex is Politics/Christopher Isherwood's Kind/Pink Triangle and Yellow Star/Tennessee Williams: Someone to Laugh at the Squares With/Oscar Wilde on the Skids Again/Maugham's Half and Half/The Birds and the Bees are from *UNITED STATES 1952-1992* Copyright 1993 by Gore Vidal. Reprinted by permission of Random House, Inc. "J'accuse" Copyright © 1998 by Gore Vidal. Originally published in *The Advocate*. Reprinted by permission of the author. Interview by John Mitzel and Steven Abbott published in *Gay Sunshine Interviews*, Volume 1, edited by Winston Leyland. Published by Gay Sunshine Press, San Francisco 1978. Copyright 1978 by Steven Abbott and John Mitzel. Reprinted by permission of John Mitzel, Steven Abbott and Winston Leyland. Interview by Steven Abbott and Thom Willenbecher published in *Gay Sunshine Interviews*, Volume 1, edited by Winston Leyland. Published by Gay Sunshine Press, San Francisco 1978. Copyright 1978 by Winston Leyland. Reprinted by permission of Winston Leyland and Steven Abbott. "The Sadness of Gore Vidal" copyright 1992 by Larry Kramer. Originally published in *QW* (Maer Roshan, Editor), October 4 1992. Reprinted by permission of Larry Kramer.

Vidal, Gore, 1925-
Gore Vidal: sexually speaking : collected sex writings / Gore Vidal. — 1st ed.
      p.   cm.
    ISBN 1-57344-082-5 (cloth)
    1. Vidal, Gore, 1925- —Interviews. 2. American literature—20th century—History and criticism. 3. Authors, American—20th century—Interviews. 4. English literature—History and criticism.
    5. Homosexuality and literature. 6. Sex in literature. 7. Sex I. Title.
PS3543.I26A6 1999
818'.5409—dc21   99-13533
                                                          CIP

Contents

Preface • 9

ESSAYS

Sex and the Law • 13

The Sexus of Henry Miller • 23

Pornography • 29

Doc Reuben • 42

Women's Liberation: Feminism and Its Discontents • 57

Eleanor Roosevelt • 70

Christopher Isherwood's Kind • 84

Sex Is Politics • 97

Pink Triangle and Yellow Star • 115

Tennessee Williams: Someone to Laugh at the Squares With • 133

Oscar Wilde: On the Skids Again • 147

Maugham's Half & Half • 155

The Birds and the Bees • 180

J'accuse! • 186

INTERVIEWS

Introduction by Donald Weise • 191

The *Fag Rag* Interview by John Mitzel and Steven Abbott • 194

The *Gay Sunshine* Interview by Steven Abbott and
Tom Willenbecher • 219

The Sadness of Gore Vidal: An Interview by Larry Kramer • 252

Index • 273

Preface

The last few years of Tennessee Williams' life were not made happier by the demands of gay militants who thought it imperative that our country's only great playwright should dedicate himself exclusively in his plays to gay characters and situations. I admired his response to this sort of dull bigotry: "Why should I limit my audience any more than it is already?" After decades of being well and truly bashed by heteros, Williams had ceased to have much of any audience; only after his death by misadventure did his works, in revival, begin to take off. But the underlying sentiment of his gay critics strikes me as sinister. Is the gay condition so unique that in every aspect of life, particularly as shown in art, that other ways of living-loving must become marginal? It never occurred to his critics that he was not, like Proust, say, turning homos into heteros in order to be read or performed. Tennessee knew much more about men-women than he did about men-men (he experienced his first homosexual adventure in the Sloan Street YMCA in his mid-twenties after serving much time in hetero-land). Yet for decades any fag writer, particularly in the theater, was thought to be traducing good family values by showing the horrors of fag life while pretending that he was writing about heteros. For the morbidly inclined, read *The New York Review of Books* piece called, "Albee Damned" by the odious homophobe, Philip Roth.

The confusion that there are two teams—one good, straight; one bad, gay—is not helped by reversing the adjectives. It is the virtue of a great writer like Tennessee to know that there is only one team, the human, and the rest is politics.

I have tried, without much luck, to make the human declaration over the years. Unfortunately, Americans are so twisted from birth in their sexual attitudes and superstitions that very little reality can get through to them. Nevertheless, I have kept at it in essays over the years. In a piece called "Sex Is Politics" I thought, as it was to be published in an anniversary issue of *Playboy* aglitter with names, that I might delimit my audience and speak to the world in untold millions of copies.

I was living in the Hollywood Hills at the time. *Now* I shall get some reaction, I thought. But there was none, not a letter, postcard, comment from a friend. Eventually, I discovered that I had had two readers only. One was an elderly security guard at the opening of a Warner Brothers film. He had liked the piece. The other was Elaine May, an old friend. "You're so positive!" This from the woman who once said, "I love a moral problem so much more than a real problem." I was so thrilled by her praise that I forgot to ask her why she was reading *Playboy*.

Gore Vidal
Ravello, Italy
March 1999

ESSAYS

Sex and the Law

In 1963, H. L. A. Hart, Oxford Professor of Jurisprudence, gave three lectures at Stanford University. In these lectures (published by the Stanford University Press as *Law, Liberty and Morality*) Professor Hart attempted to answer an old question: Is the fact that certain conduct is by common standards immoral a sufficient cause to punish that conduct by law? A question which leads him to what might be a paradox: "Is it morally permissible to enforce morality as such? Ought immorality as such to be a crime?" Philosophically, Professor Hart inclines to John Stuart Mill's celebrated negative. In *On Liberty*, Mill wrote, "The only purpose for which power can rightfully be exercised over any member of a civilized community against his will is to prevent harm to others"; and to forestall the arguments of the paternally minded, Mill added that a man's own good, either physical or moral, is not sufficient warrant. He cannot rightfully be compelled to do or forbear because it will be better for him to do so, because it will make him happier, because in the opinions of others, to do so would be wise or even right.

Now it would seem that at this late date in the Anglo-American society, the question of morality and its relation to the law has been pretty much decided. In general practice, if not in particular statute, our society tends to keep a proper distance between the two. Yet national crisis may, on occasion, bring out the worst in the citizenry. While our boys were Over There, a working majority of the Congress decided that drink was not only bad for morals but bad for health. The result was Prohibition. After a dozen years of living with the Great Experiment, the electorate finally realized that moral legislation on such a scale is impossible to enforce. A lesson was learned and one would have thought it unlikely that the forces which created the Volstead Act could ever again achieve a majority. But today strange things are happening in the American Empire, as well as in the Kingdom across the water where Professor Hart detects a revival of what he calls "legal moralism," and he finds alarming certain recent developments.

In the days of the Star Chamber, to conspire to corrupt public morals was a common-law offense. Needless to say, this vague catchall turned out to be a useful instrument of tyranny and it was not entirely abandoned in England until the eighteenth century. Now it has been suddenly revived as a result of the 1961 case *Shaw* v. *Director of Public Prosecutions*. Shaw was an enterprising pimp who published a magazine called *Ladies Directory*, which was just that. Despite this useful contribution to the gallantry of England, Shaw was found guilty of three offenses: publishing an obscene article, living on the earnings of prostitutes, and conspiring to corrupt public morals. The last offense delighted the legal moralists. There was much satisfied echoing of the eighteenth-century Lord Mansfield's statement, "Whatever is *contra bonos mores et decorum* the principles of our laws prohibit and the King's Court as the general censor and guardian of the public morals is bound to restrain and punish." As a result of the decision against Mr. Shaw, the possibilities of banning a book like *Lady Chatterley's Lover* on the imprecise grounds that it will corrupt public morals (themselves ill-defined) are endless and alarming. Though various American states still retain "conspiring to corrupt" statutes, they are largely cherished as relics of our legal origins in the theocratic code of Oliver Cromwell. The last serious invoking of this principle occurred in 1935 when the Nazis solemnly determined that anything was punishable if it was deserving of punishment according "to the fundamental conceptions of penal law and sound popular feeling."

Defining immorality is of course not an easy task, though English judges and American state legislatures seem not to mind taking it on. Lord Devlin, a leader of the legal moralists, has said that "the function of the criminal law is to enforce a moral principle and nothing else." How does Lord Devlin arrive at a moral principle? He appeals to the past. What is generally said to be wrong is wrong, while "a recognized morality is as necessary to society's existence as a recognized government." Good. But Lord Devlin does not acknowledge that there is always a considerable gap between what is officially recognized as good behavior and what is in actual fact countenanced and practiced. Though adultery in England is thought to be morally wrong, there are no statutes under which a man may be punished for sleeping with someone else's wife. Adultery is not a legal offense, nor does it presumably arouse in the public "intolerance, indignation, and disgust," the three emotions which Lord Devlin insists are inevitably evoked by those acts which offend the accepted morality. Whenever this triad is present, the law must punish. Yet how is one to measure "intolerance, indignation, and disgust"? Without an appeal to Dr. Gallup, it would be difficult to decide what, if anything, the general public really thinks about these matters. Without a referendum, it is anyone's guess to what degree promiscuity, say, arouses disgust in the public. Of course Lord Devlin is not really arguing for this sort of democracy. His sense of right and wrong is based on what he was brought up to believe was right and wrong, as prescribed by church and custom.

In the realm of sexual morals, all things take on a twilight shade. Off and on for centuries, homosexuality has aroused the triple demon in the eyes of many. But a majority? It would be surprising if it did, knowing what we now know about the extent—if not the quality— of human sexual behavior. In any case, why should homosexual acts between consenting adults be considered inimical to the public good? This sort of question raises much heat, and the invoking of "history." According to Lord Devlin, "the loosening of moral bonds is often the first stage of [national] disintegration." Is it? The periods in history which are most admired by legal moralists tend to be those vigorous warlike times when a nation is pursuing a successful and predatory course of military expansion, such as the adventures of the Spartans and Alexander, of Julius Caesar and Frederick of Prussia. Yet a reading of history ought to convince Lord Devlin that these militaristic societies were not only brutish and "immoral" by any standard but also startlingly homosexual. Yet what was morally desirable in a clean-limbed Spartan army officer is now punished in Leicester Square. Obviously public attitudes have changed since those vigorous days. Does that then mean that laws should alter as old prejudices are replaced by new? In response to public opinion, the Emperor Justinian made homosexuality a criminal offense on the grounds that buggery, as everyone knew, was the chief cause of earthquakes.

With the decline of Christianity, western moralists have more and more used the state to punish sin. One of Lord Devlin's allies, J. G. Stephen, in *Liberty, Equality, Fraternity*, comes straight to the point. Referring to moral offenders, he writes, "The feeling of hatred and the desire of vengeance are important elements to human nature which ought, in such cases, to be satisfied in a regular public and legal manner." There is the case not only for capital punishment but for public hangings, all in the name of the Old Testament God of vengeance. Or as Lord Goddard puts it, "I do not see how it can be either non-Christian, or other than praiseworthy, that the country should be willing to avenge crime." Yet Mr. Stephen also realizes that for practical purposes "you cannot punish anything which public opinion as expressed in the common practice of society does not strenuously and unequivocally condemn. To be able to punish a moral majority must be overwhelming." But is there such a thing as moral majority in sexual matters? Professor Hart thinks not. "The fact that there is lip service to an official sexual morality should not lead us to neglect the possibility that in sexual, as other matters, there may be a number of mutually tolerant moralities, and that even where there is some homogeneity of practice and belief, offenders may be viewed not with hatred or resentment, but with amused contempt or pity."

In the United States the laws determining correct human behavior are the work of the state legislatures. Over the years these assemblies have managed to make a complete hash of things, pleasing no one. The present tangled codes go back to the founding of the country. When the Cromwells fell, the disgruntled Puritans left England for Holland (not because they were persecuted for their religious beliefs but because they were forbidden to persecute others for *their* beliefs). Holland took them in, and promptly turned them out. Only North America was left. Here, as lords of the wilderness, they were free to create the sort of quasi-theocratic society they had dreamed of. Rigorously persecuting one another for religious heresies, witchcraft, sexual misbehavior, they formed that ugly polity whose descendants we are. As religious fundamentalists, they were irresistibly drawn to the Old Testament God at his most forbidding and cruel, while the sternness of St. Paul seemed to them far more agreeable than the occasional charity of Jesus. Since adultery was forbidden by the Seventh Commandment and fornication was condemned in two of St. Paul's memos, the Puritans made adultery and fornication criminal offenses even though no such laws existed in England, before or after Cromwell's reign. As new American states were formed, they modelled their codes on those of the original states. To this day, forty-three states will punish a single act of adulterous intercourse, while twenty-one states will punish fornications between unmarried people. In no other western country is fornication a criminal offense. As for adultery, England, Japan, and the Soviet Union have no such statutes. France and Italy will punish adultery under special conditions (e.g., if the man should establish the mistress in the family home). Germany and Switzerland punish adultery only if a court can prove that a marriage has been dissolved because of it.

In actual practice, the state laws are seldom invoked, although two hundred and forty-two Bostonians were arrested for adultery as recently as 1948. These statutes are considered "dead-letter laws" and there are those who argue that since they are so seldom invoked, why repeal them? One answer came in 1917 when a number of racketeers were arrested by the Federal government because they had taken girl friends to Florida, violating the Mann Act as well as the local fornication-adultery statutes. This case (*Caminetti* v. *U.S.*) set a dangerous precedent. Under a busy Attorney General, the "dead-letter laws" could be used to destroy all sorts of dissidents, villainous or otherwise.

Rape is another offense much confused by state laws. During the Thirties, out of 2,366 New York City indictments for rape, only eighteen percent were for forcible rape. The remaining eighty-two percent were for statutory rape, a peculiar and imprecise crime. For instance, in Colorado it is statutory rape if intercourse takes place between an unmarried girl under eighteen and a man over eighteen. In practice this means that a boy of nineteen who has an affair with a consenting girl of seventeen is guilty of statutory rape. All the girl needs to do is to accuse her lover of consensual relations and he can be imprisoned for as long as fifty years. There are thousands of "rapists" serving time because, for one reason or another, they were found guilty of sexual intercourse with a willing partner.

In nearly every state fellatio, cunnilingus, and anal intercourse are punished. Not only are these acts forbidden between men, they are forbidden between men and women, within as well as without wedlock. As usual, the various state laws are in wild disarray. Ohio deplores fellatio but tolerates cunnilingus. In another state, sodomy is punished with a maximum twenty-year sentence, while fellatio calls for only three years, a curious discrimination. Deviate sexual acts between consenting adults are punished in most states, with sentences running from three years to life imprisonment. Of the other countries of the West, only the Federal German Republic intrudes itself upon consenting adults.

Elsewhere in the field of moral legislation, twenty-seven states forbid sexual relations and/or marriage between the white race and its "inferiors": blacks, American Indians, Orientals. And of course our narcotics laws are the scandal of the world. With the passage in 1914 of the Harrison Act, addiction to narcotics was found to be not the result of illness or bad luck but of sin, and sin must of course be punished by the state. For half a century the Federal government has had a splendid time playing cops and robbers. And since you cannot have cops without robbers, they have created the robbers by maintaining that the sinful taking of drugs must be wiped out by law. As a result, the government's severity boosts the price of drugs, makes the game more desperate for addicts as well as pushers, and encourages crime which in turn increases the payroll of the Narcotics Bureau. This lunatic state of affairs could exist only in a society still obsessed by the idea that the punishing of sin is the responsibility of the state. Yet in those countries where dope addiction is regarded as a matter for the doctor and not the police, there can be no criminal traffic in drugs. In all of England there are 550 drug addicts. In New York City alone there are 23,000 addicts.

Theoretically, the American separation of church and state should have left the individual's private life to his conscience. But this was not to be the case. The states promptly took it upon themselves to regulate the private lives of the citizens, flouting, many lawyers believe, the spirit if not the letter of the Constitution. The result of this experiment is all around us. One in eight Americans is mentally disturbed, and everywhere psychiatry flourishes. Our per capita acts of violence are beyond anything known to the other countries of the West. Clearly the unique attempt to make private morality answerable to law has not been a success. What to do?

On April 25, 1955, a committee of the American Law Institute presented a Model Penal Code (tentative draft No. 4) to the Institute, which was founded some forty years ago "to promote the clarification and simplification of the law and its better adaptation to social needs." This Code represented an attempt to make sense out of conflicting laws, to remove "dead-letter laws" which might, under pressure, be used for dark ends, and to recognize that there is an area of private sexual morality which is no concern of the state. In this the Code echoed the recommendation of the British Wolfenden Report, which said: "Unless a deliberate attempt is to be made by society, acting through the agency of the law, to equate the sphere of crime with that of sin, there must remain a realm of private morality and immorality which is, in brief and crude terms, not the law's business." The drafters of the Code proposed that adultery and sodomy between consenting adults be removed from the sphere of the law on the grounds that "the Code does not attempt to use the power of the state to enforce purely moral or religious standards. We deem it inappropriate for the government to attempt to control behavior that has no substantial significance except as to the morality of the actor. Such matters are best left to religious, educational and other influences." The Committee's recommendation on adultery was accepted. But on sodomy, Judge John J. Parker spoke for the legal moralists: "There are many things that are denounced by the criminal civil code in order that society may know that the state disapproves. When we fly in the face of public opinion, as evidenced by the code of every state in this union, we are not proposing a code which will commend itself to the thoughtful." Judge Parker was answered by Judge Learned Hand, who said, "Criminal law which is not enforced practically is much worse than if it was not on the books at all. I think homosexuality is a matter of morals, a matter very largely of taste, and it is not a matter that people should be put in prison about." Judge Hand's position was upheld by the Institute.

As matters now stand, only the state of Illinois has attempted to modify its sex laws. As of 1962 there is no longer any penalty in Illinois for the committing of a deviate sexual act. On the other hand, an "open and notorious" adulterer can still be punished with a year in prison and fornication can be punished with six months in prison. So it is still taken for granted that the state has the right to regulate private behavior in the interest of public morality.

One postwar phenomenon has been the slowness of the liberal community to respond to those flaws in our society which might be corrected by concerted action. It would seem to me that a change in the legal codes of the fifty American states might be an interesting occupation for the liberally inclined. As the laws stand, they affect nearly everyone; implemented, they would affect millions. Originally, the United States made a brave distinction between church and state. But then we put within the legal province of the states that which was either the concern of religion or of the moral conscience of the individual. The result has caused much suffering. The state laws are executed capriciously and though in time they may fade away, without some organized effort they could continue for generations. In fact, there are signs today that the legal conservatives are at work strengthening these laws. In Florida the administration has distributed an astonishing pamphlet denouncing homosexualists in terms of seventeenth-century grandeur. In Dallas a stripper named Candy Barr was given an unprecedented fifteen-year prison term, ostensibly because she was found with marijuana in her possession but actually because she was a sinful woman. In the words of a Dallas lawyer (Warren Leslie in *Dallas, Public and Private*), the jury was "showing the world they were in favor of God, heaven, and sending to hell-fire a girl who violated their sense of morality."

In these lowering days, there is a strong movement afoot to save society from sexual permissiveness. Guardians of the old-time virtue would maintain what they believe to be the status quo. They speak of "common decency" and "accepted opinion." But do such things really exist? And if they do, are they "right"? After all, there is no position so absurd that you cannot get a great many people to assume it. Lord Maugham, a former Lord Chancellor (where do they find them?), was convinced that the decline of the Roman Empire was the result of too frequent bathing. Justinian *knew* there was a causal link between buggery and earthquakes, while our grandparents, as Professor Steven Marcus recently reminded us, believed that masturbation caused insanity. I suspect that our own faith in psychiatry will seem as touchingly quaint to the future as our grandparents' belief in phrenology seems now to us. At any given moment, public opinion is a chaos of superstition, misinformation, and prejudice. Even if one could accurately interpret it, would that be a reason for basing the law upon a consensus?

Neither Professor Hart nor the legal moralists go that far. The conservatives are very much aware that they are living in an age of "moral decline." They wish to return to a stern morality like that of Cato or of Calvin. Failing that, they will settle for maintaining existing laws, the harsher the better. Professor Hart, on the other hand, believes that between what the law says people ought to do in their private lives and what they in fact do, there is a considerable division. To the degree that such laws ought, ideally, to conform with human practice, he is a democrat. In answering those who feel that despite what people actually do, they ought not to do it, he remarks that this may be true, yet "the use of legal punishment to freeze into immobility the morality dominant at a particular time in a society's existence may possibly succeed, but even where it does it contributes nothing to the survival of the animating spirit and formal values of social morality and may do much harm to them."

There is some evidence that by fits and starts the United States is achieving a civilization. Our record so far has not been distinguished, no doubt because we had a bad beginning. Yet it is always possible to make things better—as well as worse. Various groups are now at work trying to make sense of the fifty state codes. New York and

California are expected to have improved codes by the end of this decade. But should there be a sudden renewal of legal moralism, attempts to modify and liberalize will fail. What is needed, specifically, is a test case before the Supreme Court which would establish in a single decision that "sin," where it does not disturb the public order, is not the concern of the state. This conception is implicit in our Constitution. But since it has never been tested, our laws continue to punish the sinful as though the state were still an arm of Church Militant. Although a Great Society is more easily attained in rhetoric than in fact, a good first step might be the removal from our statute books of that entirely misplaced scarlet letter.

Partisan Review
Summer 1965

The Sexus of Henry Miller

In 1949 Henry Miller sent his friend Lawrence Durrell the two volumes of *Sexus* that together comprise one of the seven sections of his long-awaited masterwork, *The Rosy Crucifixion* (Rosicrucian?). The other parts are titled *Nexus, Plexus,* and presumably anything else that ends in "exus." Durrell's reaction to *Sexus* has been published in that nice book, *Lawrence Durrell and Henry Miller: A Private Correspondence*: "I must confess I'm bitterly disappointed in [*Sexus,*] despite the fact that it contains some of your very best writing to date. But, my dear Henry, the moral vulgarity of so much of it is artistically painful. These silly meaningless scenes which have no *raison d'être,* no humor, just childish explosions of obscenity—what a pity, what a terrible pity for a major artist not to have a critical sense enough to husband his force, to keep his talent aimed at the target. What on earth possessed you to leave so much twaddle in?"

Miller's response was serene and characteristic. "I said it before and I repeat it solemnly: I am writing exactly what I want to write and the way I want to do it. Perhaps it's twaddle, perhaps not.... I am trying to reproduce in words a block of my life which to me has the utmost significance—every bit of it. Not because I am infatuated with my own ego. You should be able to perceive that only a man without ego could write thus about himself. (Or else I am really crazy. In which case, pray for me.)"

Sexus is a very long book about a character named Henry Miller (though at times his first name mysteriously changes to Val) who lives in Brooklyn (circa 1925) with a wife and daughter; he works for the Cosmodemonic Telegraph Company of North America (Western Union) and conducts an affair with a dance-hall girl named Mara (whose first name changes to Mona halfway through and stays Mona). In the course of six hundred and thirty-four pages, the character Henry Miller performs the sexual act many times with many different women, including, perversely, his wife, whom he does not much like. By the end of the book he has obtained a divorce and Mara-Mona becomes his second or perhaps third wife, and he dreams of freedom in another land.

Because of Miller's hydraulic approach to sex and his dogged use of four-letter words, *Sexus* could not be published in the United States for twenty-four years. Happily, the governors of the new American Empire are not so frightened of words as were the custodians of the old Republic. *Sexus* can now be dispensed in our drugstores, and it will do no harm, even without prescription.

Right off, it must be noted that only a total egotist could have written a book which has no subject other than Henry Miller in all his sweet monotony. Like shadows in a solipsist's daydream, the other characters flit through the narrative, playing straight to the relentless old exhibitionist whose routine has not changed in nearly half a century. Pose one: Henry Miller, sexual athlete. Pose two: Henry Miller, literary genius and life force. Pose three: Henry Miller and the cosmos (they have an understanding). The narrative is haphazard. Things usually get going when Miller meets a New Person at a party. New Person immediately realizes that this is no ordinary man. In fact, New Person's whole life is often changed after exposure to the hot radiance of Henry Miller. For opening the door to Feeling, Miller is then praised by New Person in terms which might turn the head of God— but not the head of Henry Miller, who notes each compliment with the gravity of the recording angel. If New Person is a woman, then she is due for a double thrill. As a lover, Henry Miller is a national resource, on the order of Yosemite National Park. Later, exhausted by his unearthly potency, she realizes that for the first time she has met

Man...one for whom *post coitum* is not *triste* but rhetorical. When lesser men sleep, Miller talks about the cosmos, the artist, the sterility of modern life. Or in his own words: "...our conversations were like passages out of *The Magic Mountain*, only more virulent, more exalted, more sustained, more provocative, more inflammable, more dangerous, more menacing, and much more, ever so much more, exhausting."

Now there is nothing inherently wrong with this sort of book-making. The literature of self-confession has always had an enormous appeal, witness the not entirely dissimilar successes of Saints Augustine and Genet. But to make art of self-confession it is necessary to tell the truth. And unless Henry Miller is indeed God (not to be ruled out for lack of evidence to the contrary), he does not tell the truth. Everyone he meets either likes or admires him, while not once in the course of *Sexus* does he fail in bed. Hour after hour, orgasm after orgasm, the great man goes about his priapic task. Yet from Rousseau to Gide the true confessors have been aware that not only is life mostly failure, but that in one's failure or pettiness or wrongness exists the living drama of the self. Henry Miller, by his own account, is never less than superb, in life, in art, in bed. Not since the memoirs of Frank Harris has there been such a record of success in the sack. Nor does Miller provide us with any sort of relief. One could always skip Frank Harris's erotic scenes in favor of literary and political gossip. But Miller is much too important for gossip. People do not interest him. Why should they? They are mere wedding guests: he is the Ancient Mariner.

At least half of *Sexus* consists of tributes to the wonder of Henry Miller. At a glance men realize that he *knows*. Women realize that he *is*. Mara-Mona: "I'm falling in love with the strangest man on earth. You frighten me, you're so gentle...I feel almost as if I were with a god." Even a complete stranger ("possibly the countess he had spoken of earlier") is his for the asking the moment she sees him. But, uniquely, they both prefer to chat. The subject? Let the countess speak for herself: "Whoever the woman is you love, I pity her...Nobody can hold you for long...You make friends easily, I'm sure. And yet there is no one whom you can really call your friend. You are alone. You will always be alone." She asks him to embrace her. He does, chastely. Her life is now changed. "You have helped, in a way...You always help, indirectly. You can't help radiating energy, and that is something. People lean on you, but you don't know why." After two more pages of this keen analysis, she tells him, "Your sexual virility is only the sign of a greater power, which you haven't begun to use." She never quite tells him what this power is, but it must be something pretty super because everyone else can also sense it humming away. As a painter friend (male) says, "I don't know any writer in America who has greater gifts than you. I've always believed in you—and I will even if you prove to be a failure." This is heady praise indeed, considering that the painter has yet to read anything Miller has written.

Miller is particularly irresistible to Jews: "You're no Goy. You're a black Jew. You're one of those fascinating Gentiles that every Jew wants to shine up to." Or during another first encounter with a Jew (Miller seems to do very well at first meetings, less well subsequently): "I see you are not an ordinary Gentile. You are one of those lost Gentiles—you are searching for something...With your kind we are never sure where we stand. You are like water—and we are rocks. You eat us away little by little—not with malice, but with kindness..." Even when Miller has been less than loyal in his relations with others, he is forgiven. Says a friend: "You don't seem to understand what it means to give and take. You're an intellectual hobo...You're a gangster, do you know that?" He chuckled. "Yes, Henry, that's what you are—you're a spiritual gangster." The chuckle saves the day for lovable Henry.

Yet Henry never seems to do anything for anyone, other than to provide moments of sexual glory which we must take on faith. He does, however, talk a lot and the people he knows are addicted to his conversation. "Don't stop talking now...please," begs a woman whose life is being changed, as Henry in a manic mood tells her all sorts of liberating things like "Nothing would be bad or ugly or evil— if we really let ourselves go. But it's hard to make people understand that." To which the only answer is that of another straight man in the text who says, "You said it, Henry. Jesus, having you around is like getting a shot in the arm." For a man who boasts of writing nothing but the truth, I find it more than odd that not once in the course of a long narrative does anyone say, "Henry, you're full of shit." It is possible, of course, that no one ever did, but I doubt it.

Interlarded with sexual bouts and testimonials are a series of prose poems in which the author works the cosmos for all it's worth. The style changes noticeably during these arias. Usually Miller's writing is old-fashioned American demotic, rather like the prose of one of those magazines Theodore Dreiser used to edit. But when Miller climbs onto the old cracker barrel, he gets very fancy indeed. Sentences swell and billow, engulfing syntax. Arcane words are put to use, often accurately: ectoplasmic, mandibular, anthropophagous, terrene, volupt, occipital, fatidical. Not since H. P. Lovecraft has there been such a lover of language. Then, lurking pale and wan in this jungle of rich prose, are the Thoughts: "Joy is founded on something too profound to be understood and communicated: To be joyous is to be a madman in a world of sad ghosts." Or: "Only the great, the truly distinctive individuals resemble one another. Brotherhood doesn't start at the bottom, but at the top." Or: "Sex and poverty go hand in hand." The interesting thing about the Thoughts is that they can be turned inside out and the effect is precisely the same: "Sex and affluence go hand in hand," and so on.

In nearly every scene of *Sexus* people beg Miller to give them The Answer, whisper The Secret, reveal The Cosmos; but though he does his best, when the rosy crucial moment comes he invariably veers off into platitude or invokes high mysteries that can be perceived only through Feeling, never through thought or words. In this respect he is very much in the American grain. From the beginning of the United States, writers of a certain kind, and not all bad, have been bursting with some terrible truth that they can never quite articulate. Most often it has to do with the virtue of feeling as opposed to the vice of thinking. Those who try to think out matters are arid, sterile, anti-life, while those who float about in a daffy daze enjoy copious orgasms and the happy knowledge that they are the salt of the earth. This may well be true but Miller is hard put to prove it, if only because to make a case of any kind, cerebration is necessary, thereby betraying the essential position. On the one hand, he preaches the freedom of the bird, without attachments or the need to justify anything in words, while on the other hand, he feels obligated to write long books in order to explain the cosmos to us. The paradox is that if he really meant what he writes, he would not write at all. But then he is not the first messiah to be crucified upon a contradiction.

It is significant that Miller has had a considerable effect on a number of writers better than himself—George Orwell, Anaïs Nin, Lawrence Durrell, to name three at random—and one wonders why. Obviously his personality must play a part. In the letters to Durrell he is a most engaging figure. Also, it is difficult not to admire a writer who has so resolutely gone about his own business in his own way without the slightest concession to any fashion. And though time may have turned the Katzenjammer Kid into Foxy Grandpa, the old cheerful anarchy remains to charm.

Finally, Miller helped make a social revolution. Forty years ago it was not possible to write candidly of sexual matters. The door was shut. Then the hinges were sprung by D. H. Lawrence, and Miller helped kick it in. Now other doors need opening (death is the new obscenity). Nevertheless, at a certain time and in a certain way, Henry Miller fought the good fight, for which he deserves not only our gratitude but a permanent place of honor in that not inconsiderable company which includes such devoted figures as Havelock Ellis, Alfred C. Kinsey, and Marie C. Stopes.

Book Week
August 1, 1965

Pornography

The man and the woman make love; attain climax; fall separate. Then she whispers, "I'll tell you who I was thinking of if you'll tell me who you were thinking of." Like most sex jokes, the origins of this pleasant exchange are obscure. But whatever the source, it seldom fails to evoke a certain awful recognition, since few lovers are willing to admit that in the sexual act to create or maintain excitement they may need some mental image as erotic supplement to the body in attendance. One perverse contemporary maintains that when he is with A he thinks of B and when he is with B he thinks of A; each attracts him only to the degree that he is able simultaneously to evoke the image of the other. Also, for those who find the classic positions of "mature" lovemaking unsatisfactory yet dare not distress the beloved with odd requests, sexual fantasy becomes inevitable and the shy lover soon finds himself imposing mentally all sorts of wild images upon his unsuspecting partner, who may also be relying on an inner theater of the mind to keep things going; in which case, those popular writers who deplore "our lack of communication today" may have a point. Ritual and magic also have their devotees. In one of Kingsley Amis's fictions, a man mentally conjugates Latin verbs in order to delay orgasm as he waits chivalrously for his partner's predictably slow response. While another considerate lover (nonfictional) can only reduce tempo by thinking of a large loaf of sliced white bread, manufactured by Bond.

Sexual fantasy is as old as civilization (as opposed to as old as the race), and one of its outward and visible signs is pornographic literature, an entirely middle-class phenomenon, since we are assured by many investigators (Kinsey, Pomeroy, et al.) that the lower orders seldom rely upon sexual fantasy for extra-stimulus. As soon as possible, the uneducated man goes for the real thing. Consequently he seldom masturbates, but when he does he thinks, we are told, of *nothing at all*. This may be the last meaningful class distinction in the West.

Nevertheless, the sex-in-the-head middle classes that D. H. Lawrence so despised are not the way they are because they want deliberately to be cerebral and anti-life; rather they are innocent victims of necessity and tribal law. For economic reasons they must delay marriage as long as possible. For tribal reasons they are taught that sex outside marriage is wrong. Consequently the man whose first contact with a woman occurs when he is twenty will have spent the sexually most vigorous period of his life masturbating. Not unnaturally, in order to make that solitary act meaningful, the theater of his mind early becomes a Dionysian festival, and should he be a resourceful dramatist he may find actual lovemaking disappointing when he finally gets to it, as Bernard Shaw did. One wonders whether Shaw would have been a dramatist at all if he had first made love to a girl at fourteen, as nature intended, instead of at twenty-nine, as class required. Here, incidentally, is a whole new line of literary-psychological inquiry suitable for the master's degree: "Characteristics of the Onanist as Dramatist." Late coupling and prolonged chastity certainly help explain much of the rich dottiness of those Victorians whose peculiar habits planted thick many a quiet churchyard with Rose La Touches.

Until recently, pornography was a small cottage industry among the grinding mills of literature. But now that sex has taken the place of most other games (how many young people today learn bridge?), creating and packaging pornography has become big business, and though the high courts of the American Empire cannot be said to be very happy about this state of affairs, they tend to agree that freedom of expression is as essential to our national life as freedom of meaningful political action is not. Also, despite our governors' paternalistic bias, there are signs that they are becoming less intolerant in sexual matters. This would be a good thing if one did not suspect that they may regard sex as our bread and circuses, a means of keeping us off the political streets, in bed and out of mischief. If this is so, we may yet observe the current President in his mad search for consensus settling for the consensual.

Among the publishers of pornography ("merchants of smut," as they say at the FBI), Maurice Girodias is uniquely eminent. For one thing, he is a second-generation peddler of dirty books (or "d.b.'s," as they call them on Eighth Avenue). In the 1930s his English father, Jack Kahane, founded the Obelisk Press in Paris. Among Kahane's authors were Anaïs Nin, Lawrence Durrell, Cyril Connolly, and of course Henry Miller, whose books have been underground favorites for what seems like a century. Kahane died in 1939 and his son, Maurice Girodias (he took his mother's name for reasons not given), continued Kahane's brave work. After the war, Girodias sold Henry Miller in vast quantities to easily stimulated GIs. He also revived *Fanny Hill*. He published books in French. He prospered. Then the terror began. Visionary dictatorships, whether of a single man or of the proletariat, tend to disapprove of irregular sex. Being profoundly immoral in public matters, dictators compensate by insisting upon what they think to be a rigorous morality in private affairs. General de Gaulle's private morality appears to have been registered in his wife's name. In 1946 Girodias was prosecuted for publishing Henry Miller. It was France's first prosecution for obscenity since the trial of *Madame Bovary* in 1844. Happily, the world's writers rallied to Miller's defense, and since men of letters are taken solemnly in France, the government dropped its charges.

In a preface to the recently published *The Olympia Reader*, Girodias discusses his business arrangements at length; and though none of us is as candid about money as he is about sex, Girodias does admit that he lost his firm not as a result of legal persecution but through incompetence, a revelation that gives him avant-garde status in the new pornography of money. Girodias next founded the Olympia Press, devoted to the creation of pornography, both hard and soft core. His adventures as a merchant of smut make a nice story. All sorts of writers, good and bad, were set to work turning out books, often written to order. He would think up a title (e.g., *With Open Mouth*) and advertise it; if there was sufficient response, he would then commission someone to write a book to go with the title. Most of his writers used pseudonyms. Terry Southern and Mason Hoffenberg wrote *Candy* under the name of Maxwell Kenton. Christopher Logue wrote *Lust* under the name of Count Palmiro Vicarion, while Alex Trocchi, as Miss Frances Lengel, wrote *Helen and Desire*. Girodias also published Samuel Beckett's *Watt*, Vladimir Nabokov's *Lolita*, and J. P. Donleavy's *The Ginger Man*; perversely, the last three authors chose not to use pseudonyms.

Reading of these happy years, one recalls a similar situation just after the Second War when a number of New York writers were commissioned at so many cents a page to write pornographic stories for a United States Senator. The solon, as they say in smutland, never actually met the writers but through a go-between he guided their stories: a bit more flagellation here, a touch of necrophilia there.... The subsequent nervous breakdown of one of the Senator's pornographers, now a celebrated poet, was attributed to the strain of not knowing which of the ninety-six Senators he was writing for.*

In 1958 the Fourth French Republic banned twenty-five of Girodias's books, among them *Lolita*. Girodias promptly sued the Ministry of the Interior and, amazingly, won. Unfortunately, five months later, the General saw fit to resume the grandeur of France. De Gaulle was back; and so was Madame de Gaulle. The Minister of the Interior appealed the now defunct Fourth Republic's decision and was upheld. Since then, censorship has been the rule in France. One by one Girodias's books, regardless of merit, have been banned. Inevitably, André Malraux was appealed to and, inevitably, he responded with that elevated double-talk which has been a characteristic of what one suspects will be a short-lived Republic. Girodias is currently in the United States, where he expects to flourish. Ever since our Puritan republic became a gaudy empire, pornography has been a big business for the simple reason that when freedom of

---

*David Ignatius Walsh (Dem., Mass.).

expression is joined with the freedom to make a lot of money, the dream of those whose bloody footprints made vivid the snows of Valley Forge is close to fulfillment and that happiness which our Constitution commands us to pursue at hand.

The Olympia Reader is a collection of passages from various books published by Maurice Girodias since 1953. Reading it straight through is a curiously disjointed experience, like sitting through a program of movie trailers. As literature, most of the selections are junk, despite the presence of such celebrated contemporary figures as Nabokov, Genet and Queneau; and of the illustrious dead, Sade and Beardsley.

Pornography is usually defined as that which is calculated to arouse sexual excitement. Since what arouses X repels Y, no two people are apt to respond in quite the same way to the same stimulus. One man's meat, as they say, is another man's poison, a fact now recognized by the American judiciary, which must rule with wearisome frequency on obscenity. With unexpected good sense, a judge recently observed that since the books currently before him all involved ladies in black leather with whips, they could not be said to corrupt the generality, since a taste for being beaten is hardly common and those who are aroused by such fantasies are already "corrupted" and therefore exempt from laws designed to protect the young and usual. By their nature, pornographies cannot be said to proselytize, since they are written for the already hooked. The worst that can be said of pornography is that it leads not to "antisocial" sexual acts but to the reading of more pornography. As for corruption, the only immediate victim is English prose. Mr. Girodias himself writes like his worst authors ("Terry being at the time in acute financial need...") while his moral judgments are most peculiar. With reverence, he describes his hero Sir Roger Casement (a "superlative pederast," whatever that is) as "politically confused, emotionally unbalanced, maudlin when depressed and absurdly naive when in his best form; but he was exceptionally generous, he had extraordinary courage and a simple human wisdom which sprang from his natural goodness." Here, Mr. Girodias demonstrates a harmony with the age in which he lives. He may or may not have described Sir Roger accurately, but he has certainly drawn an accurate portrait of the Serious American Novelist, 1966.

Of the forty selections Mr. Girodias has seen fit to collect, at least half are meant to be literature in the most ambitious sense, and to the extent that they succeed, they disappoint; Beckett's *Watt*, Queneau's *Zazie*, Donleavy's *The Ginger Man* are incapable of summoning up so much as the ghost of a rose, to appropriate Sir Thomas Browne's handsome phrase. There is also a good deal of Henry Miller, whose reputation as a pornographer is largely undeserved. Though he writes a lot about sex, the only object he seems ever to describe is his own phallus. As a result, unless one lusts specifically for the flesh of Henry Miller, his works cannot be regarded as truly edifying. Yet at Miller's best he makes one irritably conscious of what it is like to be inside his skin, no mean feat...the pornographic style, incidentally, is contagious: the stately platitude, the arch paraphrase, the innocent line which starts suddenly to buck with unintended double meanings.

Like the perfect host or madam, Mr. Girodias has tried to provide something for everyone. Naturally there is a good deal of straightforward heterosexual goings-on. Mr. Girodias gives us several examples, usually involving the seduction of an adolescent male by an older woman. For female masochists (and male sadists) he gives us *Story of O*. For homosexual sadists (and masochists) *The Gaudy Image*. For negrophiles (and phobes) *Pinktoes*, whose eloquent author, Chester Himes, new to me, has a sense of humor which sinks his work like a stone. For anal eroticists who like science fiction there are passages from William Burroughs's *Naked Lunch* and *The Soft Machine*. For devotees of camp, new to the scene, the thirty-three-year-old *The Young and Evil* by Charles Henri Ford and Parker Tyler is a pioneer work and reads surprisingly well today. Parenthetically, it is interesting to note the role that clothes play in most of these works, camp, kinky, and straight. Obviously, if there is to be something for everyone, the thoughtful entrepreneur must occasionally provide an old sock or pair of panties for the fetishist to get, as it were, his teeth into. But even writers not aiming at the fetishist audience make much of the ritual taking off and putting on of clothes, and it is significant that the bodies thus revealed are seldom described as meticulously as the clothes are.

Even Jean Genet, always lyric and vague when celebrating cock, becomes unusually naturalistic and detailed when he describes clothes in an excerpt from *The Thief's Journal*. Apparently when he was a boy in Spain a lover made him dress up as a girl. The experiment was a "failure because "Taste is required...I was already refusing to have any. I forbade myself to. Of course I would have shown a great deal of it." Nevertheless, despite an inadequate clothes sense, he still tells us far more about the *travesti manqué* than he ever tells us about the body of Stilitano for whom he lusted.

In most pornography, physical descriptions tend to be sketchy. Hard-core pornographers seldom particularize. Inevitably, genitals are massive, but since we never get a good look at the bodies to which they are attached, the effect is so impersonal that one soon longs to read about those more modest yet entirely tangible archetypes, the girl and boy next door, two creatures far more apt to figure in the heated theater of the mind than the voluptuous grotesques of the pulp writer's imagination. Yet by abstracting character and by keeping his human creatures faceless and vague, the pornographer does force the reader to draw upon personal experience in order to fill in the details, thereby achieving one of the ends of all literary art, that of making the reader collaborator.

As usual, it is the Marquis de Sade (here represented by a section from *Justine*) who has the most to say about sex—or rather the use of others as objects for one's own pleasure, preferably at the expense of theirs. In true eighteenth-century fashion, he explains and explains and explains. There is no God, only Nature, which is heedless of the Good as well as of the Bad. Since Nature requires that the strong violate the weak and since it is demonstrably true that Nature made women weak and men strong, therefore...and so on. The Marquis's vision—of which so much has been made in this century—is nothing but a rather simpleminded Manicheism, presented with more passion than logic. Yet in his endless self-justification (un-Natural this: Nature never apologizes, never explains) Sade's tirades often strike the Marlovian note: "It is Nature that I wish to outrage. I should like to spoil her plans, to block her advance, to halt the course of the stars, to throw down the globes that float in space—to destroy everything that serves her, to protect everything that harms her, to cultivate everything that irritates her—in a word to insult all her works." But he stops considerably short of his mark. He not only refused to destroy one of her more diverting creations, himself, but he also opposed capital punishment. Even for a French *philosophe*, Sade is remarkably inconsistent, which is why one prefers his letters to his formal argument. Off duty he is more natural and less Natural. While in the Bastille he described himself as possessing an "extreme tendency in everything to lose control of myself, a disordered imagination in sexual matters such as has never been known in this world, an atheist to the point of fanaticism—in two words there I am, and so once again kill me or take me like that, because I shall never change." Latter-day diabolists have tried to make of his "disordered imagination in sexual matters" a religion and, as religions go, it is no more absurd than that of the crucified tripartite man-god. But though Nature is indeed nonhuman and we are without significance except to ourselves, to make of that same indifferent Nature an ally in behavior which is, simply, harmful to human society is to be singularly vicious.

Yet it is interesting to note that throughout all pornography, one theme recurs: the man or woman who manages to capture another human being for use as an unwilling sexual object. Obviously this is one of the commonest of masturbatory daydreams. Sade's originality was to try, deliberately, to make his fantasies real. But he was no Gilles de Rais. He lacked the organizational sense, and his actual adventures were probably closer to farce than to tragedy, more Charlie Chaplin trying to drown Martha Raye than Ilse Koch castrating her paramours at Buchenwald. Incidentally, it is typical of our period that the makers of the play *Marat/Sade* were much admired for having perversely reduced a splendid comic idea to mere tragedy.

Mr. Girodias's sampler should provide future sociologists with a fair idea of what sex was like at the dawn of the age of science. They will no doubt be as amused as most of us are depressed by the extent to which superstition has perverted human nature (not to mention thwarted Nature). Officially the tribal norm continues. The family is the central unit of society. Man's function is to impregnate woman in order to make children. Any sexual act that does not lead to the making of a child is untribal, which is to say antisocial. But though these assumptions are still held by the mass of human society in the West, the pornographers by what they write (as well as by what they omit to mention) show that in actual fact the old laws are not only broken (as always) but are being questioned in a new way.

Until this generation, even nonreligious enemies of irregular sexuality could sensibly argue that promiscuity was bad because it led to venereal disease and to the making of unwanted babies. In addition, sex was a dirty business since bodies stank and why should any truly fastidious person want to compound the filth of his own body's corruption with that of another? Now science has changed all that. Venereal disease has been contained. Babies need not be the result of the sexual act ("I feel so happy and safe now I take the pill"), while improved bathing facilities together with the American Mom's relentless circumcision of boys has made the average human body a temptingly hygienic contraption suitable for all sorts of experiment. To which the moralists can only respond: Rome born again! Sexual license and excessive bathing, as everyone knows, made the Romans effete and unable to stand up to the stalwart puritan savages from the German forests whose sacred mission was to destroy a world gone rotten. This simplistic view of history is a popular one, particularly among those who do not read history. Yet there *is* a basic point at issue and one that should be pondered.

Our tribal standards are an uneasy combination of Mosaic law and the warrior sense of caste that characterized those savage tribesmen who did indeed engulf the world of cities. The contempt for people in trade one still finds amongst the Wasp aristocracy, the sense of honor (furtive but gnawing), the pride in family, the loyalty to class, and (though covert) the admiration for the military virtues and physical strength are all inherited not from our civilized predecessors who lived in the great cities but from their conquerors, the wandering tribesmen, who planted no grain, built no cities, conducted no trade, yet preyed successfully upon those who did these contemptible, unmanly things. Today of course we are all as mixed in values as in blood, but the unstated assumption that it is better to be physically strong than wise, violent than gentle, continent than sensual, landowner or coupon clipper than shopkeeper, lingers on as a memorial to those marauding tribes who broke into history at the start of the Bronze Age and whose values are with us still, as the Gallup Poll attested recently, when it revealed that the President's war in Vietnam is most popular in the South, the most "tribal" part of the United States. Yet the city is the glory of our race, and today in the West, though we are all city dwellers, we still accept as the true virtue the code of our wild conquerors, even though our actual lives do not conform to their laws, nor should they, nor should we feel guilty because they don't.

In ten thousand years we have learned how to lengthen human lives but we have found no way to delay human puberty. As a result, between the economics of the city and the taboos of the tribe we have created a monstrous sexual ethic. To mention the most notorious paradox: It is not economically convenient for the adolescent to marry; it is not tribally correct for him to have sex outside of marriage. Solutions to this man-made problem range from insistence upon total chastity to a vague permissiveness which, worriedly, allows some sexuality if those involved are "sincere" and "mature" and "loving." Until this generation, tribal moralists could argue with perfect conviction that there was only one correct sexual equation: man plus woman equals baby. All else was vice. But now that half the world lives with famine—and all the world by the year 2000, if Pope Paul's as yet unborn guests are allowed to attend (in his unhappy phrase) the "banquet of life"—the old equation has been changed to read: man plus woman equals baby equals famine. If the human race is to survive, population will have to be reduced drastically, if not by atomic war then by law, an unhappy prospect for civil liberties but better than starving. In any case, it is no longer possible to maintain that those sexual acts which do not create (or simulate the creation of) a child are unnatural; unless, to strike the eschatological note, it is indeed Nature's will that we perish through overpopulation, in which case reliable hands again clutch the keys of Peter.

Fortunately, the pornographers appear to be on the side of survival. They make nothing of virginity deflowered, an important theme for two thousand years; they make nothing of it for the simple reason we make little of it. Straightforward adultery no longer fascinates the pornographer; the scarlet letter has faded. Incest, mysteriously, seldom figures in current pornographies. This is odd. The tribal taboo remains as strong as ever, even though we now know that when members of the same family mate the result is seldom more cretinous or more sickly than its parents. The decline of incest as a marketable theme is probably due to today's inadequate middle-class housing. In large Victorian houses with many rooms and heavy doors, the occupants could be mysterious and exciting to one another in a way that those who live in rackety developments can never hope to be. Not even the lust of a Lord Byron could survive the fact of Levittown.

Homosexuality is now taken entirely for granted by pornographers because we take it for granted. But though there is considerable awareness nowadays of what people actually do, the ancient somewhat ambivalent hostility of the tribe persists; witness *Time* magazine's recent diagnosis of homosexuality as a "pernicious sickness" like influenza or opposing the war in Vietnam. Yet from the beginning, tribal attitudes have been confused on this subject. On the one hand, nothing must be allowed to deflect man the father from his procreative duty. On the other hand, man the warrior is more apt than not to perform homosexual acts. What was undesirable in peace was often a virtue in war, as the Spartans recognized, inventing the buddy system at the expense of the family unit. In general, it would seem that the more warlike the tribe, the more opportunistic the sexual response. "You know where you can find your sex," said that sly chieftain Frederick the Great to his officers, "—in the barracks." Of all the tribes, significantly, the Jews alone were consistently opposed not only to homosexuality but to any acknowledgment of the male as an erotic figure (cf. II Maccabees 4: 7-15). But in the great world of pre-Christian cities, it never occurred to anyone that a homosexual act was less "natural" than a heterosexual one. It was simply a matter of taste. From Archilochus to Apuleius, this acceptance of the way people actually are is implicit in what the writers wrote. Suetonius records that of his twelve emperors, eleven went with equal ease from boys to girls and back again without Suetonius ever finding anything remarkable in their "polymorphous perverse" behavior. But all that, as Stanley Kauffmann would say, happened in a "different context."

Nevertheless, despite contexts, we are bisexual. Opportunity and habit incline us toward this or that sexual object. Since additional children are no longer needed, it is impossible to say that some acts are "right" and others "wrong." Certainly to maintain that a homosexual act in itself is antisocial or neurotic is dangerous nonsense, of the sort that the astonishing Dr. Edmund Bergler used to purvey when he claimed that he would "cure" homosexuals, as if this was somehow desirable, like changing Jewish noses or straightening Negro hair in order to make it possible for those who have been so altered to pass more easily through a world of white Christians with snub noses.

Happily, in a single generation, science has changed many old assumptions. Economics has changed others. A woman can now easily support herself, independent of a man. With the slamming of Nora's door, the family ceased to be the essential social unit. Also, the newly affluent middle class can now pursue other pleasures. In the film *The Collector*, a lower-class boy captures an educated girl and after alternately tormenting and boring her, he says balefully, "If more people had more time and money, there would be a lot more of this." This got an unintended laugh in the theater, but he is probably right. Sexual experiment is becoming more open. A placid Midwestern town was recently appalled to learn that its young married set was systematically swapping wives. In the cities, group sex is popular, particularly among the young. Yet despite the new freedoms that the pornographers reflect (sadly for them, since their craft must ultimately wither away), the world they show, though closer to human reality than that of the tribalists, reveals a new illness: the powerlessness that most people feel in an overpopulated and overorganized society.

The sado-masochist books that dominate this year's pornography are not the result of a new enthusiasm for the *vice anglais* so much as a symptom of helplessness in a society where most of the male's aggressive-creative drive is thwarted. The will to prevail is a powerful one, and if it is not fulfilled in work or in battle, it may find an outlet in sex. The man who wants to act out fantasies of tying up or being tied up is imposing upon his sex life a power drive which became socially undesirable once he got onto that escalator at IBM that will take him by predictable stages to early retirement and the medically prolonged boredom of sunset years. Solution of this problem will not be easy, to say the least.

Meanwhile, effort must be made to bring what we think about sex and what we say about sex and what we do about sex into some kind of realistic relationship. Indirectly, the pornographers do this. They recognize that the only sexual norm is that there is none. Therefore, in a civilized society law should not function at all in the area of sex except to protect people from being "interfered with" against their will.

Unfortunately, even the most enlightened of the American state codes (Illinois) still assumes that since adultery is a tribal sin it must be regarded as a civil crime. It is not, and neither is prostitution, that most useful of human institutions. Traditionally, liberals have opposed prostitution on the ground that no one ought to be forced to sell his body because of poverty. Yet in our Affluency, prostitution continues to flourish for the simple reason that it is needed. If most men and women were forced to rely upon physical charm to attract lovers, their sexual lives would be not only meager but in a youth-worshipping country like America painfully brief. Recognizing this state of affairs, a Swedish psychologist recently proposed state brothels for women as well as for men, in recognition of the sad biological fact that the middle-aged woman is at her sexual peak at a time when she is no longer able to compete successfully with younger women. As for the prostitutes themselves, they practice an art as legitimate as any other, somewhere between that of masseur and psychiatrist. The best are natural healers and, contrary to tribal superstition, they often enjoy their work. It is to the credit of today's pornographer that intentionally or not, he is the one who tells us most about the extraordinary variety of human sexual response. In his way he shows us as we are, rather like those Fun House mirrors which, even as they distort and mock the human figure, never cease to reflect the real thing.

The New York Review of Books
March 31, 1966

Doc Reuben

*Everything you always wanted to know about sex**
Explained by David Reuben, M.D.
**But were afraid to ask*

The title of the current number-one nonfiction best seller is cute as a bug's ear, and we know what Freud thought of those who were cute about sex. ("Very uptight"—Sigmund Freud, M.D.). If a jocose approach to sexual matters is a mask for unease, then David Reuben, M.D. ("currently in private psychiatric practice in San Diego, California"), is in a state of communicable panic and I would be most unwilling to have him privately practice psychiatry on me, even in San Diego, the Vatican of the John Birch Society.

David Reuben, M.D., is a relentlessly cheery, often genuinely funny writer whose essential uncertainty about sex is betrayed by a manner which shifts in a very odd way from night-club comedian to reform rabbi, touching en route almost every base except the scientific. Essentially he is a moralist, expressing the hang-ups of today's middle-aged, middle-class urban American Jews, hang-ups which are not (as I shall attempt to show) necessarily those of the gentile population or, for that matter, of the rising generation of American Jews.

Yes, I am going to talk about class and race-religion, two unmentionables in our free land, and I am going to make a case that Jewish family patterns, sexual taboos, and superstitions are often very different from those of the rest of the population, black, white, and yellow, Roman Catholic, Protestant and Moslem. For gentile readers much of the charm of *Portnoy's Complaint* was its exoticism. And despite those ecumenical reviewers who insist that *everyone's* mother is a Jewish mother, the truth is that Mrs. Portnoy was the result of a specific set of historical circumstances, not applicable to anyone else, including the next generation of American Jews, if we are to believe in her child Alexander's rebellion. Certainly his son (assuming he has not entirely wasted his posterity) will probably resemble next-door neighbor George Apley III rather more than father or grandfather.

I mention Alexander Portnoy because David Reuben, M.D., is his contemporary and they have a good deal in common. But where Portnoy's creator is a highly talented artist often able to view objectively the prejudices and tribal taboos of his mother's ghetto culture, Dr. Reuben is still very much in her thrall. Essentially he is not a man of science but a moderately swinging rabbi who buttresses his prejudices with pious quotations from the Old Testament (a single reference to the New Testament is inaccurate); surprisingly, the only mental therapist he mentions is Freud—in order to set him straight.

But then Dr. Reuben seems not to have been affected at all by the discipline of science. He explodes with snappy generalities ("All children at the time of puberty develop pimples") and opinions ("All prostitutes hate men") and statistics which he seems to have made up ("Seventy to eighty percent of Americans engage in fellatio and cunnilingus"). He makes no attempt to prove anything; he merely states his prejudices and enthusiasms as though they were in some way self-evident. It is possible that his advice to middle-aged, middle-class Jewish heterosexuals is useful, but they make up a very small part of the population he now wants to convert to his notions of "mature" sexuality. Certainly a white Protestant will find much of what he has to say inscrutable, while a black will no doubt regard him as something from outer space (that is to say, suburbia) and yet another good reason for replacing Jerusalem with Mecca.

At two points Dr. Reuben is at odds with Moses. He thinks Onan was quite a guy, and his lonely practice particularly useful in toning up those of our senior citizens whose wheelchairs will not accommodate two people; and he has a positively Updikean enthusiasm for cunnilingus. Dr. Reuben would like everyone to indulge in this chivalrous practice—except women, of course: Lesbianism is "immature." He is also sufficiently American to believe that more of everything is best. At times he sounds not unlike the late Bruce Barton extolling God as a super-salesman. "Success in the outside world breeds success in the inside world of sex," sermonizes Dr. Reuben. "Conversely, the more potent a man becomes in the bedroom, the more potent he is in business." Is God a super-salesman? You bet!—and get this—*God eats it, too!*

On those rare occasions when Dr. Reuben is not proselytizing, he can be most instructive, particularly when he describes what happens to the body during orgasm (I assume he is correct about the plumbing), and as he lists all the things that take place between the first thought of sex (D. H. Lawrence, apparently, was wrong: sex is all in the head) and final emission, the male reader is certain to be impotent for the next twenty-four hours ("You will never again," said Leo Tolstoi wickedly, "step on a crack without thinking of a white bear"). Dr. Reuben also has a good plan for eliminating venereal disease by a mass inoculation of the entire population, which he only slightly spoils by suggesting that we use "our gigantic Civil Defense network," which was set up for "just such a mass medical program (in case of bacteriological warfare). This would be a wonderful opportunity for a dry run which might pay off in case of a real war." Well, he does live in San Diego.

Dr. Reuben is also a liberal on abortion, and informative on the subject of contraceptives. He finds something a bit wrong with all the present methods and suspects that the eventual solution will be a morning-after pill for women—as a Jewish patriarch he believes that woman, the lesser vessel, should bear the responsibility. He is also filled with wonderful lore, some of which I hope is true. Want to know the best nonmedical contraceptive? "Coca-Cola. Long a favorite soft drink, it is, coincidentally, the best douche available. A Coke contains carbolic acid which kills the sperm and sugar which explodes the sperm cells...The six-ounce bottle is just the right size for one application." Yes, but won't it rot her teeth?

Between mature guys and gals, anything goes (though anal pene-
tration of the gal leaves Doc a bit queasy). Male impotence and
female frigidity he recognizes as hazards, but psychiatry, he is quick
to point out, will work wonders. He is a remorseless self-advertiser.
Every few pages he gives us a commercial with brisk dialogue and
characters named Emily who suffer from frigidity until...But let's listen in on Emily and her doctor after some months of treatment. Is
Emily frigid now? Lordy no! Emily is fucking like a minx. "I'm happy
to say, Doctor, this is just a social call. I wanted to tell you how happy
I am. I don't know what it's done for other people but psychiatry did
what Mother Nature couldn't do—it made a woman out of me!"
Music up and out.

Or take the case of Joni, the beautiful airline stewardess who
couldn't achieve the big O no matter how hard she (he) tried. After
being told that the values she had learned as a girl on a farm in Iowa
(Christian puritanism) were not applicable to a flying bunny, she was
able in a matter of months to write her doctor "at Christmastime"
(when, presumably, all thoughts flow toward the orgasm), "I may
have been a stewardess, but I really 'won my wings' in the psychiatrist's office." To one who locates psychiatry somewhere between
astrology and phrenology on the scale of human gullibility, the cold-
blooded desire to make money by giving one's fellows (at best) obvious advice and (at worst) notions even sillier than the ones that made
them suffer smacks of *Schadenfreude*.

Along with testimonials to the efficacy of his art, Dr. Reuben has
a good deal to say about many subjects, and since he never attempts
to prove anything, his opinions must be taken as just that. Some
examples. "Orgasm among nymphomaniacs is as rare as orgasm
among prostitutes." To which any liberal arts professor would scrib-
ble in the margin, "prove." For Dr. Reuben's instruction, the only
bona fide nymphomaniac I ever went to bed with promptly produced
a splendid series of orgasms of the variety known as "skimming." In
fact, she enjoyed having orgasms so much that she thought it fun to
have sex with a lot of different people, thus betraying her immaturity. Three point two times a week year in and year out with the same
mature and loving mate ought to have been quite enough for the
saucy shiksa.

Then there is Smiling Jack, who suffers from premature ejaculation. Why? *Because he wants to punish women.* "The smile is characteristic of men with premature ejaculation—they are all profusely apologetic but their regrets have a hollow ring." Fast comer, wipe that smile off your face before you stretch out on Dr. Reuben's couch.

"Blind girls become particularly adept at secret masturbation. They..." No. You had better read this section for yourself. At least the author had the courtesy to wait until Helen Keller was dead before rushing into print with the news. Then "The chap who pays to see two ladies perform homosexually also has his problems, as do the father and son who patronize the same hustler." A breath-taking non sequitur, as usual unprovable and also, as usual, an echo of Mosaic law: Thou shalt not look upon thy father's nakedness.

The looniest of Dr. Reuben's folklore is "Food seems to have a mysterious fascination for homosexuals. Many of the world's greatest chefs have been homosexuals." (Who? I'm really curious. Not Brillat-Savarin, not Fanny Farmer.) "Some of the country's best restaurants are run by homosexuals" (Those two at Twenty One?). "Some of the fattest people are homosexuals" (King Farouk? Orson Welles? President Taft?). "The exact reason is complex...." It certainly is, since there is no evidence one way or the other. But if there were, Dr. Reuben had best find himself a friendly shrink because he makes at least eight references in his book to the penis as food, usually "limp as a noodle"; in fact, food is seldom far from the good doctor's mind when he contemplates genitalia—no doubt for a very complex reason (when I met him three years ago in San Diego he was round as a...well, butterball; since then, according to the dustjacket photo, he has "matured" and lost weight).

But Reuben the folklorist is nothing compared to Reuben the statistician. "At least seventy-five to eighty-five percent of [prostitutes'] clients want to have their penises sucked." "Ninety-nine percent of johns refuse to wear condoms [with prostitutes]." "Only about one tenth of [aging] females choose celibacy." "Chronic or repeated impotence probably affects about thirty to forty percent of men at any given time." And of course those 70 to 80 percent of men who engage in cunnilingus. Since two can play these games, I shall now open my own private files to the public. Right off, 92 percent of those men who get cancer of the tongue have practiced cunnilingus from once to 3309 times in their lives. Those who practice fellatio, however, are not only better dressed but will take at least one long trip in the coming year. Ninety-six percent of those who practice sixty-nine (for Dr. Reuben's heteros a must) periodically complain of a sense of suffocation. Finally, all major American novelists after forty occasionally have orgasm without a full erection. Further statistics on this poignant condition will be revealed as soon as I have heard from Saul, Vladimir and Mary.

In favor of contraception, abortion, masturbation, oral sex between male and female, Dr. Reuben is up-to-date and a source of comfort to his reformed congregation (though the orthodox must be grimly looking about for some useful anathema to lob his way). On circumcision he is orthodox—nature wanted the glans penis covered but Jehovah knew better (our rabbi quotes from both Genesis and Exodus to support this profitable—for doctors—mutilation); on prostitution he is orthodox but tries not to be; on homosexuality he is Mosaic—it is a bad business strictly for immature freaks. Bisexuality does not exist for reasons he and his mentor the late Dr. Bergler never quite give, though they have a lot of opinions which, in their confident American way, they present as facts.

Parenthetically, the collapse of responsible commentary in the United States is as noticeable in a pseudoscience like psychiatry as it is, say, in literary criticism. No one need *prove* anything; simply state private opinion as public fact, preferably in lurid terms. It is now a national characteristic and part of the general cretinizing effect certain dour biologists (accused, accurately, of elitism) regard as a concomitant of promiscuous breeding and overpopulation.

To his credit, Dr. Reuben realizes the practical uses and pleasures of prostitution, an arrangement necessary to the well-being of many millions of men (and women) since the dawn of money, and he is forced to admit that most of the usual arguments against it are not only hypocritical but inaccurate. Nevertheless, looking up from his well-thumbed Old Testament, he is obliged to remind us that " 'harlots' are mentioned forty-four times in the Bible, 'whores' and 'whore mongers' are featured fifty-three times, and committing 'whoredoms' is mentioned eight times."

He then makes his only allusion to the New Testament. Apparently "[it] began where the Old Testament left off and commenced a religious campaign against prostitution which took on all the attributes of a Crusade...." As J. C.'s numerous readers know, his only reference to prostitution was a proposal that the fallen Mary Magdalene be shown charity. Even St. Paul was not a pornophobe; he was a chiliast who believed the day of judgment was at hand and so thought it wise to keep oneself in a state of ceremonial purity—in other words, no sex of any kind (even mature); but if such continence was unbearable then "it is better to marry than to burn."

It should be noted that in matters of history (excepting always Old Testament studies) and etymology Dr. Reuben is usually wrong. He tells us that the word pornography "comes from two Greek words, *pornos*, meaning dirty, and *graphos*, meaning words." *Graphos* of course means "writing" not "words." *Pornos* does not mean "dirty"; it means "harlot." Though I do not think Dr. Reuben has any Greek, if he did it would be a marvelous tribute to the unconscious mind that he confuses "harlot" with "dirty." He also thinks that homosexual sadists "filled the ranks of Hitler's Gestapo and SS." After the purge of Ernst Roehm and his friends in 1934, only banal heterosexual sadists were recruited by the Gestapo and SS. By 1940 homosexualists were being carted off to concentration camps along with Jews, gypsies, and communists. The text is full of misprints (as if anyone cares), bad grammar, misspellings (on page 142 "syphillitic").

While acknowledging the Old Testament's harsh line on prostitution, our cruise director finds peculiarly contemptible the moralizing of those "ministers and moral educators who couldn't be farther removed from practical knowledge of the subject if they lived on the moon." Although Dr. Reuben is robust in his attacks on Protestant clergymen, neither Roman Catholic priest nor Jewish rabbi is ever noted as a hypocritical enemy of life. Obviously Dr. Reuben knows a militant minority when he sees one. But though he is right in blaming a good deal of what is wrong with our sexual ethos on the Protestant founders, he ought, in all fairness, to note that later arrivals haven't been much help either.

To Dr. Reuben's credit, he puts at rest the myth that prostitutes are wicked people because they spread venereal disease. Of 4700 women arrested for prostitution in New York City (1966), 619 had gonorrhea and only four had syphilis. Not a bad record considering their line of work and the harassment they are subject to. He also reminds us that where prostitution is legal, sex crimes diminish. Finally, "most girls become prostitutes because they like it." But then he can't leave that reasonable opinion alone (those 105 Old Testament cracks about "whores" obviously prey on him). Two paragraphs later we are told that "in prostitution no one's happy." Then Dr. Reuben erupts in a torrent of tribal wisdom worthy of any Baptist divine working out of the Oral Roberts Tabernacle. "All prostitutes have at least one thing in common—they hate men." They are doomed to this sad state unless "some dramatic change like psychiatric treatment intervenes." Unexpectedly "their genitals are usually in better condition than those of the average woman." But unfortunately (for men) "the majority of prostitutes are female homosexuals in their private lives."

This, incidentally, is a beloved post-Freudian myth, quite unproven but perennially exciting to men who want to believe that the women they rent deeply hate them and only go to bed with them because they lack money. It is the ultimate charade in the power fantasy which drives so many men (you are tied up and helpless, my proud beauty), including homosexualists who try, not always vainly, to make that one "totally" heterosexual male either because he needs money or must yield to physical force. To say that all female prostitutes are really Lesbians is to succumb to a pleasant if rather silly daydream.

But then Dr. Reuben the rabbi sooner or later does in Dave the swinger. Harlots must, finally, suffer for their evil ways; therefore few "achieve orgasm even in the privacy of their own bedrooms" (a slightly confusing statement: where do they work? They can't all be represented by Al Fresco), but then how can they be expected to have mature orgasms when the only source of "love for a prostitute is her pimp...who provides her with what little emotional warmth he is capable of"? Value judgment. Prove. But then there is no superstition about prostitutes that Dr. Reuben does not offer us as "scientific" fact. Mrs. Portnoy would be proud of Alexander's nice contemporary, particularly when he tells us that the relationship between prostitute and customer is simply "masturbation in a vagina" (a slight contradiction since earlier he told us that 75 to 85 percent of the johns are blown).

Although none of this is provable one way or the other (the nice thing about a pseudoscience like psychiatry is that one can pose any hypothesis upon which to build if not a science a religion), and assuming that a good deal of commercial sex is a kind of joyless masturbation, one is tempted to point out that the same is true of marriage in which, as time passes, the man (and now women are beginning to make the same confession) is constantly forced to rely on inner newsreels in order to make love to a body that no longer excites him yet because of law and tribal custom he must pretend to respond to for thirty or forty or, if Dr. Reuben is counseling him, seventy years of mature sexuality.

In the course of "proving" that a majority of prostitutes are Lesbians and so (naturally) unhappy, Dr. Reuben reveals the bedrock upon which all his superstitions finally rest. "Just as one penis plus one penis equals nothing, one vagina plus another vagina still equals zero." There it is. Dr. Reuben believes in what Roman Catholics term "natural law"—everything is created for a *single* natural purpose. Penis plus vagina equals continuation of the species. Unfortunately the big natural lawyer in the sky slightly confused matters by combining our divine instruments of conception with those of excretion, a source of chagrin and shame to the perennial puritan. Our genitals have always done double duty and cannot be said strictly to have only one sacred function from which all else is deviation, wicked or not, depending on who is doing the moralizing.

Yet from Moses to Freud (despite his discontents) to Dr. Reuben, Judaeo-Christian doctrine has been remarkably unchanging. Man and woman are joined together in a special covenant to bring into the world children; and as it has been since the Bronze Age, so shall it be not only in our Age of Plastic but for all time to come. Those who transgress this law shall be punished, if not with death by stoning then with a mild rash due to neurosis brought on by immature (that is, unholy) attitudes.

It is not an overstatement to say that a belief in this ancient covenant has made a hell of Western man's life on earth (try to find a hotel room in which to make love in any American state; a few seedy places exist but by and large the entire society is resolutely determined to keep from carnal knowledge of one another those not joined together by the Jewish/Christian God). Worse, the ancient covenant's injunction to be fruitful and multiply (Dr. Reuben surprisingly omits this text. It is Genesis 1: 28) has now brought the human race to what may well be a most unpleasant coda as too many people destroy not only the biosphere which supports us but the society which sustains us.

On the subject of homosexuality, Dr. Reuben tries to be a good sport. Yet at heart he is angry with the homosexualist who perversely refuses to enter into a penis-vagina relationship. It would be so easy to straighten him out. If he would only visit "a psychiatrist who knows how to cure homosexuality, he has every chance of becoming a happy, well-adjusted heterosexual." I wonder if Dr. Reuben might be got up on a charge of violating the fair advertising practices act— on the ground that no such psychiatrist exists. It is true that the late Dr. Bergler enjoyed announcing "cures," but since no one knows what a homosexualist is (as opposed to a homosexual act), much less what the psychic life (as opposed to the sex life) of any of his patients was like, his triumphs must be taken on faith.

However, it should be noted that anyone so disturbed by society's condemnation of his natural sexual instinct that he would want to pervert it in order to conform would, no doubt, be a candidate for some kind of "conversion" at the hands of a highly paid quack. Yet to change a man's homosexual instinct is as difficult (if not impossible) as changing a man's heterosexual instinct, and socially rather less desirable since it can hardly be argued, as it used to be—the clincher, in fact, of the natural lawyers—that if everyone practiced homosexuality the race would die out. The fact of course is that not everyone would, at least exclusively, and the race currently needs no more additions.

As a religious rather than a scientific man, Dr. Reuben believes that there is something wicked (he would say sick) about the homosexual act. Therefore those who say they really enjoy it must be lying. He also believes implicitly a set of old queens' tales that any high school boy in Iowa (if not the Bronx) could probably set him straight on. "Most homosexuals at one time or another in their lives act out some aspect of the female role." Aside from his usual inability to define anything (what is a male role? a female role?), he seems to mean that a man who enjoys relations with his own sex is really half a man, a travesty of woman.

This is not the case. The man involved in a homosexual act is engaged in a natural male function; he is performing as a man, and so is his partner. That there are men who think of themselves as women is also a fact, as the visitor to any queer bar will have noticed (those Bette Davis types are with us from Third Avenue to Hong Kong), but they are a tiny minority, not unlike those odd creatures who think of themselves as 100 percent he-men on the order of Lyndon Johnson, another small and infinitely more depressing minority, which of course includes the thirty-sixth President.

Dr. Reuben is also horrified by what he thinks to be the promiscuity of all homosexuals. But then "homosexuals thrive on danger," he tells us, and of course their "primary interest is the penis, not the person." As usual no evidence is given. He takes as fact the prejudices of his race-religion-country, and, most important, as I shall point out, class. Reading him on homosexuality, I was reminded of the lurid anti-Semitic propaganda of the Thirties: All Jews love money. All Jews are sensualists with a penchant for gentile virgins. All Jews are involved in a conspiracy to take over the financial and cultural life of whatever country they happen to be living in. Happily, Dr. Reuben is relatively innocent of making this last charge. The Homintern theory, however, is a constant obsession of certain journalists and crops up from time to time not only in the popular press but in the pages of otherwise respectable literary journals. Fag-baiting is the last form of minority baiting practiced at every level of American society.

Dr. Reuben tends to gloss over the social pressures which condition the life of anyone who prefers, occasionally or exclusively, the company of his own sex. Homosexuals seldom settle down to cozy mature domesticity for an excellent reason: society forbids it. Two government workers living together in Washington, D.C., would very soon find themselves unemployed. They would be spied on, denounced secretly, and dismissed. Only a bachelor entirely above suspicion like J. Edgar Hoover can afford to live openly with another man. In any case, homosexual promiscuity differs from heterosexual only in the atmosphere of fear in which the homosexualist must operate. It is a nice joke if a Louisiana judge is caught in a motel with a call girl. It is a major tragedy if a government official with a family is caught in a men's room.

For someone like Dr. Reuben who believes that there is no greater sin than avoidance of "heterosex—penis and vagina," two men who do live together must, somehow, be wretched. "Mercifully for both of them, the life expectancy of their relationship together is brief." Prove? I wrote for the tenth time in the margin. But we are beyond mere empiricism. We are now involved in one of the major superstitions of our place and time and no evidence must be allowed to disturb simple faith.

Dr. Kinsey (dismissed by Dr. Reuben as a mere biologist) did try to find out what is actually going on. Whatever Kinsey's shortcomings as a researcher, he revealed for the first time the way things are. Everyone is potentially bisexual. In actual practice a minority never commits a homosexual act, others experiment with their own sex but settle for heterosexuality, still others swing back and forth to a greater or lesser degree, while another minority never gets around to performing the penis-vagina act. None of this is acceptable to either Dr. Bergler or Dr. Reuben because they *know* that there is no such thing as bisexuality. Therefore Dr. Kinsey's findings must be discredited. To the rabbinical mind, any man who admits to having enjoyed sexual relations with another man must be, sadly, consigned to the ranks of Sodom. That the same man spends the rest of his sex life in penis-vagina land means nothing because, having enjoyed what he ought not to have enjoyed, his relations with women are simply playacting. Paradoxically, in the interest of making money, the mental therapists are willing to work with any full-time homosexualist who has never had a penis-vagina relationship because deep down they know he does not enjoy men no matter what he says. This is the double standard with a vengeance.

Driving through Wyoming, a Jewish friend of mine picked up a young cowhand and had sex with him. Dr. Reuben will be pleased to note that my friend was, as usual, guilt-ridden; so much so that the boy finally turned to his seducer and with a certain wonder said, "You know, you guys from the East do this because you're sick and we do it because we're horny." My friend has never recovered from this insight into that polymorphic goyisher world best revealed some years ago in Boise, Idaho, where a number of businessmen were discovered frolicking with the local high school boys. Oddly enough (to the innocent), as husbands and fathers, the businessmen were all long-time homesteaders in penis-vagina land. So what were they up to? Bisexuality? No, it does not exist. Evidence dismissed, just as all accounts of other cultures are also unacceptable. Turks, Greeks, Moslems...Well, as one critic likes to say, that is another context (disgusting lot is what he means). I would suggest, however, that a recent book by Brian W. Aldiss, *The Hand-Reared Boy,* be admitted as evidence.

Mr. Aldiss is an English heterosexual—well, he *pretends* to be one, has wife and children—and he tells us in fascinating detail what it was like to go to a second-rate public school just before the Second World War. Admittedly all Americans think all Englishmen are fags, so I daresay this interesting account of a seventeen-year-old who has full sexual relationships with other boys as well as a mature penis-vagina relationship with a girl will be dismissed on the ground that seventeen is a man for all practical purposes, and so he could not do both whole-heartedly. Yet he did. In this Mr. Aldiss tends to resemble his American counterparts, a world obviously alien to the Dr. Reubens, who cannot accept the following simple fact of so many lives (certainly my own): that it is possible to have a mature sexual relationship with a woman on Monday, and a mature sexual relationship with a man on Tuesday, and perhaps on Wednesday have both together (admittedly you have to be in good condition for this).

Now I am sure that Dr. Reuben would not like for 100-percent heterosexualists to be advised on their behavior by 100-percent homosexualists, so may I, diffidently, suggest that until Dr. Reuben has had a full and mature relationship with a man, he ought not to speak of what he does not know. Finally, realizing that at the deepest level, no rabbi can take this sort of blunt talk from a foreskinned dog (Bernard Malamud's loving phrase), I suggest that he read that grandest of Anti-Rabbis, Paul Goodman. He will learn a lot about the naturalness of bisexuality, and in a Jewish context.

It is ironic (and dismaying) that Dr. Reuben's collection of tribal taboos and reactionary nostrums should be popular just when the entire concept of the family is undergoing a radical revision.

Population continues to double at shorter and shorter intervals. Famine is now chronic in half the world. If the race is to continue, we must limit human breeding by law. That is the simple fact of our present condition. Once we have acted to regulate population (I am assuming that this will be done: mass suicide is not a characteristic of our race), most people will not have children to raise. Without children, there will be no reason for men and women to enter into lifetime contracts with one another and marriage, as we have known it, will be at an end. Certainly that curious institution is already in a state of advanced decay in America, witness the underlying theme of all the how-to sex books (including Dr. Reuben's): how to stay sexually interested in your mate long after nature has ceased to make either of you attractive to the other.

Needless to say, even if all governments were to act promptly to limit population, marriage would not end at once or (in some forms) ever entirely vanish, but once it ceases to be the central fact of our society, to that extent women will be for the first time in recorded history freed from a particularly debasing relationship in which they are relentlessly conditioned by the Dr. Reubens to be brainless, enticing bunnies whose reward for making a good home in which to raise their husbands' children through a series of wonderful orgasms. The most startling thing about the women's liberation movement is not its ferocity (and ghastly rhetoric) but the fact that it took so long to surface. It is certainly true that women are half-citizens even in the relatively liberated West. From birth they are programmed by the tribalists to serve men, raise children, and be (if they are interested in True Maturity) geishas, as we are told by "J" (a pseudonym for Dr. Reuben? Or for the sly Professor James Moran?) in *The Sensuous Woman,* a volume every bit as fatuous as Dr. Reuben's compendium of tribal taboos. "J" sees woman's job as not only how to get HIM in the sack but how to keep him excited, a job she admits is not easy within marriage since ardor sooner or later flags. Nevertheless, by unexpectedly redoing the bedroom in sexy shades, a new hair style, exotic perfumes, ravishing naughty underwear, an unexpected blow job with a mouth full of cream of wheat, *somehow* a girl who puts her mind to it can keep him coming back for more year after year after year. As far as I know, no one in tribal lore has ever asked the simple question: Why bother? Why not move on?

Finally, it is to be hoped that with the reduction of population by law and the consequent abandoning of the family unit, men and women will be able for the first time to confront one another as equals, no longer resorting to the sick game in which the man thinks the woman means to trap him into a legal arrangement and the woman thinks she is wrong not to want to capture him and sign herself up for a lifetime of dull subservience. In any case, new things are happening as yet undreamed of in the office of David Reuben, M.D. We are coming either to a better understanding of our sexual nature, or to the race's end. Certainly, either is preferable to the way things are.

The New York Review of Books
June 4, 1970

Women's Liberation:
Feminism and Its Discontents

Every schoolboy has a pretty good idea of what the situation was down at Sodom but what went on in Gomorrah is as mysterious to us as the name Achilles took when he went among women. Or was. Thanks to Eva Figes, author of *Patriarchal Attitudes*, we now know what Gomorrheans are up to. Miss Figes quotes from an eighth-century Palestinian midrash which tries to explain the real reason for the Flood (one of the better jokes in the Old Testament). Apparently passage on the Ark was highly restricted. "Some authorities say that according to God's orders, if the male lorded it over the female of his own kind, both were admitted but not otherwise."

The Founding Father had strong views on the position of woman (under the man) and one of the few mistakes he ever admitted to was the creation of Lilith as a mate for Adam. Using the same dust as his earthly replica...but let us hear it in his own words, rabbinically divined in the fifth century.

Adam and Lilith never found peace together; for when he wished to lie with her, she took offense at the recumbent posture he demanded. "Why must I lie beneath you?" she asked. "I also was made from dust, and am therefore your equal."

Because Adam tried to compel her obedience by force, Lilith, in a rage, uttered the magic name of God, rose into the air and left him.

The outcast Lilith is still hanging about the *Zeitgeist*, we are told, causing babies to strangle in their sleep, men to have wet dreams, and Kate Millett, Betty Friedan, Germaine Greer, and Eva Figes to write books.

The response to *Sexual Politics, Feminine Mystique*, etcetera, has been as interesting as anything that has happened in our time, with the possible exception of Richard Nixon's political career. The hatred these girls have inspired is to me convincing proof that their central argument is valid. Men do hate women (or as Germaine Greer puts it: "Women have very little idea of how much men hate them") and dream of torture, murder, flight.

It is no accident that in the United States the phrase "sex and violence" is used as one word to describe acts of equal wickedness, equal fun, equal danger to that law and order our masters would impose upon us. Yet equating sex with violence does change the nature of each (words govern us more than anatomy), and it is quite plain that those who fear what they call permissiveness do so because they know that if sex is truly freed of taboo it will lead to torture and murder because that is what *they* dream of or, as Norman Mailer puts it, "Murder offers us the promise of vast relief. It is never unsexual."

There has been from Henry Miller to Norman Mailer to Phyllis Schafly a logical progression. The Patriarchalists have been conditioned to think of women as, at best, breeders of sons; at worst, objects to be poked, humiliated, killed. Needless to say, their reaction to Women's Liberation has been one of panic. They believe that if women are allowed parity with men they will treat men the way men have treated women and that, even they will agree, has not been very well or, as Cato the Censor observed, if woman be made man's equal she will swiftly become his master.

Patriarchalists know that women are dangerously different from men, and not as intelligent (though they have their competencies: needlework, child-care, detective stories). When a woman does show herself to be superior at, say, engineering, Freud finessed that anomaly by reminding us that since she is a bisexual, like everyone else, her engineering skill simply means that she's got a bit too much of the tomboy in her, as W. C. Fields once remarked to Grady Sutton on a similar occasion.

Women are not going to make it until the Patriarchalists reform, and that is going to take a long time. Meanwhile the current phase of the battle is intense and illuminating. Men are on the defensive, shouting names; they think that to scream "dyke" is enough to make the girls burst into tears, but so far they have played it cool. Some have even admitted to a bit of dyking now and then along with warm mature heterosexual relationships of the deeply meaningful fruitful kind that bring much-needed children into the world ("Good fucks make good babies"—N. Mailer). I love you Marion and I love you too, Marvin. The women are responding with a series of books and position papers that range from shrill to literature. In the last category one must place Eva Figes who, of the lot, is the only one whose work can be set beside John Stuart Mill's celebrated review of the subject and not seem shoddy or self-serving.

In effect, the girls are all writing the same book. Each does a quick biological tour of the human body, takes on Moses and St. Paul, congratulates Mill, savages Freud (that mistake about vaginal orgasm has cost him glory), sighs over Marx, roughs up the Patriarchalists, and concludes with pleas for child-care centers, free abortions, equal pay, and—in most cases—an end to marriage. These things seem to be well worth accomplishing. And even the enemy are now saying that of course women should be paid the same as men for the same work. On that point alone Women's Lib has already won an important battle because, until recently, the enemy was damned if a woman was going to be paid as much as he for the same job.

Figes begins her short, elegant work with an attempt to define masculine and feminine. Is there any real difference between male and female other than sexual gear? Figes admits to the systematic fluctuation of progesterone levels during the woman's menstrual cycle and pregnancy, and these fluctuations make for "moods," which stop with menopause. Yet Figes makes a most telling point when she observes that although there is little or no hormonal difference between girls and boys before puberty, by the age of four or five boys are acting in a very different manner from girls. Since there is no hormonal explanation for this, the answer is plainly one of indoctrination.

What Figes is saying and what anyone who has ever thought with any seriousness about the human estate knows is that we are, or try to be, what our society wants us to be. There is nothing innate in us that can be called masculine or feminine. We have certain common drives involving survival. Yet our drive toward procreation, oddly enough, is not as powerful as our present-day obsession with sex would lead us to believe.

Of all mammals, man is the only one who must be taught how to mate. In open societies this is accomplished through observation but in a veiled, minatory, Puritan society, sex is a dirty secret, the body shameful, and making love a guilty business, often made dreadful through plain ignorance of what to do. Yet the peripheral male and female roles are carefully taught us. A little girl is given a doll instead of a chemistry set. That she might not like dolls, might prefer a chemistry set, will be the start of a nice neurosis for her, a sense of guilt that she is not playing the part society wants her to play. This arbitrary and brutal shaping of men and women has filled the madhouses of the West, particularly today when the kind of society we still prepare children for (man outside at work, woman at home with children) is no longer the only possibility for a restless generation.

Figes quotes Lévi-Strauss. "Men do not act as members of a group, in accordance with what each feels as an individual; each man feels as a function of the way in which he is permitted or obliged to act. Customs are given as external norms before giving rise to internal sentiments, and these non-sentiment norms determine the sentiments of individuals as well as the circumstances in which they may, or must, be displayed." One sees this in our society's emphasis on what Hemingway called "grace under pressure," or that plain old-fashioned patriotism which so often means nothing more than persuading a man to kill a man he does not know. To get him to do this the society must with its full weight pervert the normal human instinct not to kill a stranger against whom he has no grudge.

This kind of conditioning is necessary for the maintenance of that acquisitive, warrior society to which we belong, a society which now appears to be cracking up in the United States, to the despair of the

Patriarchalists, not to mention those financial interests whose profits depend upon the exploitation and conquest of distant lands and markets. Concentrating on social pressures, Figes has written a book concerned with those external norms "which give rise to internal sentiments, with the organization of emotions into sentiments."

For those who like to remind the girls that no woman wrote anything in the same class as *Paradise Lost* or painted anything like the Sistine Chapel or composed *Don Carlos* (in the novel the girls hold their own), Figes observes that women were not expected to do that sort of thing and so did not. It is easy for a talented boy to be a sculptor because there are other males whom he can identify with and learn from. But society does everything to discourage a girl from making the attempt; and so she stifles as best she can whatever secret yearning she might have to shape stone, and gets on with the dishes.

In recent years, however, women have begun to invade fields traditionally assigned to men. Eventually, the boys will have to face the fact that the arts and sciences are not masculine or feminine activities, but simply human ones. Incidentally, all the girls have a go at one Otto Weininger, a nineteenth-century *philosophe* who at twenty-three wrote a book to prove that women were incapable of genius, then killed himself. The girls tend unkindly to cackle over that.

Figes does the obligatory chapters on Moses and St. Paul, those proud misogynists whose words have caused so much misery down the millennia. The hatred of women that courses through both Old and New Testaments is either lunatic or a mask for something else. What were the Patriarchs so afraid of? Is Robert Graves right after all? Was there really a Great Mother cult the Patriarchs destroyed? Were the attacks on woman political in origin? to discredit the Great Mother and her priestesses? We shall never know.

Perhaps it is simply guilt. People don't like their slaves very much. Women were—and in some cases still are—slaves to men, and attempts to free slaves must be put down. Also, as Figes puts it, "Human beings have always been particularly slow to accept ideas that diminish their own absolute supremacy and importance." For men, "like all people who are privileged by birth and long tradition, the idea of sharing could only mean giving up."

According to Figes, "The rise of capitalism is the root cause of the modern social and economic discrimination against women, which came to a peak in the last century." She remarks upon the degree of equality women enjoyed in Tudor times. From Portia to Rosalind, women existed as people in their own right. But with the simultaneous rise of Puritanism and industry, woman was more and more confined to the home—when she was not exploited in the factories as a cheap source of labor. Also, the Puritan tide (now only beginning to ebb) served to remind man that woman was unclean, sinful, less than he, and the cause of his fall. It was in those years that Patriarchalism was born, emigrated to America, killed Indians, enslaved blacks, conned women with sonorous good manners to get them into the wilderness, then tried to dominate them but never quite succeeded: a woman in a covered wagon with a rifle on her lap is going to be a formidable opponent, as the American woman has proved to be, from Daisy Miller to Kate Millett (a name James would have savored, weakly changing "i" to "a").

What does the American woman want? is the plaintive cry. Doesn't she kill off her husbands with mantis-abandon, inherit the money, become a Mom to Attis-like sons, dominate primary education (most American men are "feminized" in what they would regard as the worst sense of that word by being brought up almost entirely by women and made to conform to American female values which are every bit as twisted as American male values)?

Yet the American woman who seems to have so much is still very much a victim of patriarchal attitudes—after all, she is made to believe that marriage is the most important thing in life, a sentiment peculiarly necessary to a capitalist society in which marriage is still the employer's best means of controlling the employee. The young man with a child and pregnant wife is going to do as he is told. The young man or woman on his own might not be so tractable. Now that organized religion is of little social significance, the great corporations through advertising (remember "Togetherness"?) and hiring policies favor the married, while looking with great suspicion on the bachelor who might be a Commie Weirdo Fag or a Pro-Crypto dyke. As long as marriage (and Betty Friedan's *Feminine Mystique*) are central to our capitalism (and to its depressing Soviet counterpart) neither man nor woman can be regarded as free to be human.

"In a society where men have an overriding interest in the acquisition of wealth, and where women themselves have become a form of property, the link between sexuality and money becomes inextricable." This is grim truth. Most men buy their wives, though neither party would admit to the nature of the transaction, preferring such euphemisms as Marvin is a good provider and Marion is built. Then Marion divorces Marvin and takes him to the cleaners, and he buys with whatever is left a younger model. It is money, not sex, that Puritans want. After all, the English word for "coming" used to be "spending": you spend your seed in the woman's bank and, if the moon is right, nine months later you will get an eight-pound dividend.

Needless to say, if you buy a woman you don't want anyone else using her. To assure your rights, you must uphold all the taboos against any form of sex outside marriage. Figes draws an interesting parallel between our own society and the Mainus, as reported by Margaret Mead.

> There was such a close tie between women and property that adultery was always a threat to the economic system. These people devalued sex, were prudish, and tended to equate the sex act with the excretory functions and, perhaps most significant of all, had commercial prostitution which is rare in primitive societies.

Rousseau is briskly dealt with by the girls: his rights of man were just that, for men. He believed women "should reign in the home as a minister reigns in the state, by contriving to be ordered to do what she wants." Darwin? According to Figes, "Darwin was typically a creature of his age in seeing the class and economic struggles as a continuation of the evolutionary one." In this struggle woman was *hors de combat*. "The chief distinction in the intellectual powers of the two sexes is shown by man attaining to a higher eminence, in whatever he takes up, than woman can attain, etc." Schopenhauer found woman "in every respect backward, lacking in reason and true morality...a kind of middle step between the child and the man, who is the true human being."

Figes finds a link between anti-feminism and anti-Semitism. It is called Nietzsche. "Man should be trained for war and woman for the recreation of the warrior: all else is folly." Like the effeminate Jews, women subvert the warrior ideal, demanding sympathy for the poor and the weak. Hitler's reaction to this rousing philosophy has not gone unnoticed.

Like her fellow polemicists, Figes is at her most glittering with Freud...one almost wrote "poor Freud," as Millett calls him. Apparently Freud's gravest limitation was an inability to question the status quo of the society into which he was born. Politically, he felt that "it is just as impossible to do without control of the mass by a minority as it is to dispense with coercion in the work of civilization. For the masses are lazy and unintelligent."

To Freud, civilization meant a Spartan denial of pleasure in the present in order to enjoy solvency and power in middle age. Unhappily, the main line of Freudian psychoanalysis has served well the status quo by insisting that if one is not happy with one's lot, a better adjustment to society must be made because society is an unalterable fact, not to be trifled with or changed. Now, of course, every assumption about the rights of society as opposed to those of the individual is in question, and Freud's complacency seems almost as odd to us as his wild notion that clitoral excitement was a wicked (immature) thing in a grown woman, and the longer she resisted making the transfer from the tiny pseudopenis to the heavenly inner space of the vagina (Erik Erikson is not in the girls' good books either) the sicker she would become.

One would like to have been a fly on the wall of that Vienna study as one woman after another tearfully admitted to an itch that would not go away, despite the kindly patriarch's attempts to get to the root of the problem. It is a nice irony that the man who said that anatomy is destiny took no trouble to learn woman's anatomy. He did *know* that the penis was the essential symbol and fact of power and primacy; otherwise (and his reasoning was circular) why would girls envy boys' having penises? Why would little boys suffer from fears of castration if they did not instinctively know that the penis is a priceless sign of God the Father, which an envious teeth-lined cunt might want to snap off? Figes's response to Freud's circle is reasonable.

In a society not sexually repressive little boys would be unlikely to develop castration fears; in a society where all the material rewards did not go to those endowed with penises there would be no natural envy of that regalia.

The Patriarchs' counterattack is only now gathering momentum. So far Figes appears to be unknown to United Statesmen, but Millett has been attacked hereabouts with a ferocity usually reserved for major novelists. She should feel important. The two principal spokesmen to weigh in so far are Norman Mailer and Irving Howe. Mailer's answer to Millett ("The Prisoner of Sex" in *Harper's*) gave the impression of being longer than her book *Sexual Politics*. Part of this is due to a style which now resembles H. P. Lovecraft rather more than the interesting, modest Mailer of better days. Or as Emma Cockburn (excellent name for a Women's Libber) pointed out, Mailer's thoughts on sex read like three days of menstrual flow.

Mailer begins by reminding the reader who he is. This is cunning and necessary in a country with no past. We learn of marriages, children, prizes (the Nobel is almost at hand), the great novel he will one day write, the rejection of *Time's* offer to put him on the cover which Millett then gets for, among other things, attacking him. His credits given, he counterattacks, says she writes like a tough faggot, a literary Mafiosa, calls her comrade and commissar. He then makes some excellent points on her disingenuous use of quotations from Miller and Lawrence (she has a tendency to replace those qualifying phrases which make the Patriarchs seem human with three dots).

But Mailer's essential argument boils down to the following points. Masturbation is bad and so is contraception because the whole point to sex between man and woman is conception. Well, that's what the Bible says, too. He links homosexuality with evil. The man who gives in to his homosexual drives is consorting with the enemy. Worse, not only does he betray moral weakness by not fighting those drives but he is a coward for not daring to enter into competition with other Alpha males for toothsome females. This is dizzy but at least a new thought. One of the many compliments Mailer has tendered the Patriarchs over the years is never having succumbed to whatever homosexual urges they might have had. Now, to his shock, instead of getting at least a Congressional Medal of Honor for hero-ism, he sees slowly descending upon his brow an unmistakable dunce cap. All that hanging about boxers, to no good end!

Finally, Mailer's attitude toward woman is pretty much that of any VFW commander in heartland America. He can never under-stand that a woman is not simply a creature to be used for breeding (his "awe" at the thought of her procreative function is blarney), that she is as human as he is, and that he is dangerous to her since did not the Lord thy God say, "In sorrow thou shalt bring forth children. And thy desire shall be thy husband. And he shall rule over thee." Which brings us to Figes's remark, "We cannot be iconoclasts, we cannot relinquish the old gods because so much has been sacrificed to them." Irving Howe's tone is apoplectic. He *knows* what the relations between men and women ought to be and no Millett is going to change his mind or pervert other women if he can do anything about it—which is to write a great deal on the subject in a magazine piece called "The Middle Class Mind of Kate Millett." Astonishingly enough, the phrase "middle class" is used in a pejorative sense, not the most tactful thing to do in a middle-class country. Particularly when one is not only middle class oneself but possessed of a brow that is just this side of high.

Anyway, Howe was aroused enough to address to her a series of *ad hominem (ad hysteram?)* insults that are startling even by the vicious and mindless standards of New York bookchat writing. Millett is "squalid," "feckless," "morally shameful," a failed scholar, a female impersonator, and so on. But Howe is never able to take on the essential argument of the girls. Men have enslaved women, made them second-rate citizens, made them hate themselves (this to me is the worst of all...I'm a man's woman, says the beauty complacently, I don't like other women; meaning, I don't like myself), and now that woman is beginning to come alive, to see herself as the equal of man, Rabbi Howe is going to strike her down for impertinence, just as the good Christian knows that "it is shameful for women to speak in church."

Howe has always had an agreeable gift for literary demolition and his mind, though hardly of the first quality, is certainly good by American academic standards. But now watch him tie himself in a knot. Millett makes the point, as Figes does, that the Nazis were anti-woman and pro-family. Woman was breeder, man was warrior. Now Irving doesn't want the Nazis to be so "sensible," so much like himself. He writes:

> The comedy of all this is that Miss Millett prints, at one point, a footnote quoting from a book by Joseph Folsom. "The Nazis have always wanted to strengthen the family as an instrument of the state. *State interest is always paramount.* Germany does not hesitate to turn a husband against a wife or children against parents when political loyalty is involved." (Emphasis added.) Miss Millett prints this footnote but clearly does not understand it: otherwise she would recognize how completely it undermines her claim that in the totalitarian countries the "sexual counterrevolution" consisted in the reinforcement of the family.

This passage would make a good test question for a class in logic. Find where Howe misses or distorts the point to the Folsom footnote. Point one: the Nazis strengthened the family yet put the state first. All agreed? What does this mean? It means that, on occasion, Nazis would try to turn members of a family against one another *"when political loyalty is involved."* (Emphasis added.) O.K.? Well, class, how many people are politically subversive in any country at any time? Not many, alas; therefore Millett's point still stands that the Nazis celebrated old-time family virtues except in cases of suspected subversion.

Howe's piece is full of this sort of thing and I can only assume that his usually logical mind has been unhinged by all these unnatural girls. Howe ends with a celebration of the values of his immigrant parents in the Depression years. Apparently his mother was no more a drudge than his father (but why in a good society should either be a drudge?), and they were happy in the old-time Mosaic, St. Pauline, Freudian way, and…well, this hymn to tribal values was rather better sung by the judge in the movie version of *Little Murders*.

Those who have been treated cruelly will treat others cruelly. This seems to be a fact of our condition. The Patriarchs have every reason to be fearful of woman's revenge should she achieve equality. He is also faced with the nightmare (for him) of being used as a sexual object or, worse, being ignored (the menacing cloud in the middle distance is presently no larger than a vibrator). He is fighting back on every front.

Take pornography. Though female nudes have been usually acceptable in our Puritan culture, until recently the male nude was unacceptable to the Patriarchs. After all, the male—any male—is a stand-in for God, and God wears a suit at all times, or at least jockey shorts. Now, thanks to randy Lilith, the male can be shown entirely nude but, say the American censors, never with an erection. The holy of holies, the totem of our race, the symbol of the Patriarchs' victory over the Great Mother must be respected. Also, as psychologists point out, though women are not as prone to stimulus through looking at pictures as men (is this innate or the result of conditioning?), they are more excited by pictures of the male erect than of the male at ease. And excitement of course is bad for them, gives them ideas, makes them insatiable; even the ancient Greeks, though freer in sexual matters than we, took marriage seriously. As a result, only unmarried girls could watch naked young men play because young girls ought to be able to look over a field which married women had better not know about.

Today we are witnessing the breakup of patterns thousands of years old. The patriarchal response is predictable: if man on top of woman has been the pattern for all our known history, it must be right. This of course was the same argument he made when the institution of slavery was challenged. After all, slavery was quite as old an institution as marriage. With the rejection of the idea of ownership of one person by another at the time of our Civil War, Women's Lib truly began. If you could not own a black man, you could not own a woman either. So the war began. Needless to say, the forces of reaction are very much in the saddle (in every sense), and women must fight for their equality in a system which wants to keep them in manageable family groups, buying consumer goods, raising future consumers, until the end of time—or the world's raw resources, which is rather closer at hand.

Curiously enough, not even Figes senses what is behind this new restiveness, this new desire to exist not as male or female but as human. It is very simple: we are breeding ourselves into extinction. We cannot feed the people now alive. In thirty-seven years the world's population will double unless we have the "good luck" to experience on the grandest scale famine, plague, war. To survive we must stop making babies at the current rate, and this can only be accomplished by breaking the ancient stereotypes of man the warrior, woman the breeder. The patriarchal roar is that of our tribal past, quite unsuitable, as the old Stalinists used to say, to new necessities.

Figes feels that a change in the economic system will free women (and men) from unwanted roles. I have another idea. Free the sexes first and the system will have to change. There will be no housewife to be conned into buying things she does not need. But all this is in the future. The present is the battleground, and the next voice you hear will be that of a patriarch, defending his attitudes—on a stack of Bibles.

The New York Review of Books
July 22, 1971

Eleanor Roosevelt

*N*icholas and Alexandra. Now *Eleanor and Franklin*. Who's next for the tandem treatment? *Dick and Pat? J. Edgar and Clyde?* Obviously there is a large public curious as to what goes on in the bedrooms of Winter Palace and White House, not to mention who passed whom in the corridors of power. All in all, this kind of voyeurism is not a bad thing in a country where, like snakes, the people shed their past each year ("Today nobody even remembers there *was* a Depression!" Eleanor Roosevelt exclaimed to me in 1960, shaking her head at the dullness of an audience we had been jointly trying to inspire). But though Americans dislike history, they do like soap operas about the sexual misbehavior and the illnesses—particularly the illnesses—of real people in high places: "Will handsome, ambitious Franklin ever regain the use of his legs? Tune in tomorrow."

The man responsible for the latest peek at our masters, off-duty and on, is Joseph Lash. A journalist by trade, a political activist by inclination, an old friend of Eleanor Roosevelt as luck would have it (hers as well as his), Mr. Lash has written a very long book. Were it shorter, it would have a smaller sale but more readers. Unfortunately, Mr. Lash has not been able to resist the current fashion in popular biography: he puts in everything. The Wastebasket School leaves to the reader the task of arranging the mess the author has collected.

Bank balances, invitations to parties, funerals, vastations in the Galerie d'Apollon—all are presented in a cool democratic way. Nothing is more important than anything else. At worst the result is "scholarly" narrative; at best, lively soap opera. No more does prophet laurel flower in the abandoned Delphi of Plutarch, Johnson, Carlyle, Strachey: Ph.D. mills have polluted the sacred waters.

Objections duly noted, I confess that I found *Eleanor and Franklin* completely fascinating. Although Mr. Lash is writing principally about Eleanor Roosevelt, someone I knew and admired, I still think it impossible for anyone to read his narrative without being as moved as I was. After all, Eleanor Roosevelt was a last (*the* last? the *only?*) flower of that thorny Puritan American conscience which was, when it was good, very, very good, and now it's quite gone things are horrid.

A dozen years ago, Mrs. Roosevelt asked me to come see her at Hyde Park. I drove down to Val-Kill cottage from where I lived on the Hudson. With some difficulty, I found the house. The front door was open. I went inside. "Anybody home?" No answer. I opened the nearest door. A bathroom. To my horror, there in front of the toilet bowl, stood Eleanor Roosevelt. She gave a startled squeak. "Oh, *dear!*" Then, resignedly, "Well, now you know *everything.*" And she stepped aside, revealing a dozen gladiolas she had been arranging in the toilet bowl. "It does keep them fresh." So began our political and personal acquaintance.

I found her remarkably candid about herself and others. So much so that I occasionally made notes, proud that I alone knew the truth about this or that. Needless to say, just about every "confidence" she bestowed on me appears in Mr. Lash's book and I can testify that he is a remarkably accurate recorder of both her substance and style. In fact, reading him is like having her alive again, hearing that odd, fluting yet precise voice with its careful emphases, its nervous glissade of giggles, the great smile which was calculated not only to avert wrath but warn potential enemies that here was a lioness quite capable of making a meal of anyone.

Then there were those shrewd, gray-blue eyes which stared and stared at you when you were not looking at her. When you did catch her at it, she would blush—even in her seventies the delicate gray skin would grow pink—giggle, and look away. When she was not interested in someone she would ask a polite question; then remove her glasses, which contained a hearing aid, and nod pleasantly—assuming she did not drop into one of her thirty-second catnaps.

The growing up of Eleanor Roosevelt is as interesting to read about as it was, no doubt, hard to have lived through. Born plain. Daughter of an alcoholic father whom she adored. Brought up by a sternly religious maternal grandmother in a house at Tivoli, New York, some thirty miles north of Hyde Park, where her cousin Franklin was also growing up, a fatherless little boy spoiled by his mother, the dread Sara Delano, for forty years the constant never-to-be-slain dragon in Eleanor's life.

Long after the death of Mrs. James (as Sara Delano Roosevelt was known to the Valley), Eleanor would speak of her with a kind of wonder and a slight distention of the knotty veins at her temples. "Only once did I ever *openly* quarrel with Mrs. James. I had come back to Hyde Park to find that she had allowed the children to run wild. Nothing I'd wanted done for them had been done. 'Mama,' I said" (accent on the second syllable, incidentally, in the French fashion), " 'you are *impossible!*' " "And what did she say?" I asked. "Why, nothing." Mrs. Roosevelt looked at me with some surprise. "You see, she was a grande dame. She never noticed *anything* unpleasant. By the next day she'd quite forgotten it. But of course I couldn't. I forgive..." One of her favorite lines, which often cropped up in her conversation as well as—now—in the pages of Mr. Lash's book, "but I *never* forget."

But if Mrs. James was to be for Eleanor a life's antagonist, her father was to be the good—if unlikely—angel, a continuing spur to greatness, loved all the better after death. Elliott Roosevelt was charming and talented (many of his letters are remarkably vivid and well-written) and adored by everyone, including his older brother Theodore, the President-to-be. Elliott had everything, as they say; unfortunately, he was an alcoholic. When his drinking finally got out of control, the family sent him south; kept him away from Eleanor and her young brother Hall (himself to be an alcoholic). During these long absences, father and daughter exchanged what were, in effect, love letters, usually full of plans to meet. But when those rare meetings did take place, he was apt to vanish and leave her sitting alone at his club until, hours later, someone remembered she was there and took her home.

Yet in his letters, if not in his life, Elliott was a Puritan moralist—with charm. He wanted his daughter, simply, to be good. It is hard now to imagine what being good is, but to that generation there was not much ambiguity about the word. As Eleanor wrote in 1927, in a plainly autobiographical sketch,

> She was an ugly little thing, keenly conscious of her deficiencies, and her father, the only person who really cared for her, was away much of the time; but he never criticized her or blamed her, instead he wrote her letters and stories, telling her how he dreamed of her growing up and what they would do together in the future, but she must be truthful, loyal, brave, well-educated, or the woman he dreamed of would not be there when the wonderful day came for them to fare forth together. The child was full of fears and because of them lying was easy; she had no intellectual stimulus at that time and *yet she made herself as the years went on into a fairly good copy of the picture he painted.*

As it turned out, Eleanor did not fare forth with her father Elliott but with his cousin Franklin, and she was indeed all the things her father had wanted her to be, which made her marriage difficult and her life work great.

In 1894, Elliott died at 313 West 102nd Street, attended by a mistress. The ten-year-old Eleanor continued to live in the somber house at Tivoli, her character forming in a way to suggest that something unusual was at work. The sort of world she was living in could hardly have inspired her to write, as she did at fourteen:

> Those who are ambitious & make a place & a name in the great world for themselves are nearly always despised & laughed at by lesser souls who could not do as well & all they do for the good of men is construed into wrong & yet they do the good and they leave their mark upon the ages & if they had had no ambition would they have ever made a mark?

This was written in the era of Ward McAllister, when the best circles were still intent on gilding the age with bright excess. Eleanor was already unlike others of her class and time.

The turning point—the turning on—of her life occurred at Allenswood, an English school run by the formidable Mlle. Souvestre, a freethinker (doubtless shocking to Eleanor, who remained a believing Christian to the end of her days) and a political liberal. Readers of *Olivia* know the school through the eyes of its author, Dorothy Bussy—a sister of Lytton Strachey. Allenswood was a perfect atmosphere in which to form a character and "furnish a mind." The awkward withdrawn American girl bloomed, even became popular. Some of Eleanor's essays from this period are very good. On literature:

"The greatest men often write very badly and all the better for them. It is not in them that we look for perfect style but in the secondary writers (Horace, La Bruyère)—one must know the masters by heart, adore them, try to think as they do and then leave them forever. For technical instruction there is little of profit to draw from the learned and polished men of genius."

So exactly did Flaubert speak of Balzac (but it is unlikely that Eleanor could have read that report of dinner Chez Magny). She perfected her French, learned Italian and German, and became civilized, according to the day's best standards.

Nearly eighteen, Eleanor returned to America. It was 1902: a time of great hope for the Republic. Uncle Theodore was the youngest President in history. A reformer (up to a point), he was a bright example of the "right" kind of ambition. But Tivoli was no more cheerful than before. In fact, life there was downright dangerous because of Uncle Vallie, a splendid alcoholic huntsman who enjoyed placing himself at an upstairs window and then, as the family gathered on the lawn, opening fire with a shotgun, forcing them to duck behind trees (in the Forties there was a young critic who solemnly assured us that America could never have a proper literature because the country lacked a rich and complex class system!). It is no wonder that Eleanor thought the Volstead Act a fine thing and refused to serve drink at home for many years.

Eleanor came out, as was expected, and suffered from what she considered her ungainly appearance. Yet she was much liked, particularly by her cousin Franklin (known to *their* cousin Alice as "The Feather Duster": "You know, the sort of person you wouldn't ask to dinner, but for afterward"). During this period, Eleanor's social conscience was stirring. She worked at a settlement house where she not only saw how the poor lived but met a generation of women reformers, many of them also active in the suffragette movement. Eleanor was a slow convert to women's rights. But a convert she became. Just as she was able to change her prejudices against Jews and blacks (she was once attacked by the NAACP for referring to the colored, as they were then known, as "darkies").

Franklin began to court her. The letters he wrote her she destroyed—no doubt, a symbolic act when she found him out in adultery. But her letters remain. They are serious (she had been nicknamed "Granny"); they are also ambitious. For a young man who had made up his mind that he would rise to the top of the world she was a perfect mate. It is a sign of Franklin's genius—if that is the word—that even in his spoiled and callow youth he had sense enough to realize what Eleanor was all about.

The marriage ceremony was fine comedy. The bride and groom were entirely overshadowed by Uncle Ted. Eleanor was amused, Franklin not. Mr. Lash misses—or omits—one important factor in the marriage. For all of Eleanor's virtues (not immediately apparent to the great world which Franklin always rather liked) she was a catch for one excellent reason: she was the President's niece, and not just your average run-of-the-mill President but a unique political phenomenon who had roused the country in a way no other President had since Jackson. I suspect this weighed heavily with Franklin. Certainly when it came time for him to run for office as a Democrat, many Republicans voted for him simply because his name was Roosevelt and he was married to the paladin's niece.

As the world knows, Franklin and Eleanor were a powerful political partnership. But at the personal level, the marriage must never have been happy. For one thing, Eleanor did not like sex, as she confided in later years to her daughter. Franklin obviously did. Then there was his mother. The lives of the young couple were largely managed by Mrs. James, who remained mistress of the house at Hyde Park until she died. It is poignant to read a note from Eleanor to

Franklin after the old lady's death in 1941, asking permission to move furniture around—permission generally not granted, for the place was to remain, as long as Franklin lived (and as it is now), the way his mother wanted it—and the most God-awful Victorian taste it is. But surroundings never meant much to any of the family, although Mrs. Roosevelt once told me how "Mr. Truman showed me around the White House, which he'd just redone, and he was so proud of the upstairs which looked to me *exactly* like a Sheraton Hotel!"

Franklin went to the State Senate. Eleanor learned to make speeches—not an easy matter because her voice was high, with a tendency to get out of control. Finally, she went to a voice coach. "You must tell President Kennedy. The exercises did wonders for my voice." A giggle. "Yes, I know, I don't sound *very* good but I was certainly a lot worse before, and Mr. Kennedy does need help because he talks much too fast and too high for the average person to understand him."

I remarked that in the television age it was quite enough to watch the speaker. She was not convinced. One spoke to the people in order to *educate* them. That was what politics was all about, as she was among the last to believe.

It is startling how much is known at the time about the private lives of the great. My grandfather Senator Gore's political career ended in 1936 after a collision with President Roosevelt ("This is the last relief check you'll get if Gore is reelected" was the nice tactic in Oklahoma), but in earlier times they were both in the liberal wing of the Democratic party and when Franklin came to Washington as Assistant Secretary of the Navy under Wilson, he was on friendly terms with the Senator. Washington was a small town then and everyone knew all about everyone else's private life. Not long ago Alice Longworth managed to startle even me by announcing, at a dinner party: "Daisy Harriman told me that every time she was alone with Senator Gore he would pounce on her. I could never understand why he liked her. After all, he was *blind*. But then Daisy always smelled nice."*

Meanwhile, the Gores were keeping track of the Roosevelts.

---

*My sister responded to this story by reminding Mrs. Longworth of a certain peculiar episode in the Governor's office at Albany between TR and a lady. Mrs. Longworth was not amused.

Franklin fell in love with Eleanor's young secretary, Lucy Mercer, and they conducted an intense affair (known to everyone in Washington except Eleanor who discovered the truth in the tried-and-true soap opera way: innocently going through her husband's mail when he was ill). Senator Gore used to say, "What a trial Eleanor must be! She waits up all night in the vestibule until he comes home." I never knew exactly what this meant. Now Mr. Lash tells us "the vestibule story." Angry at her husband's attentions to Lucy at a party, Eleanor went home alone but because Franklin had the keys, she spent much of the night sitting on the stoop.

Later, confronted with proof of Franklin's adultery, Eleanor acted decisively. She would give him a divorce but, she pointed out, she had five children and Lucy would have to bring them up. Lucy, a Catholic, and Franklin, a politician-on-the-make, agreed to cool it. But toward the end of his life they began to see each other again. He died with Lucy in the room at Warm Springs and Eleanor far away. Eleanor knew none of this until the day of her husband's death. From what she later wrote about that day, a certain amount of normal grief seems not to have been present.

When Franklin got polio in 1921, Eleanor came into her own. On his behalf, she joined committees, kept an eye on the political situation, pursued her own good works. When the determined couple finally arrived at the White House, Eleanor became a national figure in her own right. She had her own radio program. She wrote a syndicated column for the newspapers. She gave regular press conferences. At last she was loved, and on the grandest scale. She was also hated. But at fourteen she had anticipated everything ("It is better to be ambitious & do something than to be unambitious & do nothing").

Much of what Mr. Lash writes is new to me (or known and forgotten), particularly Eleanor's sponsorship of Arthurdale, an attempt to create a community in West Virginia where out-of-work miners could each own a house, a bit of land to grow things on, and work for decent wages at a nearby factory. This was a fine dream and a bureaucratic catastrophe. The houses were haphazardly designed, while the factory was not forthcoming (for years any industrialist who wanted to be invited to the White House had only to suggest to Eleanor that he might bring industry to Arthurdale). The right wing of course howled about socialism.

The right wing in America has always believed that those who have money are good people and those who lack it are bad people. At a deeper level, our conservatives are true Darwinians and think that the weak and the poor ought to die off, leaving the spoils to the fit. Certainly a do-gooder is the worst thing anyone can be, a societal pervert who would alter with government subsidy nature's harsh but necessary way with the weak. Eleanor always understood the nature of the enemy: she was a Puritan, too. But since she was Christian and not Manichaean, she felt obliged to work on behalf of those dealt a bad hand at birth. Needless to say, Franklin was quite happy to let her go about her business, increasing his majorities.

"Eleanor has this state trooper she lives with in a cottage near Hyde Park." I never believed that one but, by God, here the trooper is in the pages of Mr. Lash. Sergeant Earl R. Miller was first assigned to the Roosevelts in Albany days. Then he became Eleanor's friend. For many years she mothered him, was nice to his girlfriends and wives, all perfectly innocent—to anyone but a Republican. It is a curious fact of American political life that the right wing is enamored of the sexual smear. Eleanor to me: "There are actually people in Hyde Park who knew Franklin all his life and said that he did not have polio but the sort of disease you get from not living the *right* sort of life."

The left wing plays dirty pool, too, but I have no recollection of their having organized whispering campaigns of a sexual nature against Nixon, say, the way the right so often does against liberal figures. Knowing Eleanor's active dislike of sex as a subject and, on the evidence of her daughter, as a fact, I think it most unlikely she ever had an affair with anyone. But she did crave affection, and jealously held on to her friends, helped them, protected them—often unwisely. Mr. Lash describes most poignantly Eleanor's grief when she realized that *her* friend Harry Hopkins had cold-bloodedly shifted his allegiance to Franklin.

Eleanor was also faced with the President's secretary and *de facto* wife Missy Le Hand ("Everybody knows the old man's been living with her for years," said one of the Roosevelt sons to my father who had just joined the subcabinet. My father, an innocent West Pointer, from that moment on regarded the Roosevelt family arrangements as not unlike those of Ibn Saud). Yet when Missy was dying, it was Eleanor who would ring her up. Franklin simply dropped her. But then Missy was probably not surprised. She once told Fulton Oursler that the President "was really incapable of a personal friendship with anyone."

Mr. Lash writes a good deal about Eleanor's long friendship with two tweedy ladies, Marion Dickerman and Nancy Cook. For years Eleanor shared Val-Kill cottage with them; jointly they ran a furniture factory and the Todhunter School, where Eleanor taught until she went to the White House. The relationship of the three women seems unusually tangled, and Mr. Lash cannot do much with it. Things ended badly with an exchange of letters, filled with uncharacteristic bitterness on Eleanor's side. If only the author of *Olivia* could have had a go at that subject.

In a sense Eleanor had no personal life after the White House years began. She was forever on the go (and did not cease motion during the long widowhood). She suffered many disappointments from friends and family. I remember her amused description of Caroline Kennedy and what a good thing it was that the two Kennedy children would still be very young when they left the White House because, she frowned and shook her head, "It is a terrible place for young people to grown up in, continually flattered and—*used*."

I was with her the day the news broke that a son had married yet again. While we were talking, he rang her and she smiled and murmured, over and over, "Yes, dear…yes, I'm very happy." Then when she hung up, her face set like stone. "You would think that he might have told his mother *first*, before the press." But that was a rare weakness. Her usual line was "people are what they are, you can't change them." Since she had obviously begun life as the sort of Puritan who thought people not only could but must be changed, this later tolerance was doubtless achieved at some cost.

When I was selected as Democratic-Liberal candidate for Congress, Eleanor (I called her Mrs. R) was at first cool to the idea— I had known her slightly all my life (she had liked my father, detested my grandfather). But as the campaign got going and I began to move up in the polls and it suddenly looked as if, wonder of wonders, Dutchess County might go Democratic in a congressional election for the first time in fifty years (since Franklin's senatorial race, in fact), she became more and more excited. She joined me at a number of meetings. She gave a tea at Val-Kill for the women workers in the campaign. Just as the women were leaving, the telephone rang. She spoke a few minutes in a low voice, hung up, said good-by to the last of the ladies, took me aside for some political counsel, was exactly as always except that the tears were streaming down her face. Driving home, I heard on the radio that her favorite granddaughter had just been killed.

In later years, though Eleanor would talk—if asked—about the past, she was not given to strolls down memory lane. In fact, she was contemptuous of old people who lived in the past, particularly those politicians prone to the Ciceronian vice of exaggerating their contribution to history, a category in which she firmly placed that quaint Don Quixote of the cold war, Dean Acheson. She was also indifferent to her own death. "I remember Queen Wilhelmina when she came to visit during the war" (good democrat that she was, nothing royal was alien to Eleanor) "and she would sit under a tree on the lawn and commune with the dead. She would even try to get *me* interested in spiritualism but I always said: Since we're going to be dead such a long time anyway it's rather a waste of time chatting with all of them *before* we get there."

Although a marvelous friend and conscience to the world, she was, I suspect, a somewhat unsatisfactory parent. Descendants and their connections often look rather hard and hurt at the mention of her. For those well-placed by birth to do humanity's work, she had no patience if they were—ultimate sin—unhappy. A woman I know went to discuss with her a disastrous marriage; she came away chilled to the bone. These things were to be borne.

What did Eleanor feel about Franklin? That is an enigma, and perhaps she herself never sorted it out. He was complex and cold and cruel (so many of her stories of life with him would end, "And then I *fled* from the table in tears!"). He liked telling her the latest "Eleanor stories"; his sense of fun was heavy. A romantic, Mr. Lash thinks she kept right on loving him to the end (a favorite poem of the two was E. B. Browning's "Unless you can swear, 'For life, for death,'/Oh, fear to call it loving!"). But I wonder. Certainly he hurt her mortally in their private relationship; worse, he often let her down in their public partnership. Yet she respected his cunning even when she deplored his tactics.

I wonder, too, how well she understood him. One day Eleanor told me about something in his will that had surprised her. He wanted one side of his coffin to be left open. "Well, we hadn't seen the will when he was buried and of course it was too late when we did read it. But what *could* he have meant?" I knew and told her: "He wanted, physically, to get back into circulation as quickly as possible, in the rose garden." She looked at me as if this were the maddest thing she had ever heard.

I suspect the best years of Eleanor's life were the widowhood. She was on her own, no longer an adjunct to his career. In this regard, I offer Mr. Lash an anecdote. We were four at table: Mrs. Tracy Dows, Mrs. Roosevelt her uncle David Gray (our wartime Ambassador to Ireland), and myself. Eleanor began: "When Mr. Joe Kennedy came back from London, during the war…" David Gray interrupted her. "Damned coward, Joe Kennedy! Terrified they were going to drop a bomb on him." Eleanor merely grinned and continued. "Anyway he came back to Boston and gave that *unfortunate* interview in which he was…well, somewhat *critical* of us."

She gave me her teacher's smile, and an aside. "You see, it's a very funny thing but whatever people say about us we almost always hear. I don't know *how* this happens but it does." David Gray scowled. "Unpleasant fellow, that Joe. Thought he knew everything. Damned coward." I said nothing, since I was trying to persuade Eleanor to support the wicked Joe's son at the Democratic convention; something she could not, finally, bring herself to do.

"Well, *my* Franklin said, 'We better have him down here'—we were at Hyde Park—'and see what he has to say.' So Mr. Kennedy arrived at Rhinecliff on the train and I met him and took him straight to Franklin. Well, ten minutes later one of the aides came and said, 'The President wants to see you right away.' This was unheard of. So I *rushed* into the office and there was Franklin, white as a sheet. He asked Mr. Kennedy to step outside and then he said, and his voice was *shaking*, 'I never want to see that man again as long as I live." David Gray nodded: "Wanted us to make a deal with Hitler." But Eleanor was not going to get into that. "Whatever it was, it was *very* bad. Then

Franklin said, 'Get him out of here,' and I said, 'But, dear, you've invited him for the weekend, and we've got guests for lunch and the train doesn't leave until two,' and Franklin said, 'Then you drive him around Hyde Park and put him on that train,' and I did and it was the most dreadful four hours of my life!" She laughed. Then, seriously: "I wonder if the *true* story of Joe Kennedy will ever be known."

To read Mr. Lash's book is to relive not only the hopeful period in American life (1933-40) but the brief time of world triumph (1941-45). The book stops, mercifully, with the President's death and the end of Eleanor and Franklin (Mr. Lash is correct to put her name first; of the two she was greater). Also, the end of...what? American innocence? Optimism? From 1950 on, our story has been progressively more and more squalid. Nor can one say it is a lack of the good and the great in high places: they are always there when needed. Rather the corruption of empire has etiolated the words themselves. Now we live in a society which none of us much likes, all would like to change, but no one knows how. Most ominous of all, there is now a sense that what has gone wrong for us may be irreversible. The empire will not liquidate itself. The lakes and rivers and seas will not become fresh again. The arms race will not stop. Land ruined by insecticides and fertilizers will not be restored. The smash-up will come.

To read of Eleanor and Franklin is to weep at what we have lost. Gone is the ancient American sense that whatever is wrong with human society can be put right by human action. Eleanor never stopped believing this. A simple faith, no doubt simplistic—but it gave her a stoic serenity. On the funeral train from Georgia to Washington: "I lay in my berth all night with the window shade up, looking out at the countryside he had loved and watching the faces of the people at stations, and even at the crossroads, who came to pay their last tribute all through the night. The only recollection I clearly have is thinking about 'The Lonesome Train,' the musical poem about Lincoln's death. ('A lonesome train on a lonesome track/Seven coaches painted black/A slow train, a quiet train/Carrying Lincoln home again...'). I had always liked it so well—and now this was so much like it."

I had other thoughts in 1962 at Hyde Park as I stood alongside the thirty-third, the thirty-fourth, the thirty-fifth, and the thirty-sixth

Presidents of the United States, not to mention all the remaining figures of the Roosevelt era who had assembled for her funeral (unlike the golden figures in Proust's last chapter, they all looked if not smaller than life smaller than legend—so many shrunken March of Time dolls soon to be put away). Whether or not one thought of Eleanor Roosevelt as a world ombudsman or as a chronic explainer or as a scourge of the selfish, she was like no one else in her usefulness. As the box containing her went past me, I thought, well, that's that. We're really on our own now.

The New York Review of Books
November 18, 1971

Christopher Isherwood's Kind

In 1954 I had lunch with Christopher Isherwood at MGM. He told me that he had just written a film for Lana Turner. The subject? Diane de Poitiers. When I laughed, he shook his head. "Lana can do it," he said grimly. Later, as we walked about the lot and I told him that I hoped to get a job as a writer at the studio since I could no longer live on my royalties as a novelist (and would not teach), Christopher gave me as melancholy a look as those bright—even harsh—blue eyes can affect. "Don't," he said with great intensity, posing against the train beneath whose wheels Greta Garbo as Anna Karenina made her last dive, "become a hack like me." But we both knew that this was play-acting. Like his friend Aldous Huxley (like William Faulkner and many others), he had been able to write to order for movies while never ceasing to do his own work in his own way. Those whom Hollywood destroyed were never worth saving. Not only has Isherwood written successfully for the camera, he has been, notoriously, in his true art, *the* camera.

"I am a camera." With those four words at the beginning of the novel *Goodbye to Berlin* (1939), Christopher Isherwood became famous. Because of those four words he has been written of (and sometimes written off) as a naturalistic writer, a recorder of surfaces, a film director *manqué*. Although it is true that, up to a point,

Isherwood often appears to be recording perhaps too impartially the lights, the shadows, the lions that come within the area of his vision, he is never without surprises; in the course of what looks to be an undemanding narrative, the author will suddenly produce a Polaroid shot of the reader reading, an alarming effect achieved by the sly use of the second person pronoun. You never know quite where *you* stand in relation to an Isherwood work.

During the half century that Christopher Isherwood has been more or less at the center of Anglo-American literature, he has been much scrutinized by friends, acquaintances, purveyors of book-chat. As memoirs of the Twenties, Thirties, Forties now accumulate, Isherwood keeps cropping up as a principal figure, and if he does not always seem in character, it is because he is not an easy character to fix upon the page. Also, he has so beautifully invented himself in the Berlin stories, *Lions and Shadows, Down There on a Visit,* and now *Christopher and His Kind,* that anyone who wants to snap yet again this lion's shadow has his work cut out for him. After all, nothing is harder to reflect than a mirror.

To date the best developed portrait of Isherwood occurs in Stephen Spender's autobiography *World Within World* (1951). Like Isherwood, Spender was a part of that upper-middle-class generation which came of age just after World War I. For the lucky few able to go to the right schools and universities, postwar England was still a small and self-contained society where everyone knew everyone else. In fact, English society was simply an extension of school. But something disagreeable had happened at school just before the Isherwoods and Spenders came on stage. World War I had killed off the better part of a generation of graduates, and among the graduated dead was Isherwood's father. There was a long shadow over the young...of dead fathers, brothers; also of dead or dying attitudes. Rebellion was in the air. New things were promised.

In every generation there are certain figures who are who they are at an early age: stars *in ovo*. People want to know them; imitate them; destroy them. Isherwood was such a creature and Stephen Spender fell under his spell even before they met.

At nineteen Spender was an undergraduate at Oxford; another undergraduate was the twenty-one-year-old W. H. Auden. Isherwood himself (three years Auden's senior) was already out in the world; he had got himself sent down from Cambridge by sending up a written examination. He had deliberately broken out of the safe, cozy university world, and the brilliant but cautious Auden revered him. Spender writes how, "according to Auden, [Isherwood] held no opinions whatever about anything. He was wholly and simply interested in people. He did not like or dislike them, judge them favorably or unfavorably. He simply regarded them as material for his Work. At the same time, he was the Critic in whom Auden had absolute trust. If Isherwood disliked a poem, Auden destroyed it without demur."

Auden was not above torturing the young Spender: "Auden withheld the privilege of meeting Isherwood from me." Writing twenty years later, Spender cannot resist adding, "Isherwood was not famous at this time. He had published one novel, *All the Conspirators*, for which he had received an advance of £30 from his publishers, and which had been not very favorably reviewed." But Isherwood was already a legend, as Spender concedes, and worldly success has nothing to do with legends. Eventually Auden brought them together. Spender was not disappointed:

> He simplified all the problems which entangled me, merely by describing his own life and his own attitudes towards these things.... Isherwood had a peculiarity of being attractively disgusted and amiably bitter.... But there was a positive as well as negative side to his beliefs. He spoke of being Cured and Saved with as much intensity as any Salvationist.

In Isherwood's earliest memoir, *Lions and Shadows* (1938), we are given Isherwood's first view of Spender, a sort of reverse-angle shot (and known to Spender when he wrote *World Within World*): "[Spender] burst in upon us, blushing, sniggering loudly, contriving to trip over the edge of the carpet—an immensely tall, shambling boy of nineteen, with a great scarlet poppy-face, wild frizzy hair, and eyes the violent color of bluebells." The camera turns, watching it all. "In an instant, without introductions, we were all laughing and talking at the top of our voices...He inhabited a world of self-created and absorbing drama, into which each new acquaintance was immediately conscripted to play a part. [Spender] illuminated you" (the second person now starts to take hold: the film's *voice-over* has begun its aural seduction) "like an expressionist producer, with the crudest and most eccentric of spot-lights: you were transfigured, became grandiose, sinister, brilliantly ridiculous or impossibly beautiful, in accordance with his arbitrary, prearranged conception of your role." *You, spot-light, producer....*

In *The Whispering Gallery,* the publisher and critic John Lehmann describes his first meeting with Spender in 1930 and how he "talked a great deal about Auden, who shared (and indeed had inspired) so many of his views, and also about a certain young novelist Christopher Isherwood, who, he told me, had settled in Berlin in stark poverty and was an even greater rebel against the England we lived in than he was...." When Lehmann went to work for Leonard and Virginia Woolf at the Hogarth Press, he got them to publish Isherwood's second novel, *The Memorial.*

Lehmann noted that the generation's Novelist

> was much shorter than myself, he nevertheless had a power of dominating which small people of outstanding intelligence or imaginative equipment often possess. One of my favorite private fancies has always been that the most ruthless war that underlies our civilized existence...is the war between the tall and the short.

Even so, "It was impossible not to be drawn to him.... And yet for some months after our first meeting...our relations remained rather formal: perhaps it was the sense of alarm that seemed to hang in the air when his smile was switched off, a suspicion he seemed to radiate that one might after all be in league with the 'enemy,' a phrase which covered everything he had, with a pure hatred, cut himself off from in English life...."

In 1931 a cold transatlantic eye was turned upon both Isherwood and Spender. The twenty-year-old Paul Bowles presented himself to Isherwood in Berlin. "When I came to Isherwood," Bowles records in *Without Stopping,* "he said he would take me himself to Spender." Bowles did not approve of Spender's looking and acting the part of a poet: "Whether Spender wrote poetry or not seemed relatively unimportant; that at all costs the fact should not be evident was what should have mattered to him." Bowles acknowledges that this primness reflected the attitudes of his Puritan family and background. "I soon found that Isherwood with Spender was a very different person from Isherwood by himself." But then the camera and its director are bound to alter according to light, weather, cast. "Together they were overwhelmingly British, two members of a secret society constantly making references to esoteric data not available to outsiders." This strikes me as an accurate and poignant description of the difference between American and English writers. The English tend to play off (and with) one another; while the Americans are, if not Waldenized solitaries, Darwinized predators constantly preying upon one another. I think it significant that when Paul Bowles came to write *his* autobiography, he chose a prose style not unlike that of Julius Caesar's report on how he laid waste Gaul.

"At all our meetings I felt that I was being treated with good-humored condescension. They accepted Aaron [Copland], but they did not accept me because they considered me too young and uninteresting; I never learnt the reason, if there was one, for this exclusion by common consent." Bowles describes a British girl he met with Isherwood. She was called Jean Ross "(When Christopher wrote about her later, he called her Sally Bowles)."

In *Christopher and His Kind*, Isherwood sets up the by now obligatory reverse-angle shot: "(Sally Bowles's second name was chosen for her by Christopher because he liked the sound of it and also the looks of its owner, a twenty-year-old American whom he met in Berlin in 1931. The American thought Christopher treated him with 'good-humored condescension'; Christopher thought the American aloof....)" Apparently, there was a near-miss in Berlin.

Christopher and His Kind describes Isherwood's life from 1929 to 1939. The narrative (based on diaries and written, generally, in the third person) takes up where *Lions and Shadows* ends with "twenty-four-year-old Christopher's departure from England on March 14, 1929, to visit Berlin for the first time in his life." The book ends a decade later when Isherwood emigrates to the United States. Of *Lions and Shadows*, Isherwood says that it describes his "life between the ages of seventeen and twenty-four. It is not truly autobiographical, however. The author conceals important facts about himself...and gives his characters fictitious names." But "The book I am now going to write will be as frank and factual as I can make it, especially as far as I myself am concerned." He means to be sexually candid; and he is. He is also that rarest of creatures, the objective narcissist; he sees himself altogether plain and does not hesitate to record for us the lines that the face in the mirror has accumulated, the odd shadow that flaws character.

I have just read the two memoirs in sequence and it is odd how little Isherwood has changed in a half century. The style is much the same throughout. The shift from first to third person does not much alter the way he has of looking at things and it is, of course, the *precise* way in which Isherwood perceives the concrete world that makes all the difference. He is particularly good at noting a physical appearance that suggests, through his selection of nouns, verbs, a psychic description. This is from *Lions and Shadows*:

> [Chalmers] had grown a small moustache and looked exactly my idea of a young Montmartre poet, more French than the French. Now he caught sight of us, and greeted me with a slight wave of the hand, so very typical of him, tentative, diffident, semi-ironical, like a parody of itself. Chalmers expressed himself habitually in fragments of gestures, abortive movements, half-spoken sentences....

Then the same sharp eye is turned upon the narrator:

> Descending the staircase to the dining-room, I was Christopher Isherwood no longer, but a satanically proud, icy, impenetrable demon; an all-knowing, all-pardoning savior of mankind; a martyr-evangelist of the tea-table, from which the most atrocious drawing-room tortures could wring no more than a polite proffer of the buttered scones.

This particular *auteur du cinéma* seldom shoots a scene without placing somewhere on the set a mirror that will record the *auteur* in the act of filming.

At the time of the publication of *Lions and Shadows* in 1938, Isherwood was thirty-four years old. He had published three novels: *All the Conspirators, The Memorial, Mr. Norris Changes Trains.* With Auden he had written the plays *The Dog Beneath the Skin* and *The Ascent of F6.* Finally, most important of all, the finest of his creations had made a first appearance in *Mr. Norris Changes Trains*; with no great fuss or apparent strain, Isherwood had invented Isherwood. The Isherwood of the Berlin stories is a somewhat anodyne and enigmatic narrator. He is looking carefully at life. He does not commit himself to much of anything. Yet what might have been a limitation in a narrator, the author, rather mysteriously, made a virtue of.

Spender describes Isherwood in Berlin as occasionally "depressive, silent or petulant. Sometimes he would sit in a room with Sally Bowles or Mr. Norris without saying a word, as though refusing to bring his characters to life." But they were very much *his* characters. He lived "surrounded by the models for his creations, like one of those portraits of a writer by a bad painter, in which the writer is depicted meditating in his chair whilst the characters of his novels radiate round him under a glowing cloud of dirty varnish...." Isherwood had rejected not only the familiar, cozy world of Cambridge and London's literary life but also the world of self-conscious aestheticism. He chose to live as a proletarian in Berlin where, Spender tells us, "He was comparatively poor and almost unrecognized. His novel, *All the Conspirators,* had been remaindered," Spender notes yet again. Nevertheless, Spender realized that Isherwood

> was more than a young rebel passing through a phase of revolt against parents, conventional morality, and orthodox religion.... He was on the side of the forces which make a work of art, even more than he was interested in art itself.... His hatred of institutions of learning and even of the reputation attached to some past work of art, was really hatred of the fact that they came between people and their direct unprejudiced approach to one another.

In *Lions and Shadows* Isherwood writes of school, of friendships, of wanting to be...well, Isherwood, a character not yet entirely formed. Auden appears fairly late in the book though early in Isherwood's life: they were together at preparatory school. Younger than Isherwood, Auden wanted "to become a mining engineer.... I remember him chiefly for his naughtiness, his insolence, his smirking tantalizing air of knowing disreputable and exciting secrets." Auden was on to sex and the others were not.

Auden and Isherwood did not meet again for seven years. "Just before Christmas, 1925, a mutual acquaintance brought him in to tea. I found him very little changed." Auden "told me that he wrote poetry nowadays: he was deliberately a little over-casual in making this announcement. I was very much surprised, even rather disconcerted." But then, inevitably, the Poet and the Novelist of the age formed an alliance. The Poet had further surprises for the Novelist. Auden's "own attitude to sex, in its simplicity and utter lack of inhibition, fairly took my breath away. He was no Don Juan: he didn't run around hunting for his pleasures. But he took what came to him with a matter-of-factness and an appetite as hearty as that which he showed when sitting down to dinner."

Art and sex: the two themes intertwine in Isherwood's memoirs but in the first volume we do not know what the sex was all about: the reticences of the Thirties forbade candor. Now in *Christopher and His Kind*, Isherwood has filled in the blanks; he is explicit about both sex and love. Not only did the Poet and the Novelist of that era lust for boys, there is some evidence that each might have echoed Marlowe's mighty line: I have found that those who do not like tobacco and boys are fools.

"The book I am now going to write will be as frank and factual as I can make it, especially as far as I myself am concerned." Then the writer shifts to the third person: "At school, Christopher had fallen in love with many boys and been yearningly romantic about them. At college he had at last managed to get into bed with one. This was due entirely to the initiative of his partner, who, when Christopher became scared and started to raise objections, locked the door and sat down firmly on Christopher's lap." For an American twenty-two years younger than Christopher, the late development of the English of that epoch is astonishing. In Washington, D.C., puberty arrived at ten, eleven, twelve, and sex was riotous and inventive between consenting paeds. Yet Tennessee Williams (fourteen years my senior) reports in his *Memoirs* that neither homo- nor heterosexuality began for him until his late twenties. On the other hand, he did not go to a monosexual school as I did, as Isherwood and his kind did.

Isherwood tells us that "other experiences followed, all of them enjoyable but none entirely satisfying. This was because Christopher was suffering from an inhibition, then not unusual among upper-class homosexuals; he couldn't relax sexually with a member of his own class or nation. He needed a working-class foreigner." Germany was the answer. "To Christopher, Berlin meant Boys." Auden promptly introduced him to the Cosy Corner, a hangout for proletarian youths, and Christopher took up with a blond named Bubi, "the first presentable candidate who appeared to claim the leading role in Christopher's love myth."

John Lehmann's recently published "novel" *In the Purely Pagan Sense* overlaps with Isherwood's memoirs not only in time and place but in a similar sexual preoccupation. "I was obsessed," writes Lehmann's narrator, "by the desire to make love with boys of an entirely different class and background...." This desire for differentness is not unusual: misalliance has almost always been the name of the game hetero or homo or bi. But I suspect that the upper-middle-class man's desire for youths of the lower class derives, mainly, from fear of his own class. Between strongly willed males of the Isherwood-Auden sort, a sexual commitment could lead to a psychic defeat for one of the partners.

The recently published memoirs of Isherwood's contemporary Peter Quennell *(The Marble Foot)* describe how an upper-class *heterosexual* English writer was constantly betrayed by women of his own class. Apparently, Quennell is much too tender, too romantic, too...well, feminine to avoid victimization by the ladies. A beautiful irony never to be understood by United States-men given to the joys of the sexual majority is that a homosexualist like Isherwood cannot with any ease enjoy a satisfactory sexual relationship with a woman because he himself is so entirely masculine that the woman presents no challenge, no masculine hardness, no exciting *agon*. It is the heterosexual Don Juan (intellectual division) who is the fragile, easily wounded figure, given to tears. Isherwood is a good deal less "feminine" (in the pre-women's lib sense of the word) than Peter Quennell, say, or Cyril Connolly or our own paralyzingly butch Ernest Hemingway.

Isherwood describes his experiments with heterosexuality: "She was five or six years older than [Christopher], easygoing, stylish, humorous....He was surprised and amused to find how easily he could relate his usual holds and movements to his unusual partner. He felt curiosity and the fun of playing a new game. He also felt a lust which was largely narcissistic...." Then: "He asked himself: Do I now want to go to bed with more women and girls? Of course not, as long as I can have boys. Why do I prefer boys? Because of their shape and their voices and their smell and the way they move. And boys can be romantic. I can put them into my myth and fall in love with them. Girls can be absolutely beautiful but never romantic. In fact, their utter lack of romance is what I find most likeable about them." There is a clear-eyed healthiness (if not great accuracy) about all this.

Then Isherwood moves from the personal to the general and notes the lunatic pressure that society exerts on everyone to be heterosexual, to deny at all costs a contrary nature. Since heterosexual relations proved to be easy for Isherwood, he could have joined the majority. But he was stopped by Isherwood the rebel, the Protestant saint who declared with the fury of a Martin Luther: "even if my nature were like theirs, I should still have to fight them, in one way or another. If boys didn't exist, I should have to invent them." Isherwood's war on what he has called, so aptly, "the heterosexual dictatorship" has been unremitting and admirable.

In Berlin Isherwood settled down with a working-class boy named Heinz and most of *Christopher and His Kind* has to do with their life together during the time when Hitler came to power and the free and easy Berlin that had attracted Isherwood turned ugly. With Heinz (whose papers were not in order), Isherwood moved restlessly about Europe: Copenhagen, Amsterdam, the Canary Islands, Brussels. In the end Heinz was trapped in Germany, and forced to serve in World War II. Miraculously, he survived. After the war, Isherwood met Heinz and his wife—as pleasant an end as one can imagine to any idyll of that neo-Wagnerian age.

Meanwhile, Isherwood the writer was developing. It is during this period that the Berlin stories were written; also, *Lions and Shadows.* Also, the collaboration with Auden on the last of the verse plays. Finally, there is the inevitable fall into the movies...something that was bound to happen. In *Lions and Shadows* Isherwood describes how "I had always been fascinated by films.... I was a born film fan....The reason for this had, I think, very little to do with 'Art' at all; I was, and still am, endlessly interested in the outward appearance of people— their facial expressions, their gestures, their walk, their nervous tricks.... The cinema puts people under a microscope: you can stare at them, you can examine them as though they were insects."

Isherwood was invited to write a screenplay for the director "Berthold Viertel [who] appears as Friedrich Bergmann in the novel- ette called *Prater Violet,* which was published twelve years later." Isherwood and the colorful Viertel hit it off and together worked on a film called *Little Friend.* From that time on the best prose writer in English has supported himself by writing movies. In fact, the first Isherwood work that I encountered was not a novel but a film that he wrote called *Rage in Heaven*: at sixteen I thought it splendid. "The moon!" intoned the nutty Robert Montgomery. "It's staring at me, like a great Eye." Ingrid Bergman shuddered. So did I.

It is hard now for the young who are interested in literature (a tiny minority compared to the young who are interested in that flat- test and easiest and laziest of art forms: the movies) to realize that Isherwood was once considered "a hope of English fiction" by Cyril Connolly, and a master by those of us who grew up in World War II. I think the relative neglect of Isherwood's work is, partly, the result of his expatriation. With Auden, he emigrated to the United States just before the war began, and there was a good deal of bitter feeling at the time (they were clumsily parodied by the unspeakable Evelyn Waugh in *Put Out More Flags*). Ultimately, Auden's reputation was hardly affected. But then poets are licensed to be mad, bad, and dan- gerous to read, while prose writers are expected to be, if not respon- sible, predictable.

In America Isherwood was drawn first to the Quakers; then to Vedanta. Lately, he has become a militant spokesman of Gay

Liberation. If his defense of Christopher's kind is sometimes shrill...well, there is a good deal to be shrill about in a society so deeply and so mindlessly homophobic. In any case, none of Isherwood's moral preoccupations is apt to endear him to a literary establishment that is, variously, academic, Jewish/Christian, middle-class, and heterosexual. Yet he has written some of his best books in the United States, including the memoir at hand and the novels *A Single Man* and *A Meeting by the River*. Best of all, he still views the world aslant despite long residence in Santa Monica, a somber place where even fag households resemble those hetero couples photographed in *Better Homes and Gardens*, serving up intricate brunches 'neath the hazel Pacific sky.

What strikes me as most remarkable in Isherwood's career has not been so much the unremitting will to be his own man as the constant clarity of a prose style that shows no sign of slackness even though the author is, astonishingly, in his seventies. There is a good deal to be said about the way that Isherwood writes, particularly at a time when prose is worse than ever in the United States, and showing signs of etiolation in England. There is no excess in an Isherwood sentence. The verbs are strong. Nouns precise. Adjectives few. The third person startles and seduces, while the first person is a good guide and never coy.

Is the Isherwood manner perhaps *too* easy? Cyril Connolly feared that it might be when he wrote in *Enemies of Promise* (1938): "[Isherwood] is persuasive because he is so insinuatingly bland and anonymous, nothing rouses him, nothing shocks him. While secretly despising us he could not at the same time be more tolerant.... Now for this a price has to be paid; Herr Issyvoo" (Connolly is contemplating Isherwood's Berlin stories) "is not a dumb ox, for he is not condemned to the solidarity with his characters and with their background to which Hemingway is bound by his conception of art, but he is much less subtle, intelligent and articulate than he might be." Isherwood answered Connolly: "In conversation, Isherwood... expressed his belief in construction as the way out of the difficulty. The writer must conform to the language which is understood by the greatest number of people, to the vernacular, but his talent as a novelist will appear in the exactness of his observation, the justice of his situations and in the construction of his book."

Isherwood has maintained this aesthetic throughout a long career. When he turned his back on what Connolly termed Mandarin writing, he showed considerable courage. But the later Isherwood is even better than the early cameraman because he is no longer the anonymous, neutral narrator. He can be shocked; he can be angry.

In *Christopher and His Kind*, Isherwood wonders what attitude to take toward the coming war with Germany. "Suppose, Christopher now said to himself, I have a Nazi Army at my mercy. I can blow it up by pressing a button. The men in the army are notorious for torturing and murdering civilians—all except one of them, Heinz. Will I press the button? No—wait: Suppose I know that Heinz himself, out of cowardice or moral infection, has become as bad as they are and takes part in all their crimes? Will I press that button, even so? Christopher's answer, given without the slightest hesitation, was: Of course not." That is the voice of humanism in a bad time, and one can only hope that thanks to Christopher's life and work, his true kind will increase even as they refuse, so wisely, to multiply.

The New York Review of Books
December 9, 1976

Sex Is Politics

"But surely you do not favor the publishing of pornography?" When you hear someone say do not instead of don't, you know that you are either in court or on television. I was on television, being interviewed by two men—or persons, as they say nowadays. One was a conservative, representing the decent opinion of half a nation. One was a reactionary, representing the decent opinion of half a nation.

"Of course, I favor the publishing of—"

"You *favor* pornography?" The reactionary was distressed, appalled, sickened.

"I said the *publishing* of pornography, yes...."

"But what's the difference? I mean between being in favor of publishing pornography and pornography?"

The conservative was troubled. "Whether or not I personally like or dislike pornography is immaterial." Television is a great leveler. You always end up sounding like the people who ask the questions. "The freedom to publish *anything* is guaranteed by the First Amendment to the Constitution. That is the law. Whether you or I or anyone likes what is published is"—repetition coming up. I was tired—"is, uh, immaterial. The First Amendment guarantees us the right to say and write and publish what we want...."

Before I could make the usual exemptions for libel and for the reporting of troop movements during wartime and for that man or person who falsely yells fire in a crowded theatre (all absolutes are relative beneath the sun), the conservative struck. "But," he said, eyes agleam with what looked to be deep feeling but was actually collyrium, "the founders of the United States"—he paused, reverently; looked at me, sincerely; realized, unhappily, that I was staring at the lacing to his hairpiece (half the men who appear on television professionally are bald; why?). Nervously, he touched his forehead, and continued—"of America intended freedom of speech only for...uh, politics."

"But sex is politics," I began...and ended.

I got two blank stares. I might just as well have said that the Pelagian heresy will never take root in south Amish country. Neither the conservative nor the reactionary had ever heard anyone say anything like that before and I knew that I could never explain myself in the seven remaining in-depth minutes of air time. I was also distracted by that toupee. Mentally, I rearranged it. Pushed it farther back on his head. Didn't like the result. Tried it lower down. All the while, we spoke of Important Matters. I said that I did not think it a good idea for people to molest children. This was disingenuous. My secret hero is the late King Herod.

Sex is politics.

In the year or two since that encounter on television, I have been reminded almost daily of the fact that not only is sex politics but sex both directly and indirectly has been a major issue in this year's election. The Equal Rights Amendment, abortion, homosexuality are hot issues that affect not only the political process but the private lives of millions of people.

The sexual attitudes of any given society are the result of political decisions. In certain militaristic societies, homosexual relationships were encouraged on the ground that pairs of dedicated lovers (Thebes' Sacred Legion, the Spartan buddy system) would fight more vigorously than reluctant draftees. In societies where it is necessary to force great masses of people to do work that they don't want to do (building pyramids, working on the Detroit assembly line), marriage at an early age is encouraged on the sensible ground that if a married man is fired, his wife and children are going to starve, too. That grim knowledge makes for docility.

Although our notions about what constitutes correct sexual behavior are usually based on religious texts, those texts are invariably interpreted by the rulers in order to keep control over the ruled. Any sexual or intellectual or recreational or political activity that might decrease the amount of coal mined, the number of pyramids built, the quantity of junk food confected will be proscribed through laws that, in turn, are based on divine revelations handed down by whatever god or gods happen to be in fashion at the moment. Religions are manipulated in order to serve those who govern society and not the other way around. This is a brand-new thought to most Americans, whether once or twice or never bathed in the Blood of the Lamb.

Traditionally, Judaeo-Christianity approved of sex only between men and women who had been married in a religious ceremony. The newlyweds were then instructed to have children who would, in turn, grow up and have more children (the Reverend Malthus worried about this inverted pyramid), who would continue to serve the society as loyal workers and dutiful consumers.

For the married couple, sexual activity outside marriage is still a taboo. Although sexual activity before marriage is equally taboo, it is more or less accepted if the two parties are really and truly serious and sincere and mature...in other words, if they are prepared to do their duty by one day getting married in order to bring forth new worker-consumers in obedience to God's law, which tends to resemble with suspicious niceness the will of the society's owners.

Fortunately, nothing human is constant. Today civil marriages outnumber religious marriages; divorce is commonplace; contraception is universally practiced, while abortion is legal for those with money. But our rulers have given ground on these sexual-social issues with great reluctance, and it is no secret that there is a good deal of frustration in the board rooms of the republic.

For one thing, workers are less obedient than they used to be. If fired, they can go on welfare—the Devil's invention. Also, the fact that most jobs men do women can do and do do has endangered the old patriarchal order. A woman who can support herself and her child is a threat to marriage, and marriage is the central institution whereby the owners of the world control those who do the work.

Homosexuality also threatens that ancient domination, because men who don't have wives or children to worry about are not as easily dominated as those men who do.

At any given moment in a society's life, there are certain hot buttons that a politician can push in order to get a predictably hot response. A decade ago, if you asked President Nixon what he intended to do about unemployment, he was apt to answer, "Marijuana is a halfway house to something worse." It is good politics to talk against sin—and don't worry about non sequiturs. In fact, it is positively un-American—even Communist—to discuss a real issue such as unemployment or who is stealing all that money at the Pentagon.

To divert the electorate, the unscrupulous American politician will go after those groups not regarded benignly by Old or New Testament. The descendants of Ham are permanently unpopular with white Americans. Unhappily for the hot-button pusher, it is considered bad taste to go after blacks openly. But code phrases may be used. Everyone knows that "welfare chiseler" means nigger, as does "law and order." The first on the ground that the majority of those on welfare are black (actually, they are white); the second because it is generally believed that most urban crimes are committed by blacks against whites (actually they are committed by jobless blacks against other blacks). But poor blacks are not the only target. Many Christers and some Jews don't like poor white people very much, on the old Puritan ground that if you're good, God will make you rich. This is a familiar evangelical Christian line, recently unfurled by born-again millionaire Walter Hoving. When he found himself short $2,400,000 of the amount he needed to buy Bonwit Teller, Mr. Hoving "opened himself up to the Lord," who promptly came through with the money. "It was completely a miracle." Now we know why the rich are always with us. God likes them.

Jews are permanently unpopular with American Christers because they are forever responsible for Jesus' murder, no matter what those idolatrous wine-soaked Roman Catholics at the Second Vatican Council said. It is true that with the establishment of Israel, the Christers now have a grudging admiration for the Jew as bully. Nevertheless, in once-and-twice-born land, it is an article of faith that America's mass media are owned by Jews who mean to overthrow

God's country. Consequently, "mass media" is this year's code phrase for get the kikes, while "Save Our Children" means get the fags.

But politics, like sex, often makes for odd alliances. This year, militant Christers in tandem with militant Jews are pushing the sort of hot buttons that they think will strengthen the country's ownership by firming up the family. Apparently, the family can be strengthened only by depriving women of equal status not only in the marketplace but also in relation to their own bodies (Thou shalt not abort). That is why the defeat of the Equal Rights Amendment to the Constitution is of great symbolic importance.

Family Saviors also favor strong laws designed, ostensibly, to curtail pornography but actually intended to deny freedom of speech to those that they dislike.

Now, it is not possible for a governing class to maintain its power if there are not hot buttons to push. A few months ago, the "Giveaway of the Panama Canal" issue looked as though it were going to be a very hot button, indeed. It was thought that if, somehow, American manhood could be made to seem at stake in Panama, there was a chance that a sort of subliminal sexual button might be pushed, triggering throughout the land a howl of manly rage, particularly from ladies at church receptions: American manhood has never been an exclusively masculine preserve. But, ultimately, American manhood (so recently kneed by the Viet Cong) did not feel endangered by the partial loss of a fairly dull canal, and so that button jammed.

The issue of Cuban imperialism also seemed warm to the touch. Apparently, Castro's invincible troops are now on the march from one end of Africa to the other. If Somalia falls, Mali falls; if Mali falls....No one cares. Africa is too far away, while Cuba is too small and too near to be dangerous.

In desperation, the nation's ownership has now gone back to the tried-and-true hot buttons: save our children, our fetuses, our ladies' rooms from the godless enemy. As usual, the sex buttons have proved satisfyingly hot.

But what do Americans actually think about sex when no one is pressing a button? Recently, *Time* magazine polled a cross section of the populace. Not surprisingly, 61 percent felt that "it's getting harder and harder to know what's right and what's wrong these days." Most confused were people over 50 and under 25. Meanwhile, 76 percent said that they believed that it was "morally wrong" for a married man to be unfaithful to his wife, while 79 percent thought it wrong for a woman to cheat on her husband.

Sexual relations between teenagers were condemned by 63 percent while 34 percent felt that a young man should be a virgin on his wedding night or afternoon. Nevertheless, what people consider to be morally objectionable does not seem to have much effect on what they actually do: 55 percent of unmarried women and 85 percent of unmarried men admit to having had sex by the age of 19...no doubt, while jointly deploring teenage immorality. A worldly 52 percent think it is *not* morally wrong for an unmarried couple to live together.

Forty-seven percent thought that homosexual relations were morally wrong; 43 percent thought that they were all right: 10 percent didn't know. Yet 56 percent "would vote for legislation guaranteeing the civil rights of homosexuals." Although a clear majority thought that fags should be allowed to serve in the Army, run for office, live where they choose, Anita Bryant has done her work sufficiently well to deny them the right to teach school (48 percent against, 44 percent for) or be ministers (47 percent against, 44 percent for).

Pornography continues to be the hottest of buttons: seventy-four percent want the government to crack down on pornographers. Meanwhile, 76 percent think that that old devil permissiveness "has led to a lot of things that are wrong with the country these days."

Finally, 70 percent thought that "there should be no laws, either Federal or state, regulating sexual practice." Either this can be interpreted as a remarkable demonstration of live and let live (an attitude notoriously not shared by the current Supreme Court) or it can be nothing more than the cynical wisdom of our people who know from experience that any area the government involves itself in will be hopelessly messed up.

Despite the tolerance of the 70 percent, some 20 percent to 40 percent of the population are moral absolutists, according to the Kinsey Institute's soon-to-be-published *American Sexual Standards*. Fiercely, these zealots condemn promiscuity, adultery, homosexuality, masturbation, long hair and fluoride. Out there in the countryside (and in cities such as St. Paul and Wichita), they are the ones who most promptly respond to the politician who pushes a sex button in order to...what? Create an authoritarian society? Keep the workers docile within the confines of immutable marriage? Punish sin? Make money? Money! There is a lot of money out there on the evangelical Christian circuit and much of it is tax-exempt.

In the fall of 1977, the journalist Andrew Kopkind visited Bensenville, Illinois, in the heart of the heart of the country, in order to study those roots of grass that are now not only as high as an elephant's eye but definitely swaying to the right. *Save the Family* is this year's rallying cry. Since hardly anyone ever openly questions the value of the family in human affairs, any group that wants to save this allegedly endangered institution is warmly supported.

But to the zealots of what Kopkind calls the New Right, saving the family means all sorts of things not exactly connected with the nuclear family. Kopkind discovered that Family Saviors support "the death penalty, Laetrile, nuclear power, local police, Panama Canal, saccharin, FBI, CIA, defense budget, public prayer and real-estate growth."

Family Saviors view darkly "busing, welfare, public-employee unions, affirmative action, amnesty, marijuana, communes, gun control, pornography, the 55-mph speed limit, day-care centers, religious ecumenism, sex education, car pools and the Environmental Protection Agency." Kopkind believes that those attitudes are fairly spontaneous. He is probably right—up to a point. To get Americans to vote constantly against their own interests, however, requires manipulation of the highest order, and it starts at birth in these remarkably United States and never ends.

Until recently, it had not occurred to anyone that a profamily movement might be politically attractive. Our demagogues usually concentrate on communism versus Americanism. But Nixon's jaunts to Peking and Moscow diminished communism as an issue. Those trips also served to remind Americans that we are a fragile minority in a world where the majority is Marxist. Although communism is still a button to be pressed, it tends to tepidity.

On the other hand, to accuse your opponent of favoring any of those vicious forces that endanger the family is to do him real harm. In the past 18 months, Family Saviors have been remarkably effective.

They have defeated equal-rights ordinances for homosexualists in Dade County, St. Paul, Wichita, Eugene; obliged the House of Representatives to reverse itself on an anti-abortion bill; stalled (for a time) the Equal Rights Amendment, and so on. Sex is the ultimate politics and very soon, one way or another, every politician is going to get—as it were—into the act.

Officially, our attitudes toward sex derive from the Old and New Testaments. Even to this day, Christian fundamentalists like to say that since every single word in the good book is absolutely true, every one of God's injunctions must be absolutely true, every one of God's injunctions must be absolutely obeyed if we don't want the great plains of the republic to be studded with pillars of salt or worse. Actually, even the most rigorously literal of fundamentalists pick and choose from Biblical texts. The authors of Leviticus proscribe homo-sexuality—and so do all good Christers. But Leviticus also proscribes rare meat, bacon, shellfish, and the wearing of nylon mixed with wool. If Leviticus were to be obeyed in every instance, the garment trade would collapse.

The authors of the Old and New Testaments created not only a religious anthology but also a political order in which man is woman's eternal master (Jewish men used to pray, "I thank thee, Lord, that thou hast not created me a woman"). The hatred and fear of women that runs through the Old Testament (not to mention in the pages of our justly admired Jewish novelists) suggests that the patri-archal principle so carefully built into the Jewish notion of God must have been at one time opposed to a powerful and perhaps competi-tive matriarchal system.

Whatever the original reasons for the total subordination of woman to man, the result has been an unusually ugly religion that has caused a good deal of suffering not only in its original form but also through its later heresy, Christianity, which in due, and ironic, course was to spin off yet another heresy, communism.

The current wave of Christian religiosity that is flowing across the republic like an oil slick has served as a reminder to women that they must submit to their husbands. This is not easy, as twice-born Anita Bryant admits. She confesses to a tendency to "dump her garbage" all over her husband and master and employee, Bob Green.

But she must control herself: "For the husband is the head of the wife, even as Christ is the head of the Church" (Ephesians 5: 23). Anita also knows that because of woman's disobedience, the prototypes of the human race were excluded from the Garden of Eden.

Brooding on the Old Testament's dislike of women, Freud theorized that an original patriarchal tribe was for a time replaced by a matriarchal tribe that was then overthrown by the patriarchal Jews: the consequent "re-establishment of the primal father in his historic rights was a great step forward." This speculative nonsense is highly indicative of the way that a mind as shrewd and as original as Freud's could not conceive of a good (virtuous?) society that was not dominated by man the father.

"What do women want?" Freud once asked, plaintively. Well, Sigmund, they want equality with men. But that equality was not acceptable either to the authors of the Old Testament or to Freud himself. Today, almost 3,000 years after Moses came down from Sinai, women are approaching equality with men in the United States. But the war against woman's equality still goes on; at the moment, it is being conducted in the name of The Family.

The New Testament's Christ is a somewhat milder figure than the Jehovah of the Old Testament. Yet one is very much the son of the other, and so, presumably, nothing basic was supposed to change in the relations between the sexes. In fact, at one point, Jesus displays a positively Portnoyesque exasperation with the traditional Jewish mother. "Woman," he says to Mary, "what art thou to me?" Mary's no doubt lengthy answer has not been recorded.

As a Jew, Jesus took seriously the Ten Commandments. But he totally confused the whole business of adultery by saying that even to entertain so much as a Carter-like lust for a woman is the equivalent of actually committing adultery. Jesus also went on record as saying that whores had as good a chance of getting to heaven as IRS men. It is possible that he meant this as a joke. If so, it is the only joke in the New Testament.

To an adulteress, Jesus said, "Neither do I condemn thee," before suggesting that she stop playing around. Jesus had nothing to say about homosexuality, masturbation or the Equal Rights Amendment; but he did think the absolute world of eunuchs (Matthew 19: 10-12).

Finally, Jesus believed that the world was about to end. "But I tell you of a truth, there are some standing here, who shall not taste of death, till they see the kingdom of God" (Luke 9: 27). As far as we can tell, the world did not end in the first century A.D., and all those standing there died without having seen the kingdom.

A few years later, Saint Paul had his vision on the road to Damascus. "Both Jews and gentiles all are under sin," he—what is that best-seller verb?—shrilled. Since Paul was also convinced that the world was about to end, he believed that man must keep himself ritually pure for the day of judgment, and ritual purity required a total abstention from sex. For those who could not remain heroically chaste (to "abide even as I"), Paul rather sourly agreed that "it is better to marry than to burn"—burn with lust, by the way, not hell-fire, as some primitive Christers like to interpret that passage.

Paul also advised married men to live with their wives "as though they had none…. For the form of this world is passing away." Although this world's form did not pass away, Paul's loathing of sexuality did not pass away, either. As a result, anyone brought up in a Christian-dominated society will be taught from birth to regard his natural sexual desires as sinful, or worse.

A state of constant guilt in the citizenry is a good thing for rulers who tend not to take very seriously the religions that they impose on their subjects. Since marriage was the only admissible outlet for the sexual drive, that institution was used as a means of channeling the sexual drive in a way that would make docile the man, while the woman, humanly speaking, existed only as the repository of the sacred sperm (regarded as a manifestation of the Holy Ghost).

Woman was commanded to serve and obey her husband as totally as he, in turn, served and obeyed his temporal, Bible-quoting master. If one had set out deliberately to invent a religion that would effectively enslave a population, one could not have done much better than Judaeo-Christianity.

Curiously enough, Paul is the only Old or New Testament maven to condemn lesbianism, an activity that Queen Victoria did not believe existed and Jesus ignored. But Paul knew better. Why, even as he spoke, Roman ladies were burning "in their lust one toward another…!" Whenever Paul gets onto the subject of burning lust, he shows every sign of acute migraine.

Now, what is all this nonsense really about? Why should natural sexual desires be condemned in the name of religion? Paul would have said that since judgment day was scheduled for early next year, you should keep yourself ritually clean and ritual cleanliness amongst the Jews involved not only sexual abstinence but an eschewal of shell-fish. But Paul's hatred of the flesh is somewhat hard to understand in the light of Jesus' fairly relaxed attitude. On the other hand, Paul's dislike of homosexuality is a bit easier to understand (though never properly understood by American Christers). It derives from the Old Testament book Leviticus, the so-called Holiness Code.

Homosexual relations between heroes were often celebrated in the ancient world. The oldest of religious texts tells of the love between two men, Gilgamesh and Enkidu. When Enkidu died, Gilgamesh challenged death itself in order to bring his lover back to life. In the *Iliad*, Gilgamesh's rage is echoed by Achilles when *his* lover Patroclus dies before the walls of Troy. So intense was the love between the heroes David and Jonathan that David noted in his obituary of Jonathan, "Thy love to me was wonderful, passing the love of women." Elsewhere in the Old Testament, the love that Ruth felt for Naomi was of a sort that today might well end in the joint ownership of a ceramics kiln at Laguna Beach. Why, then, the extraordinary fuss about homosexuality in Leviticus?

Leviticus was written either during or shortly after the Jewish exile in Babylon (586-538 B.C.). The exile ended when Persia's Great King Cyrus conquered Babylon. Tolerant of all religions Cyrus let the Jews go home to Jerusalem, where they began to rebuild the temple that had been destroyed in 586. Since it was thought that the disasters of 586 might have been averted had the Jews been a bit more straitlaced in their deportment, Leviticus was drafted. It contained a very stern list of dos and don'ts. Adultery, which had been proscribed by Moses, was now not only proscribed but the adulterers were to be put to death, while "If a man...lie with mankind, as he lieth with a woman, both of them have committed an abomination" and must be put to death.

What is all this about? In earlier days, Jonathan and David were much admired. Was their celebrated love for each other an abomination? Obviously not. The clue to the mystery is the word abomination, which derives from the Hebrew word *to'ebah,* meaning idolatrous. At the time of Leviticus (and long before), the Great Goddess was worshipped throughout the Middle East. She had many names: Cybele, Astarte, Diana, Anahita. Since the Jews thought that the Great Goddess was in direct competition with their Great God, they denounced her worshipers as idolatrous, or *to'ebah,* or abominable; and particularly disapproved of the ritual sex associated with her worship. Many of Cybele's admirers castrated themselves for her glory while male and female prostitutes crowded the temple precincts, ready for action.

In Babylon, every respectable woman was obliged to go at least once in a lifetime to the temple and prostitute herself to the first pilgrim who was willing to pay her. According to Herodotus, ill-favored women were obliged to spend an awful lot of time at the temple, trying to turn that reluctant trick which would make them blessed in the eyes of the goddess.

No doubt, many Jews in Babylon were attracted, if not to the goddess's worship, to the sexual games that went on in her temples. Therefore, the authors of Leviticus made it clear that any Jew who went with a male or female temple prostitute was guilty of an idolatrous or abominable act in the eyes of the Great God Jehovah—a notoriously jealous god by his own admission. As a result, the abominations in Leviticus refer *not* to sexual acts as such but to sexual acts associated with the cult of the Great Goddess.

Elsewhere in the Old Testament, Sodom was destroyed not because the inhabitants were homosexualists but because a number of local men wanted to gang rape a pair of male angels who were guests of the town. That was a violation of the most sacred of ancient taboos: the law of hospitality. Also, gang rape, whether homosexual or heterosexual, is seldom agreeable in the eyes of any deity.

Human beings take a long time to grow up. This fact means that the tribe or the family or the commune is obliged to protect and train the young in those skills that will be needed for him to achieve a physical maturity whose sole purpose seems to be the passing on to a new generation of the sacred DNA code. The nature of life is more life. This is not very inspiring, but it is all that we know for certain that we have. Consequently, our religio-political leaders have always glorified the tribe or the family or the state at the expense of the individual. But societies change and when they do, seemingly eternal laws are superseded. Flat earth proves to be a sphere. Last year's wisdom is this year's folly.

In an overpopulated world, the Biblical injunction to be fruitful and multiply is less and less heeded. Thanks to increased automation and incontinent breeding, every industrial society in the world now has more workers than it needs. Meanwhile, housing has become so expensive that it is no longer possible for three generations of a family to live in the same house, the ideal of most Christers and strict Jews. Today the nuclear family consists of a boy for you and a girl for me in a housing development...hardly an ideal setting for either children or parents.

At this point, it would seem sensible to evolve a different set of arrangements for the human race. Certainly, fewer families would mean fewer children, and that is a good thing. Those who have a gift for parenthood (an infinitely small minority) ought to be encouraged to have children. Those without the gift ought to be discouraged. People would still live in pairs if that pleased them, but the social pressure to produce babies would be lifted.

Unhappily, the thrust of our society is still Judaeo-Christian. As a result, the single American male and the working woman are second-class citizens. A single man's median income is $11,069, while his married brother's income is $14,268 and his working sister's salary is $9,231. This is calculated discrimination. Plainly, it is better to marry than to be ill-paid.

After tax reform, this year's major political issue is Save the Family. Predictably, the Christers have been gunning for women's libbers and fags, two minorities that appear to endanger the family. Not so predictably, a number of Jews are now joining in the attack. This is odd, to say the least. Traditionally, Jews tend to a live-and-let-live attitude on the sensible ground that whenever things go wrong in any society where Jews are a minority, they will get it in the neck. So why make enemies? Unfortunately, Jewish tolerance has never really extended to homosexuality, that permanent abomination. Fag-baiting by American Jewish journalists has always been not only fashionable but, in a covert way, antigoyim.

Eighteen years ago, the busy journalist Alfred Kazin announced that homosexuality was a dead end for a writer. Apparently, fags couldn't make great literature. Today he is no longer quite so certain. In a recent issue of *Esquire*, Kazin accepted the genius of Gertrude Stein, but he could not resist mocking her lesbianism; he also felt it necessary to tell us that she was "fat, queer-looking," while her lover Alice B. Toklas was equally ugly. Although Kazin can accept—barely—the genius of an occasional fag writer, he detests what he calls "the gay mob." He is distressed that "homosexuality is being politicized and is becoming a social fact and a form of social pressure. Does the increasing impatience on all sides with the family, the oldest human institution, explain the widespread growth or emergence of homosexuality amidst so much anxiety about overpopulation?" This is one of those confused rhetorical questions whose answer is meant to be implicit in the polemical tone.

Actually, there is no such thing as a homosexual person, any more than there is such a thing as a heterosexual person. The words are adjectives describing sexual acts, not people. Those sexual acts are entirely natural; if they were not, no one would perform them. But since Judaism proscribes the abominable, the irrational rage that Kazin and his kind feel toward homosexualists has triggered an opposing rage. Gay militants now assert that there is something called gay sensibility, the outward and visible sign of a new kind of human being. Thus madness begets madness.

I have often thought that the reason no one has yet been able to come up with a good word to describe the homosexualist (sometimes known as gay, fag, queer, etc.) is because he does not exist. The human race is divided into male and female. Many human beings enjoy sexual relations with their own sex, many don't; many respond to both. This plurality is the fact of our nature and not worth fretting about.

Today Americans are in a state of terminal hysteria on the subject of sex in general and of homosexuality in particular because the owners of the country (buttressed by a religion that they have shrewdly adapted to their own ends) regard the family as their last means of control over those who work and consume. For two millennia, women have been treated as chattel, while homosexuality has been made to seem a crime, a vice, an illness.

In the *Symposium*, Plato defined the problem: "In Ionia and other places, and generally in countries which are subject to the barbarians [Plato is referring to the Persians, who were the masters of the Jews at the time Leviticus was written], the custom [homosexuality] is held to be dishonorable; loves of youths share the evil repute in which philosophy and gymnastics are held, because they are inimical to tyranny; the interests of rulers require that their subjects should be poor in spirit and that there should be no strong bond of friendship or society among them, which love, above all other motives, is likely to inspire, as our Athenian tyrants learned by experience; for the love of Aristogeiton and the constancy of Harmodius had a strength which undid their power." This last refers to a pair of lovers who helped overthrow the tyrants at Athens.

To this, our American Jews would respond: so what else would you expect from an uncircumcised Greek? While our American Christers would remind us of those scorching letters that Saint Paul mailed to the residents of Corinth and Athens.

Although the founders of our republic intended the state to be entirely secular in its laws and institutions, in actual fact, our laws are a mishmash of Judaeo-Christian superstitions. One ought never to be surprised by the intolerant vehemence of our fundamentalist Christers. After all, they started the country, and the seventeenth-century bigot Cotton Mather is more central to their beliefs than the eighteenth-century liberal George Mason, who fathered the Bill of Rights. But it is odd to observe Jews making common cause with Christian bigots.

I have yet to read anything by a Christer with an IQ above 95 that is as virulent as the journalist Joseph Epstein's statement (in *Harper's* magazine): "If I had the power to do so, I would wish homosexuality off the face of this earth. I would do so because I think that it brings infinitely more pain than pleasure to those who are forced to live with it," etc. Surely, Epstein must realize that if the word Jewry were substituted for homosexuality, a majority of American Christers would be in full agreement. No Jew ought ever to mention the removal of any minority "from the face of the earth." It is unkind. It is also unwise in a Christer-dominated society where a pogrom is never *not* a possibility.

In a recent issue of *Partisan Review*, what I take to be a Catskill hotel called the Hilton Kramer wants to know why the New York intellectuals are not offering the national culture anything "in the way of wisdom about marriage and the family, for example? Anything but attacks, and often vicious attacks, on the most elementary fealties of family life?"

The hotel is worried that for the nation at large, the New York intellectual world is represented in the pages of *The New York Review of Books* "by the likes of Gore Vidal and Garry Wills." I assume that the hotel disapproves of Wills and me because we are not Jewish. The hotel then goes on to characterize me as "proselytizing for the joys of buggery." Needless to say, I have never done such a thing, but I can see how to a superstitious and ill-run hotel anyone who has worked hard to remove consenting sexual relations from the statute books (and politics) must automatically be a salesman for abominable vices, as well as a destroyer of the family and an eater of shellfish.

Finally, dizziest of all, we have the deep thoughts of Norman Podhoretz, the editor of *Commentary*, a magazine subsidized by the American Jewish Congress. In the Sixties, Podhoretz wrote a celebrated piece in which he confessed that he didn't like niggers. Now, in the Seventies, he has discovered that he doesn't like fags, either—on geopolitical rather than rabbinical grounds.

In an article called "The Culture of Appeasement" (again in *Harper's*), Podhoretz tells us that the Vietnam caper had a bad effect on Americans because we now seem not to like war at all. Of course, "The idea of war has never been as natural or as glamorous to Americans as it used to be to the English or the Germans or the French." Podhoretz obviously knows very little American history. As recently as Theodore Roosevelt, war was celebrated as the highest of all human activities. Sadly, Podhoretz compares this year's United States to England in the Thirties when, he assures us, a powerful homosexual movement made England pacifist because the fags did not want beautiful (or even ugly?) boys killed in the trenches.

Aside from the fact that quite as many faggots like war as heterosexualists (Cardinal Spellman, Senator Joe McCarthy, General

Walker), the argument makes no sense. When the English were ready to fight Hitler, they fought. As for Vietnam, if we learned anything from our defeat so far from home, it was that we have no right to intervene militarily in the affairs of another nation.

But Podhoretz is not exactly disinterested. As a publicist for Israel, he fears that a craven United States might one day refuse to go to war to protect Israel from its numerous enemies. Although I don't think that he has much to worry about, it does his cause no good to attribute our country's alleged pacifism to a homosexual conspiracy. After all, that is the sort of mad thinking that inspired Hitler to kill not only 6,000,000 Jews but also 600,000 homosexualists.

In the late Sixties and early Seventies, the enemies of the Equal Rights Amendment set out to smear the movement as lesbian. All sorts of militant right-wing groups have since got into the act: the Ku Klux Klan, the John Birch Society, the Committee for the Survival of a Free Congress, Phyllis Schlafly's Eagle Forum, The Conservative Caucus, and dozens of other like-minded groups. Their aim is to deny equal rights to women through scare tactics. If the amendment is accepted, they warn us that lesbians will be able to marry each other, rape will be common, men will use women's toilets. This nonsense has been remarkably effective.

But then, as The Conservative Caucus's Howard Phillips told *The New Republic* with engaging candor, "We're going after people on the basis of their hot buttons." In the past year, the two hot buttons have proved to be sexual: ERA and gay rights legislation. Or "Save the Family" and "Save Our Children."

Elsewhere in the badlands of the nation, one Richard Viguerie is now the chief money raiser for the powers of darkness. In 1977, Viguerie told the *Congressional Quarterly,* "I'm willing to compromise to come to power. There aren't 50 percent of the people that share my view, and I'm willing to make concessions to come to power." That has a familiar Nuremberg ring.

Viguerie is said to have at least 10,000,000 names and addresses on file. He sends out mailings and raises large sums for all sorts of far-right political candidates and organizations. But Viguerie is not just a hustler. He is also an ideologue. "I have raised millions of dollars for the conservative movement over the years and I am not happy with the results. I decided to become more concerned with how the money is spent." He is now beginning to discuss the creation of a new political party.

Among groups that Viguerie works for and with is Gun Owners of America. He also works closely with Phyllis Schlafly, who dates back to Joe McCarthy and Barry Goldwater; currently, she leads the battle against the ERA. Another of Viguerie's clients is Utah's Senator Orrin Hatch, a proud and ignorant man who is often mentioned as a possible candidate for president if the far right should start a new political party.

Viguerie has vowed that "the organized conservative community is going to put in many times more than 3,000,000 [*sic*].... I want a massive assault on Congress in 1978. I don't want any token efforts. We now have the talent and resources to move in a bold, massive way. I think we can move against Congress in 1978 in a way that's never been conceived of."

"Move against Congress." That sounds like revolution. Anyway, it will be interesting to see whether or not Congress will be overwhelmed in November; to see whether or not those children will actually be saved; to see whether or not fealty will be sworn by all right-thinking persons to the endangered family.

Playboy
January 1979

Pink Triangle and Yellow Star

A few years ago on a trip to Paris, I read an intriguing review in *Le Monde* of a book called *Comme un Frère, Comme un Amant*, a study of "Male Homosexuality in the American Novel and Theatre from Herman Melville to James Baldwin," the work of one Georges-Michel Sarotte, a Sorbonne graduate and a visiting professor at the University of Massachusetts. I read the book, found it interesting; met the author, found him interesting. He told me that he was looking forward to the publication of his book in the United States by Anchor Press/Doubleday. What sort of response did I think he would have? I was touched by so much innocent good faith. There will be no reaction, I said, because no one outside of the so-called gay press will review your book. He was shocked. Wasn't the book serious? scholarly? with an extensive bibliography? I agreed that it was all those things; unfortunately, scholarly studies having to do with fags do not get reviewed in the United States (this was before the breakthrough of Yale's John Boswell, whose ferociously learned *Christianity, Social Tolerance and Homosexuality* obliged even the "homophobic" *New York Times* to review it intelligently). If Sarotte had written about the agony and wonder of being female and/or Jewish and/or divorced, he would have been extensively reviewed. Even a study of black literature might have got attention (Sarotte is beige), although blacks are currently something of a nonsubject in these last days of empire.

I don't think that Professor Sarotte believed me. I have not seen him since. I also have never seen a review of his book or of Roger Austen's *Playing the Game* (a remarkably detailed account of American writing on homosexuality) or of *The Homosexual as Hero in Contemporary Fiction* by Stephen Adams, reviewed at much length in England and ignored here, or of a dozen other books that have been sent to me by writers who seem not to understand why an activity of more than casual interest to more than one-third of the male population of the United States warrants no serious discussion. That is to say, no serious *benign* discussion. All-out attacks on faggots are perennially fashionable in our better periodicals.

I am certain that the novel *Tricks* by Renaud Camus (recently translated for St. Martin's Press by Richard Howard, with a preface by Roland Barthes) will receive a perfunctory and hostile response out there in bookchat land. Yet in France, the book was treated as if it were actually literature, admittedly a somewhat moot activity nowadays. So I shall review *Tricks*. But first I think it worth bringing out in the open certain curious facts of our social and cultural life.

The American passion for categorizing has now managed to create two nonexistent categories—gay and straight. Either you are one or you are the other. But since everyone is a mixture of inclinations, the categories keep breaking down; and when they break down, the irrational takes over. You *have* to be one or the other. Although our mental therapists and writers for the better journals usually agree that those who prefer same-sex sex are not exactly criminals (in most of our states and under most circumstances they still are) or sinful or, officially, sick in the head, they must be, somehow, evil or inadequate or dangerous. The Roman Empire fell, didn't it? because of the fags?

Our therapists, journalists, and clergy are seldom very learned. They seem not to realize that most military societies on the rise tend to encourage same-sex activities for reasons that should be obvious to anyone who has not grown up ass-backward, as most Americans have. In the centuries of Rome's great military and political success, there was no differentiation between same-sexers and other-sexers; there was also a lot of crossing back and forth of the sort that those

Americans who *do* enjoy inhabiting category-gay or category-straight find hard to deal with. Of the first twelve Roman emperors, only one was exclusively heterosexual. Since these twelve men were pretty tough cookies, rigorously trained as warriors, perhaps our sexual categories and stereotypes are—can it really be?—false. It was not until the sixth century of the empire that same-sex sex was proscribed by church and state. By then, of course, the barbarians were within the gates and the glory had fled.

Today, American evangelical Christians are busy trying to impose on the population at large their superstitions about sex and the sexes and the creation of the world. Given enough turbulence in the land, these natural fascists can be counted on to assist some sort of authoritarian—but never, never totalitarian—political movement. Divines from Santa Clara to Falls Church are particularly fearful of what they describe as the gay liberation movement's attempt to gain "special rights and privileges" when all that the same-sexers want is to be included, which they are not by law and custom, within the framework of the Fourteenth Amendment. The divine in Santa Clara believes that same-sexers should be killed. The divine in Falls Church believes that they should be denied equal rights under the law. Meanwhile, the redneck divines have been joined by a group of New York Jewish publicists who belong to what they proudly call "the new class" (*né arrivistes*), and these lively hucksters have now managed to raise fag-baiting to a level undreamed of in Falls Church—or even in Moscow.

In a letter to a friend, George Orwell wrote, "It is impossible to mention Jews in print, either favorably or unfavorably, without getting into trouble." But there are times when trouble had better be got into before mere trouble turns into catastrophe. Jews, blacks, and homosexualists are despised by the Christian and Communist majorities of East and West. Also, as a result of the invention of Israel, Jews can now count on the hatred of the Islamic world. Since our own Christian majority looks to be getting ready for great adventures at home and abroad, I would suggest that the three despised minorities join forces in order not to be destroyed. This seems an obvious thing to do. Unfortunately, most Jews refuse to see any similarity between their special situation and that of the same-sexers. At one level, the

Jews are perfectly correct. A racial or religious or tribal identity is a kind of fact. Although sexual preference is an even more powerful fact, it is not one that creates any particular social or cultural or religious bond between those so-minded. Although Jews would doubtless be Jews if there was no anti-Semitism, same-sexers would think little or nothing at all about their preference if society ignored it. So there *is* a difference between the two estates. But there is no difference in the degree of hatred felt by the Christian majority for Christ-killers and Sodomites. In the German concentration camps, Jews wore yellow stars while homosexualists wore pink triangles. I was present when Christopher Isherwood tried to make this point to a young Jewish movie producer. "After all," said Isherwood, "Hitler killed six hundred thousand homosexuals." The young man was not impressed. "But Hitler killed six *million* Jews," he said sternly. "What are you?" asked Isherwood. "In real estate?"

Like it or not, Jews and homosexualists are in the same fragile boat, and one would have to be pretty obtuse not to see the common danger. But obtuseness is the name of the game among New York's new class. Elsewhere, I have described the shrill fag-baiting of Joseph Epstein, Norman Podhoretz, Alfred Kazin, and the Hilton Kramer Hotel. *Harper's* magazine and *Commentary* usually publish these pieces, though other periodicals are not above printing the odd exposé of the latest homosexual conspiracy to turn the United States over to the Soviet Union or to structuralism or to Christian Dior. Although the new class's thoughts are never much in themselves, and they themselves are no more than spear carriers in the political and cultural life of the West, their prejudices and superstitions do register in a subliminal way, making mephitic the air of Manhattan if not of the Republic.

A case in point is that of Mrs. Norman Podhoretz, also known as Midge Decter (like Martha Ivers, *whisper* her name). In September of last year, Decter published a piece called "The Boys on the Beach" in her husband's magazine, *Commentary*. It is well worth examining in some detail because she has managed not only to come up with every known prejudice and superstition about same-sexers but also to make up some brand-new ones. For sheer vim and vigor, "The Boys on the Beach" outdoes its implicit model, *The Protocols of the Elders of Zion.*

Decter notes that when the "homosexual-rights movement first burst upon the scene," she was "more than a little astonished." Like so many new-class persons, she writes a stilted sort of genteel-gentile prose not unlike—but not very like, either—*The New Yorker* house style of the 1940s and 50s. She also writes with the authority and easy confidence of someone who knows that she is very well known indeed to those few who know her.

Decter tells us that twenty years ago, she got to know a lot of pansies at a resort called Fire Island Pines, where she and a number of other new-class persons used to make it during the summers. She estimates that 40 percent of the summer people were heterosexual; the rest were not. Yet the "denizens, homosexual and heterosexual alike, were predominantly professionals and people in soft marginal businesses—lawyers, advertising executives, psychotherapists, actors, editors, writers, publishers, etc." Keep this in mind. Our authoress does not.

Decter goes on to tell us that she is now amazed at the recent changes in the boys on the beach. Why have they become so politically militant—and so ill groomed? "What indeed has happened to the homosexual community I used to know—they who only a few short years ago [as opposed to those manly 370-day years] were characterized by nothing so much as a sweet, vain, pouting, girlish attention to the youth and beauty of their bodies?" Decter wrestles with this problem. She tells us how, in the old days, she did her very best to come to terms with her own normal dislike for these half-men—and half-women, too: "There were also homosexual women at the Pines, but they were, or seemed to be, far fewer in number. Nor, except for a marked tendency to hang out in the company of large and ferocious dogs, were they instantly recognizable as the men were." Well, if I were a dyke and a pair of Podhoretzes came waddling toward me on the beach, copies of Leviticus and Freud in hand, I'd get in touch with the nearest Alsatian dealer pronto.

Decter was disturbed by "the slender, seamless, elegant and utterly chic" clothes of the fairies. She also found it "a constant source of wonder" that when the fairies took off their clothes, "the largest number of homosexuals had hairless bodies. Chests, backs, arms, even legs were smooth and silky.... We were never able to determine just why there should be so definite a connection between what is nowadays called their sexual preference [previously known to right-thinking Jews as an abomination against Jehovah] and their smooth feminine skin. Was it a matter of hormones?" Here Decter betrays her essential modesty and lack of experience. In the no doubt privileged environment of her Midwestern youth, she could not have seen very many gentile males without their clothes on. If she had, she would have discovered that gentile men tend to be less hairy than Jews except, of course, when they are not. Because the Jews killed our Lord, they are forever marked with hair on their shoulders—something that no gentile man has on *his* shoulders except for John Travolta and a handful of other Italian-Americans from the Englewood, New Jersey, area.

It is startling that Decter has not yet learned that there is no hormonal difference between men who like sex with other men and those who like sex with women. She notes, "There is also such a thing as characteristic homosexual speech…it is something of an accent redolent of small towns in the Midwest whence so many homosexuals seemed to have migrated to the big city." Here one detects the disdain of the self-made New Yorker for the rural or small-town American. "Midwest" is often a code word for the flyovers, for the millions who do not really matter. But she is right in the sense that when a group chooses to live and work together, they do tend to sound and look alike. No matter how crowded and noisy a room, one can always detect the new-class person's nasal whine.

Every now and then, Decter does wonder if, perhaps, she is generalizing and whether this will "no doubt in itself seem to many of the uninitiated a bigoted formulation." Well, Midge, it does. But the spirit is upon her, and she cannot stop because "one cannot even begin to get at the truth about homosexuals without this kind of generalization. They are a group so readily distinguishable." Except of course, when they are not. It is one thing for a group of queens, in "soft, marginal" jobs, to "cavort," as she puts it, in a summer place and be "easily distinguishable" to her cold eye just as Jewish members of the new class are equally noticeable to the cold gentile eye. But it is quite another thing for those men and women who prefer same-sex sex to other-sex sex yet do not choose to be identified—and so are not. To begin to get at the truth about homosexuals, one must realize that the majority of those millions of Americans who prefer same-sex sex to other-sex sex are obliged, sometimes willingly and happily but often not, to marry and have children and to conform to the guidelines set down by the heterosexual dictatorship.

Decter would know nothing of this because in her "soft, marginal" world, she is not meant to know. She does remark upon the fairies at the Pines who did have wives and children: "They were for the most part charming and amusing fathers, rather like favorite uncles. And their wives...drank." This dramatic ellipsis is most Decterian.

She ticks off Susan Sontag for omitting to mention in the course of an essay on camp "that camp is of the essence of homosexual style, invented by homosexuals, and serving the purpose of domination by ridicule." The word "domination" is a characteristic new-class touch. The powerless are always obsessed by power. Decter seems unaware that all despised minorities are quick to make rather good jokes about themselves before the hostile majority does. Certainly Jewish humor, from the Book of Job (a laff-riot) to pre-*auteur* Woody Allen, is based on this.

Decter next does the ritual attack on Edward Albee and Tennessee Williams for presenting "what could only have been homosexual relationships as the deeper truth about love in our time." This is about as true as the late Maria Callas's conviction that you could always tell a Jew because he had a hump at the back of his neck— something Callas herself had in dromedarian spades.

Decter makes much of what she assumes to be the fags' mockery of the heterosexual men at the Pines: "Homosexuality paints them [heterosexuals] with the color of sheer entrapment," while the fags' "smooth and elegant exteriors, unmussed by traffic with the detritus of modern family existence, constituted a kind of sniggering reproach to their striving and harried straight brothers." Although I have never visited the Pines, I am pretty sure that I know the "soft marginal" types, both hetero and homo, that hung out there in the 1960s. One of the most noticeable characteristics of the self-ghettoized same-sexer is his perfect indifference to the world of the other-sexers. Although Decter's blood was always at the boil when contemplating these unnatural and immature half-men, they were, I would suspect, serenely unaware of her and her new-class cronies, solemnly worshipping at the shrine of The Family.

To hear Decter tell it, fags had nothing to complain of then, and they have nothing to complain of now: "Just to name the professions and industries in which they had, and still have, a significant presence is to define the boundaries of a certain kind of privilege: theatre, music, letters, dance, design, architecture, the visual arts, fashion at every level—from head, as it were, to foot, and from inception to retail—advertising, journalism, interior decoration, antique dealing, publishing...the list could go on." Yes. But these are all pretty "soft, marginal" occupations. And none is "dominated" by fags. Most male same-sexers are laborers, farmers, mechanics, small businessmen, schoolteachers, firemen, policemen, soldiers, sailors. Most female same-sexers are wives and mothers. In other words, they are like the rest of the population. But then it is hard for the new-class person to realize that Manhattan is not the world. Or as a somewhat alarmed Philip Rahv said to me after he had taken a drive across the United States, "My God! There are so many of them!" In theory, Rahv had always known that there were a couple of hundred million gentiles out there, but to see them, in the flesh, unnerved him. I told him that I was unnerved, too, particularly when they start showering in the Blood of the Lamb.

Decter does concede that homosexualists have probably not "established much of a presence in basic industry or government service or in such classic [new-classy?] professions as doctoring and lawyering but then for anyone acquainted with them as a group the thought suggests itself that few of them have ever made much effort in these directions." Plainly, the silly billies are too busy dressing up and dancing the hullygully to argue a case in court. Decter will be relieved to know that the percentage of same-sexers in the "classic" activities is almost as high, proportionately, as that of Jews. But a homosexualist in a key position at, let us say, the Department of Labor will be married and living under a good deal of strain because he could be fired if it is known that he likes to have sex with other men.

Decter knows that there have always been homosexual teachers, and she thinks that they should keep quiet about it. But if they keep quiet, they can be blackmailed or fired. Also, a point that would really distress her, a teacher known to be a same-sexer would be a splendid role model for those same-sexers that he—or she—is teaching. Decter would think this an unmitigated evil because men and women were created to breed; but, of course, it would be a perfect good because we have more babies than we know what to do with while we lack, notoriously, useful citizens at ease with themselves. That is what the row over the schools is all about.

Like most members of the new class, Decter accepts without question Freud's line (*Introductory Lectures on Psychoanalysis*) that "we actually describe a sexual activity as perverse if it has given up the aim of reproduction and pursues the attainment of pleasure as an aim independent of it." For Freud, perversion was any sexual activity involving "the abandonment of the reproductive function." Freud also deplored masturbation as a dangerous "primal affliction." So did Moses. But then it was Freud's curious task to try to create a rational, quasi-scientific basis for Mosaic law. The result has been not unlike the accomplishments of Freud's great contemporary, the ineffable and inexorable Mary Baker Eddy, whose First Church of Christ Scientist he was able to match with *his* First Temple of Moses Scientist.

Decter says that once faggots have "ensconced" themselves in certain professions or arts, "they themselves have engaged in a good deal of discriminatory practices against others. There are businesses and professions [which ones? She is congenitally short of data] in which it is less than easy for a straight, unless he makes the requisite gesture of propitiation to the homosexual in power, to get ahead." This, of course, was Hitler's original line about the Jews: they had taken over German medicine, teaching, law, journalism. Ruthlessly, they kept out gentiles; lecherously, they demanded sexual favors. "I simply want to reduce their numbers in these fields," Hitler told Prince Philip of Hesse. "I want them proportionate to their overall number in the population." This was the early solution; the final solution followed with equal logic.

In the 1950s, it was an article of faith in new-class circles that television had been taken over by the fags. Now I happen to have known most of the leading producers of that time and, of a dozen, the two who were interested in same-sex activities were both married to women who...did not drink. Neither man dared mix sex with business. Every now and then an actor would say that he had not got work because he had refused to put out for a faggot producer, but I doubt very much if there was ever any truth to what was to become a bright jack-o'-lantern in the McCarthy *Walpurgisnacht*.

When I was several thousand words into Decter's tirade, I suddenly realized that she does not know what homosexuality is. At some level she may have stumbled, by accident, on a truth that she would never have been able to comprehend in a rational way. Although to have sexual relations with a member of one's own sex is a common and natural activity (currently disapproved of by certain elements in this culture), there is no such thing as a homosexualist any more than there is such a thing as a heterosexualist. That is one of the reasons there has been so much difficulty with nomenclature. Despite John Boswell's attempts to give legitimacy to the word "gay," it is still a ridiculous word to use as a common identification for Frederick the Great, Franklin Pangborn and Eleanor Roosevelt. What makes some people prefer same-sex sex derives from whatever impulse or conditioning makes some people prefer other-sex sex. This is so plain that it seems impossible that our Mosaic-Pauline-Freudian society has not yet figured it out. But to ignore the absence of evidence is the basis of true faith.

Decter seems to think that yesteryear's chic and silly boys on the beach and today's socially militant fags are simply, to use her verb, "adopting" what she calls, in her tastefully appointed English, a lifestyle. On the other hand, "whatever disciplines it might entail, heterosexuality is not something adopted but something accepted. Its woes—and they have of course nowhere been more exaggerated than in those areas of the culture consciously or unconsciously influenced by the propaganda of homosexuals—are experienced as the woes of life."

"Propaganda"—another key word. "Power." "Propitiation." "Domination." What *does* the new class dream of?

Decter now moves in the big artillery. Not only are fags silly and a nuisance but they are, in their unrelenting hatred of heterosexualists, given to depicting them in their plays and films and books as a bunch of klutzes, thereby causing truly good men and women to falter—even question—that warm, mature heterosexuality that is so necessary to keeping this country great while allowing new-class persons to make it materially.

Decter is in full cry. Fags are really imitation women. Decter persists in thinking that same-sexers are effeminate, swishy, girlish. It is true that a small percentage of homosexualists are indeed effeminate, just as there are effeminate heterosexuals. I don't know why this is so. No one knows why. Except Decter. She believes that this sort "of female imitation pointed neither to sympathy with nor flattery of the female principle." Yet queens of the sort she is writing about tend to get on very well with women. But Decter can only cope with two stereotypes: the boys on the beach, mincing about, and the drab political radicals of gay liberation. The millions of ordinary masculine types are unknown to her because they are not identifiable by voice or walk and, most important, because they have nothing in common with one another except the desire to have same-sex relations. Or, put the other way around, since Lyndon Johnson and Bertrand Russell were both heterosexualists, what character traits did *they* have in common? I should think none at all. So it is with the invisible millions—now becoming less invisible—of same-sexers.

But Decter knows her Freud, and reality may not intrude: "The desire to escape from the sexual reminder of birth and death, with its threat of paternity—that is, the displacement of oneself by others—was the main underlying desire that sent those Fire Island homosexuals into the arms of other men. Had it been the opposite desire—that is, the positive attraction to the manly—at least half the boutiques, etc.," would have closed. Decter should take a stroll down San Francisco's Castro Street, where members of the present generation of fags look like off-duty policemen or construction workers. They have embraced the manly. But Freud has spoken. Fags are fags because they adored their mothers and hated their poor, hard-working daddies. It is amazing the credence still given this unproven, unprovable thesis.

Curiously enough, as I was writing these lines, expressing yet again the unacceptable obvious, I ran across Ralph Blumenthal's article in the *New York Times* (August 25), which used "unpublished letters and growing research into the hidden life of Sigmund Freud" to examine "Freud's reversal of his theory attributing neurosis in adults to sexual seduction in childhood." Despite the evidence given by his patients, Freud decided that their memories of molestation were "phantasies." He then appropriated from the high culture (a real act of hubris) Oedipus the King, and made him a complex. Freud was much criticized for this theory at the time—particularly by Sandor Ferenczi. Now, as we learn more about Freud (not to mention about the sexual habits of Victorian Vienna as reported in police records), his theory is again under attack. Drs. Milton Klein and David Tribich have written a paper titled "On Freud's Blindness." They have studied his case histories and observed how he ignored evidence, how "he looked to the child and only to the child, in uncovering the causes of psychopathology." Dr. Karl Menninger wrote Dr. Klein about these findings: "Why oh why couldn't Freud believe his own ears?" Dr. Menninger then noted, "Seventy-five per cent of the girls we accept at the Villages have been molested in childhood by an adult. And that's today in Kansas! I don't think Vienna in 1900 was any less sophisticated."

In the same week as Blumenthal's report on the discrediting of the Oedipus complex, researchers at the Kinsey Institute reported (*The Observer*, August 30) that after studying 979 homosexualists ("the largest sample of homosexuals—black and white, male and female—ever questioned in an academic study") and 477 heterosexualists, they came to the conclusion that family life has nothing to do with sexual preference. Apparently, "homosexuality is deep-rooted in childhood, may be biological in origin, and simply shows in more and more important ways as a child grows older. It is not a condition which therapy can reverse." Also, "homosexual feelings begin as much as three years before any sort of homosexual act, undermining theories that homosexuality is learned through experience." There goes the teacher-as-seducer-and-perverter myth. Finally, "Psychoanalysts' theories about smothering mum and absent dad do not stand investigation. Patients may tend to believe that they are true because therapists subtly coach them in the appropriate memories of their family life."

Some years ago, gay activists came to *Harper's*, where Decter was an editor, to demonstrate against an article by Joseph Epstein, who had announced, "If I had the power to do so, I would wish homosexuality off the face of the earth." Well, that's what Hitler had the power to do in Germany, and did—or tried to do. The confrontation at *Harper's* now provides Decter with her theme. She tells us that one of the demonstrators asked, "Are you aware of how many suicides you may be responsible for in the homosexual community?" I suspect that she is leaving out the context of this somewhat left-field *cri de coeur*. After all, homosexualists have more to fear from murder than suicide. I am sure that the actual conversation had to do with the sort of mischievous effect that Epstein's Hitlerian piece might have had on those fag-baiters who read it.

But Decter slyly zeroes in on the word "suicide." She then develops a most unusual thesis. Homosexualists hate themselves to such an extent that they wish to become extinct either through inviting murder or committing suicide. She notes that in a survey of San Francisco's homosexual men, half of them "claimed to have had sex with at least five hundred people." This "bespeaks the obliteration of all experience, if not, indeed, of oneself." Plainly Decter has a Mosaic paradigm forever in mind and any variation on it is abominable. Most men—homo or hetero—given the opportunity to have sex with 500 different people would do so, gladly; but most men are not going to be given the opportunity by a society that wants them safely married so that they will be docile workers and loyal consumers. It does not suit our rulers to have the proles tomcatting around the way that our rulers do. I can assure Decter that the thirty-fifth president went to bed with more than 500 women and that the well-known…but I must not give away the secrets of the old class or the newly-middle-class new class will go into shock.

Meanwhile, according to Decter, "many homosexuals are nowadays engaged in efforts at self-obliteration…there is the appalling rate of suicide among them." But the rate is not appreciably higher than that for the rest of the population. In any case, most who do commit—or contemplate—suicide do so because they cannot cope in a world where they are, to say the least, second-class citizens. But Decter is now entering uncharted country. She also has a point to make: "What is undeniable is the increasing longing among the homosexuals to do away with themselves—if not in the actual physical sense then at least spiritually—a longing whose chief emblem, among others, is the leather bars."

So Epstein will not be obliged to press that button in order to get rid of the fags. They will do it themselves. Decter ought to be pleased by this, but it is not in her nature to be pleased by anything that the same-sexers do. If they get married and have children and swear fealty to the family gods of the new class, their wives will...drink. If they live openly with one another, they have fled from woman and real life. If they pursue careers in the arts, heteros will have to be on guard against vicious covert assaults on heterosexual values. If they congregate in the fashion business the way that Jews do in psychiatry, they will employ only those heterosexuals who will put out for them.

Decter is appalled by the fag "takeover" of San Francisco. She tells us about the "ever deepening resentment of the San Francisco straight community at the homosexuals' defiant displays and power ['power'!] over this city," but five paragraphs later she contradicts herself: "Having to a very great extent overcome revulsion of common opinion, are they left with some kind of unappeased hunger that only their own feelings of hatefulness can now satisfy?"

There it is. *They are hateful.* They know it. That is why they want to eliminate themselves. "One thing is certain." Decter finds a lot of certainty around. "To become homosexual is a weighty act." She still has not got the point that one does not choose to have same-sex impulses; one simply has them, as everyone has, to a greater or lesser degree, other-sex impulses. To deny giving physical expression to those desires may be pleasing to Moses and Saint Paul and Freud, but these three rabbis are aberrant figures whose nomadic values are not those of the thousands of other tribes that live or have lived on the planet. Women's and gay liberation are simply small efforts to free men and women from this trio.

Decter writes, "Taking oneself out of the tides of ordinary mortal existence is not something one does from any longing to think oneself ordinary (but only following a different 'life-style')." I don't quite grasp this sentence. Let us move on to the next: "Gay Lib has been an effort to set the weight of that act at naught, to define homosexuality as nothing more than a casual option among options." Gay lib has done just the opposite. After all, people are what they are sexually not through "adoption" but because that is the way they are structured. Some people do shift about in the course of a life. Also, most of those with same-sex drives do indeed "adopt" the heterosexual life-style because they don't want to go to prison or to the madhouse or become unemployable. Obviously, there *is* an option but it is a hard one that ought not to be forced on any human being. After all, homosexuality is only important when made so by irrational opponents. In this, as in so much else, the Jewish situation is precisely the same.

Decter now gives us not a final solution so much as a final conclusion: "In accepting the movement's terms [hardly anyone has, by the way], heterosexuals have only raised to a nearly intolerable height the costs of the homosexuals' flight from normality." The flight, apparently, is deliberate, a matter of perverse choice, a misunderstanding of daddy, a passion for mummy, a fear of responsibility. Decter threads her clichés like Teclas on a string: "Faced with the accelerating round of drugs, S-M and suicide, can either the movement or its heterosexual sympathizers imagine they have done anyone a kindness?"

Although the kindness of strangers is much sought after, gay liberation has not got much support from anyone. Natural allies like the Jews are often virulent in their attacks. Blacks in their ghettos, Chicanos in their barrios, and rednecks in their pulpits also have been influenced by the same tribal taboos. That Jews and blacks and Chicanos and rednecks all contribute to the ranks of the same-sexers only increases the madness. But the world of the Decters is a world of perfect illogic.

Herewith the burden of "The Boys on the Beach": since homosexualists choose to be the way they are out of idle hatefulness, it has been a mistake to allow them to come out of the closet to the extent that they have, but now that they are out (which most are not), they will have no choice but to face up to their essential hatefulness and abnormality and so be driven to kill themselves with promiscuity, drugs, S-M and suicide. Not even the authors of *The Protocols of the Elders of Zion* ever suggested that the Jews, who were so hateful to them, were also hateful to themselves. So Decter has managed to go one step further than the Protocols' authors; she is indeed a virtuoso of hate, and thus do pogroms begin.

Tricks is the story of an author—Renaud Camus himself—who has twenty-five sexual encounters in the course of six months. Each of these encounters involves a pick-up. Extrapolating from Camus's sexual vigor at the age of 35, I would suspect that he has already passed the 500 mark and so is completely obliterated as a human being. If he is, he still writes very well indeed. He seems to be having a good time, and he shows no sign of wanting to kill himself, but then that may be a front he's keeping up. I am sure that Decter will be able to tell just how close he is to OD'ing.

From his photograph, Camus appears to have a lot of hair on his chest. I don't know about the shoulders, as they are covered, modestly, with a shirt. Perhaps he is Jewish. Roland Barthes wrote an introduction to *Tricks*. For a time, Barthes was much admired in American academe. But then, a few years ago, Barthes began to write about his same-sexual activities; he is now mentioned a bit less than he was in the days before he came out, as they say.

Barthes notes that Camus's book is a "text that belongs to literature." It is not pornographic. It is also not a Homosexual Novel in that there are no deep, anguished chats about homosexuality. In fact, the subject is never mentioned; it just is. Barthes remarks, "Homosexuality shocks less [well, he is—or was—French], but continues to be interesting; it is still at that stage of excitation where it provokes what might be called feats of discourse [see "The Boys on the Beach," no mean feat!]. Speaking of homosexuality permits those who aren't to show how open, liberal, and modern they are; and those who are to bear witness, to assume responsibility, to militate. Everyone gets busy, in different ways, whipping it up." You can say that again! And Barthes does. But with a nice variation. He makes the point that you are never allowed *not* to be categorized. But then, "say 'I am' and you will be socially saved." Hence the passion for the either/or.

Camus does not set out to give a panoramic view of homosexuality. He comments, in *his* preface, on the variety of homosexual expressions. Although there is no stigma attached to homosexuality in the French intellectual world where, presumably, there is no equivalent of the new class, the feeling among the lower classes is still intense, a memento of the now exhausted (in France) Roman Catholic Church's old dirty work ("I don't understand the French Catholics," said John Paul II). As a result, many "refuse to grant their tastes because they live in such circumstances, in such circles, that their desires are not only for themselves inadmissible but inconceivable, unspeakable."

It is hard to describe a book that is itself a description, and that is what *Tricks* is—a flat, matter-of-fact description of how the narrator meets the tricks, what each says to the other, where they go, how the rooms are furnished, and what the men do. One of the tricks is nuts; a number are very hairy—the narrator has a Decterian passion for the furry; there is a lot of anal and banal sex as well as oral and floral sex. *Frottage* flows. Most of the encounters take place in France, but there is one in Washington, D.C., with a black man. There is a good deal of comedy, in the Raymond Roussel manner.

Tricks will give ammunition to those new-class persons and redneck divines who find promiscuity every bit as abominable as same-sex relations. But that is the way men are when they are given freedom to go about their business unmolested. One current Arab ruler boasts of having ten sexual encounters a day, usually with different women. A diplomat who knows him says that he exaggerates, but not much. Of course, he is a Moslem.

The family, as we know it, is an economic, not a biological, unit. I realize that this is startling news in this culture and at a time when the economies of both East and West require that the nuclear family be, simply, God. But our ancestors did not live as we do. They lived in packs for hundreds of millennia before "history" began, a mere 5,000 years ago. Whatever social arrangements human society may come up with in the future, it will have to be acknowledged that those children who are needed should be rather more thoughtfully brought up than they are today and that those adults who do not care to be fathers or mothers should be let off the hook. This is beginning, slowly, to dawn. Hence, the rising hysteria in the land. Hence, the concerted effort to deny the human ordinariness of same-sexualists. A recent attempt to portray such a person sympathetically on television was abandoned when the Christers rose up in arms.

Although I would never suggest that Truman Capote's bright wit and sweet charm as a television performer would not have easily achieved for him his present stardom had he been a *hetero*sexualist, I do know that if he had not existed in his present form, another would have been run up on the old sewing machine because that sort of *per-*

sona must be, for a whole nation, the stereotype of what a fag is. Should some macho film star like Clint Eastwood, say, decide to confess on television that he is really into same-sex sex, the cathode tube would blow a fuse. That could never be allowed. That is all wrong. That is how the Roman Empire fell.

There is not much *angst* in *Tricks*. No one commits suicide—but there is one sad story. A militant leftist friend of Camus's was a teacher in the south of France. He taught 14-year-old members of that oldest of all the classes, the exploited laborer. One of his pupils saw him in a fag bar and spread the word. The students began to torment what had been a favorite teacher. "These are little proles," he tells Camus, "and Mediterranean besides—which means they're obsessed by every possible macho myth, and by homosexuality as well. It's all they can think about." One of the boys, an Arab, followed him down the street, screaming "Faggot!" "It was as if he had finally found someone onto whom he could project his resentment, someone he could hold in contempt with complete peace of mind."

This might explain the ferocity of the new class on the subject. They know that should the bad times return, the Jews will be singled out yet again. Meanwhile, like so many Max Naumanns (Naumann was a German Jew who embraced Nazism), the new class passionately supports our ruling class—from the Chase Manhattan Bank to the Pentagon to the Op-Ed page of *The Wall Street Journal*—while holding in fierce contempt faggots, blacks (see Norman Podhoretz's "My Negro Problem and Ours," *Commentary*, February 1963), and the poor (see Midge Decter's "Looting and Liberal Racism," *Commentary*, September 1977). Since these Neo-Naumannites are going to be in the same gas chambers as the blacks and the faggots, I would suggest a cease-fire and a common front against the common enemy, whose kindly voice is that of Ronald Reagan and whose less than kindly mind is elsewhere in the boardrooms of the Republic.

The Nation
November 14, 1981

Tennessee Williams: Someone to Laugh at the Squares With

1

Although poetry is no longer much read by anyone in freedom's land, biographies of those American poets who took terrible risks not only with their talents but with their lives, are often quite popular; and testimonies, chockablock with pity, terror and awe, provide the unread poet, if not his poetry, with a degree of posthumous fame. Ever since Hart ("Man overboard!") Crane dove into the Caribbean and all our hearts, the most ambitious of our poets have often gone the suicide route:

> There was an unnatural stillness in the kitchen which made her heart skip a beat then she saw Marvin, huddled in front of the oven; then she screamed: the head of the "finest sestina-operator of the Seventies" [*Hudson Review*, Spring 1970] had been burned to a crisp.

If nothing else, suicide really *validates*, to use lit-crit's ultimate verb, the life if not the poetry; and so sly Marvin was able to die secure in the knowledge that his emblematic life would be written about and that readers who would not have been caught dead, as it were, with the work of the finest sestina-operator of the Seventies will now fall, like so many hyenas, on the bio-bared bones of that long agony his life: high school valetudinarian. Columbia. The master's degree, written with heart's blood (on Rimbaud in *transition*). The awakening at Bread Loaf, and the stormy marriage to Linda. Precocious—and prescient—meteoric success of "On First Looking Into Delmore Schwartz's Medicine Cabinet" (*Prairie Schooner,* 1961). The drinking. The children. The pills. Pulitzer lost; Pulitzer regained. Seminal meeting with Roethke at the University of Iowa in an all-night diner. What conversation! Oh, they were titans then. But—born with one skin too few. All nerves; jangled sensibility. Lithium's failure is Lethe's opportunity. Genius-magma too radioactive for leaden human brain to hold. Oh! mounting horror as, one by one, the finest minds of a generation snuff themselves out in ovens, plastic bags, the odd river. Death and then—triumphant transfiguration as A Cautionary Tale.

By and large, American novelists and playwrights have not had to kill themselves in order to be noticed: There are still voluntary readers and restless playgoers out there. But since so many American writers gradually drink themselves to death (as do realtors, jockeys, and former officers of the Junior League), these sodden buffaloes are now attracting the sort of Cautionary Tale-spinner that usually keens over suicide-poets. Although the writer as actor in his time is nothing new, and the writer as performing self has been examined by Richard Poirier as a phenomenon ancillary to writer's writing, for the first time the self now threatens to become the sole artifact—to be written about by others who tend to erase, in the process, whatever writing the writer may have written.

Scott Fitzgerald, that most self-conscious of writers, made others conscious of himself and his crack-up through the pages known as *The Crack-Up.* Ever since then, American journalists and academics have used him as our paradigmatic Cautionary Tale on the ground that if you are young, handsome, talented, successful, and married to a beautiful woman, you will be destroyed because your life will be absolutely unbearable to those who teach and are taught. If, by some accident of fate, you are *not* destroyed, you will have a highly distressing old age like Somerset Maugham's, which we will describe in all its gamy incontinent horror. There is no winning, obviously. But then the Greeks knew that. And the rest is—Bruccoli. Today the writer need not write his life. Others will do it for him. But he must provide them with material; and a gaudy descent into drink, drugs, sex, and terminal name-dropping.

As Tennessee Williams's powers failed (drink/drugs/age), he turned himself into a circus. If people would not go to his new plays, he would see to it that they would be able to look at him on television and read about him in the press. He lived a most glamorous crack-up; and now that he is dead, a thousand Cautionary Tales are humming along the electrical circuits of a thousand word processors en route to the electrical circuits of thousands upon thousands of brains already overloaded with tales of celebrity-suffering, the ultimate consolation—and justification—to those who didn't make it or, worse, didn't even try.

In 1976, I reviewed Tennessee Williams's *Memoirs*. We had been friends from the late Forties to the early Sixties; after that, we saw very little of each other (drink/drugs), but I never ceased to be fond of what I called the Glorious Bird. Readers of my review, who have waited, I hope patiently, to find out Tennessee's reaction should know that when next we met, he narrowed his cloudy blue eyes and said, in tones that one of these biographers would call "clipped," "When your review appeared my book was number five on the nonfiction best-seller list of the *New York Times*. Within two weeks of your review, *it was not listed at all.*"

I last saw him three or four years ago. We were together on a televised Chicago talk show. He was in good form, despite a papilla on the bridge of his nose, the first sign, ever, of that sturdy rubbery body's resentment of alcohol. There were two or three other guests around a table, and the host. Abruptly, the Bird settled back in his chair and shut his eyes. The host's habitual unease became panic. After some disjointed general chat, he said, tentatively, "Tennessee, are you asleep?" And the Bird replied, eyes still shut, "No, I am not asleep but sometimes I shut my eyes when I am bored."

Two testimonials to the passion and the agony of the life of Tennessee Williams have just been published. One is a straightforward biography of the sort known as journeyman; it is called *The Kindness of Strangers* (what else?) by Donald Spoto. The other is *Tennessee: Cry of the Heart* (whose heart?) by a male sob sister who works for *Parade* magazine.

The first book means to shock and titillate in a *responsible* way (drink, drugs, "wildly promiscuous sex"); that is, the author tries, not always successfully, to get the facts if not the life straight. The second is a self-serving memoir with a Capotean approach to reality. In fact, I suspect that Crier of the Heart may indeed be the avatar of the late Caravaggio of gossip. If so, he has now taken up the fallen leper's bell, and we need not ask ever for whom it tolls.

Crier tells us that he lived with Williams, from time to time, in the Seventies. He tells us that Williams got him on the needle for two years, but that he bears him no grudge. In turn, he "radicalized" Williams during the Vietnam years. Each, we are told, really and truly hated the rich. Yet, confusingly, Crier is celebrated principally for his friendships with not one (1) but two (2) presidential sisters, Pat Kennedy Lawford and the late Ruth Carter Stapleton. He is also very much at home in counterrevolutionary circles: "A year before Tennessee died, I visited Mrs. Reagan at the White House and we had a long conversation alone in the Green Room after lunch. She asked about Tennessee, and Truman Capote, among others..." Oh, to have been a fly on that Green wall! But then when it comes to the rich and famous, Crier's style alternates between frantic to tell us the very worst and vatic as he cries up what to him is plainly the only game on earth or in heaven, Celebrity, as performed by consenting adults in Manhattan.

Since most of Crier's references to me are wrong, I can only assume that most of the references to others are equally untrue. But then words like *true* and *false* are irrelevant to this sort of venture. It is the awful plangency of the Cry that matters, and this one's a real hoot, as they used to say on the Bird Circuit.

On the other hand, responsible Mr. Spoto begins at the beginning, and I found interesting the school days, endlessly protracted, of Thomas Lanier Williams (he did not use the name Tennessee until he was twenty-eight). The first twenty years of Williams's life provided him with the characters that he would write about. There is his sister, Rose, two years older than he, who moved from eccentricity to madness. There is the mother, Edwina, who gave the order for Rose's lobotomy, on the best medical advice, or so she says; for Rose may or may not have accused the hard-drinking father, Cornelius, at war with sissy son, Tom, and relentlessly genteel wife, of making sexual advances to her, which he may or may not have made. In any case, Tom never ceased to love Rose, despite the blotting out of her personality. Finally, there was the maternal grandfather, the Reverend Dakin; and the grandmother, another beloved Rose, known as Grand.

In 1928, the Reverend Dakin took the seventeen-year-old Williams to Europe. Grandson was grateful to grandfather to the end, which did not come until 1955. Many years earlier, the reverend gave his life savings to unkind strangers for reasons never made clear. The Bird told me that he thought that his grandfather had been blackmailed because of an encounter with a boy. Later, the reverend burned all his sermons on the lawn. In time, Tennessee's sympathies shifted from his enervating mother to his now entirely absent father. These are the cards that life dealt Williams; and he played them for the rest of his life. He took on no new characters, as opposed to male lovers, who tend either to appear in his work as phantoms or as youthful versions of the crude father, impersonated, much too excitingly, by Marlon Brando.

A great deal has been made of Williams's homosexual adventures; not least, alas, by himself. Since those who write about him are usually more confused about human sexuality than he was, which is saying a lot, some instruction is now in order.

Williams was born, 1911, in the heart of the Bible belt (Columbus, Mississippi); he was brought up in St. Louis, Missouri, a town more southern than not. In 1919, God-fearing Protestants imposed Prohibition on the entire United States. Needless to say, in this world of fierce Christian peasant values anything pleasurable was automatically sin and to be condemned. Williams may not have believed in God but he certainly believed in sin; he came to sex nervously and relatively late—in his twenties; his first experiences were heterosexual; then he shifted to homosexual relations with numerous people over many years. Although he never doubted that what he liked to do was entirely natural, he was obliged to tote the usual amount of guilt of a man of his time and place and class (lower-middle-class WASP, southern-airs-and-graces division). In the end, he suffered from a sense of otherness, not unuseful for a writer.

But the guilt took a not-so-useful turn: He became a lifelong hypochondriac, wasting a great deal of psychic energy on imaginary illnesses. He was always about to die of some dread inoperable tumor. When I first met him (1948), he was just out of a Paris hospital, and he spoke with somber joy of the pancreatic cancer that would soon cause him to fall from the perch. Years later I discovered that the pancreatic cancer for which he had been hospitalized was nothing more than a half-mile or so of homely tapeworm. When he died (not of "an unwashed grape" but of suffocation caused by the inhaling of a nasal-spray top), an autopsy was performed and the famous heart ("I have suffered a series of cardiac seizures and arrests since my twelfth year") was found to be in fine condition, and the liver that of a hero.

Just as Williams never really added to his basic repertory company of actors (Cornelius and Edwina, Reverend Dakin and Rose, himself and Rose), he never picked up much information about the world during his half-century as an adult. He also never tried, consciously at least, to make sense of the society into which he was born. If he had, he might have figured out that there is no such thing as a homosexual or a heterosexual person. There are only homo- or heterosexual acts. Most people are a mixture of impulses if not practices, and what anyone does with a willing partner is of no social or cosmic significance.

So why all the fuss? In order for a ruling class to rule, there must be arbitrary prohibitions. Of all prohibitions, sexual taboo is the most useful because sex involves everyone. To be able to lock up someone or deprive him of employment because of his sex life is a very great power indeed, and one seldom used in civilized societies. But although the United States is the best and most perfect of earth's societies and our huddled masses earth's envy, we have yet to create a civilization, as opposed to a way of life. That is why we have allowed our governors to divide the population into two teams. One team is good, godly, straight; the other is evil, sick, vicious. Like the good team's sectarian press, Williams believed, until the end of his life, in this wacky division. He even went to an analyst who ordered him to give up both writing and sex so that he could be transformed into a good-team player. Happily, the analyst did not do in the Bird's beak, as Freud's buddy Fliess ruined the nose of a young lady, on the ground that only through breaking the nose could onanism be stopped in its vile track. Also, happily, the Bird's anarchy triumphed over the analyst. After a troubling session on the couch, he would appear on television and tell Mike Wallace all about the problems of his analysis with one Dr. Kubie, who not long after took down his shingle and retired from shrinkage.

Both *The Glass Menagerie* and *A Streetcar Named Desire* opened during that brief golden age (1945-1950) when the United States was everywhere not only regnant but at peace, something we have not been for the last thirty-five years. At the beginning, Williams was acclaimed by pretty much everyone; only *Time* magazine was consistently hostile, suspecting that Williams might be "basically negative" and "sterile," code words of the day for fag. More to the point, *Time's* founder, Henry Luce, had been born in China, son of a Christian missionary. "The greatest task of the United States in the twentieth century," he once told me, "will be the Christianization of China." With so mad a proprietor, it is no wonder that Time-Life should have led the press crusade against fags in general and Williams in particular.

Although Williams was able to survive as a playwright because he was supported by the drama reviewers of the *New York Times* and *Herald Tribune*, the only two newspapers that mattered for a play's success, he was to take a lot of flak over the years. After so much good-team propaganda, it is now widely believed that since Tennessee Williams liked to have sex with men (true), he hated women (untrue); as a result, his women characters are thought to be malicious caricatures, designed to subvert and destroy godly straightness.

But there is no actress on earth who will not testify that Williams created the best women characters in the modern theater. After all, he never ceased to love Rose and Rose, and his women characters tended to be either one or the other. Faced with contrary evidence, the anti-fag brigade promptly switch to their fallback position. All right, so he didn't hate women (as real guys do—the ball-breakers!) but, worse, far worse, *he thought he was a woman.* Needless to say, a biblical hatred of women intertwines with the good team's hatred of fags. But Williams never thought of himself as anything but a man who could, as an artist, inhabit any gender; on the other hand, his sympathies were always with those defeated by "the squares"; or by time, once the sweet bird of youth is flown. Or by death, "which has never been much in the way of completion."

Finally, in sexual matters (the principal interest of the two Cautionary Tales at hand), there seems to be a double standard at work. Although the heterosexual promiscuity of Pepys, Boswell, Byron, Henry Miller, and President Kennedy has never *deeply* upset any of their fans, Williams's ("feverish") promiscuity quite horrifies Mr. Spoto, and even Crier from the Heart tends to sniffle at all those interchangeable pieces of trade. But Williams had a great deal of creative and sexual energy; and he used both. Why not? And so what?

Heart's Crier describes how I took Williams to meet another sexual athlete (good-team, natch), Senator John F. Kennedy. Crier quotes the Bird, who is speaking to Mrs. Pat Lawford, Kennedy's sister and Crier's current friend: "Gore said he was invited to a lunch by Mr. Kennedy and would I like to come along? Of course I did, since I greatly admired your brother. He brought such vitality to our country's life, such hope and great style. He made thinking fashionable again." Actually, the Bird had never heard of Kennedy that day in 1958 when we drove from Miami to Palm Beach for lunch with the golden couple, who had told me that they lusted to meet the Bird. He, in turn, was charmed by them. "Now tell me again," he would ask Jack, repeatedly, "what you are. A governor or a senator?" Each time, Jack, dutifully, gave name, rank, and party. Then the Bird would sternly quiz him on America's China policy, and Jack would look a bit glum. Finally, he proposed that we shoot at a target in the patio.

While Jackie flitted about, taking Polaroid shots of us, the Bird banged away at the target; and proved to be a better shot than our host. At one point, while Jack was shooting, the Bird muttered in my ear, "Get that ass!" I said, "Bird, you can't cruise our next president." The Bird chuckled ominously: "They'll never elect those two. They are much too attractive for the American people." Later, I told Jack that the Bird had commented favorably on his ass. He beamed. "Now, that's *very* exciting," he said. But, fun and games to one side, it is, of course, tragic that both men were, essentially, immature sexually and so incapable of truly warm *mature* human relations. One could weep for what might have been.

Crier from the Heart has lots and lots of scores to settle in the course of his lament and he brings us bad news about all sorts of famous people who may have offended him. Certainly, he wears if not his heart his spleen on his sleeve. Mary Hemingway confessed to him that she and her husband Ernest were "never lovers. Mr. Hemingway was beyond that by then." Bet you didn't know that! As for the rich whom he and Tennessee so radically hate, they are finally incarnated not by the Rockefellers or by the Mellons but by a couple of hard-working overachievers called De la Renta, whose joint fortune must be a small fraction of the Bird's. To be fair, Crier has his compassionate side. A piece of trade had no money, and Tennessee was passed out. So Crier took the Bird's checkbook and "wrote out a check for six hundred dollars made out to cash, and took it downstairs to the hotel desk and had it cashed. I went back upstairs, handed Chris the money, and kissed him goodbye.

"It was the only time I ever forged Tennessee's name to a check, and I do not regret it." For such heroic continence, *canaille oblige.*

2

Thirty-seven years ago, in March 1948, Tennessee Williams and I celebrated his thirty-seventh birthday in Rome, except that he said that it was his thirty-*fourth* birthday. Years later, when confronted with the fact that he had been born in 1911 not 1914, he said, serenely, "I do not choose to count as part of my life the three years that I spent working for a shoe company." Actually, he spent ten months, not three years, in the shoe company, and the reason that he had changed his birth date was to qualify for a play contest open to those twenty-five or under. No matter. I thought him very old in 1948. But I was twenty-two in the spring of *annus mirabilis* when my novel *The City and the Pillar* was a best seller (Mr. Spoto thinks the book was published later) and his play, *A Streetcar Named Desire*, was taking the world by storm, as it still does.

I must say I was somewhat awed by Tennessee's success. Of course, he went on and on about the years of poverty but, starting with *The Glass Menagerie* (1944), he had an astonishingly productive and successful fifteen years: *Summer and Smoke* (1947), *The Rose Tattoo* (1951), *Cat on a Hot Tin Roof* (1955), *Suddenly Last Summer* (1958), *Sweet Bird of Youth* (1959). But even at that high moment in Rome, the Bird's eye was coldly realistic. "Baby, the playwright's working career is a short one. There's always somebody new to take your place." I said that I didn't believe it would happen in his case, and I still don't. The best of his plays are as permanent as anything can be in the age of Kleenex.

All his life, Tennessee wrote short stories. I have just finished reading the lot of them, some forty-six stories. The first was written when Tom was seventeen—a sister avenges her brother in lush prose in even lusher Pharaonic Egypt ("The Vengeance of Nitocris")—and published in *Weird Tales*. The last is unpublished. "The Negative" was written when Tennessee was seventy-one; he deals, as he so often came to do, with a poet, losing his mind, art; at the end, "as he ran toward this hugely tolerant receiver, he scattered from his gentleman's clothes, from their pockets, the illegibly scribbled poetry of his life."

To my mind, the short stories, and not *Memoirs*, are the true memoir of Tennessee Williams. Whatever happened to him, real or imagined, he turned into prose. Except for occasional excursions into fantasy, he sticks pretty close to life as he experienced or imagined it. No, he is not a great short-story writer like Chekhov but he has something rather more rare than mere genius. He has a narrative tone of voice that is wholly convincing. In this, he resembles Mark Twain, a very different sort of writer (to overdo understatement); yet Hannibal, Missouri, is not all that far from St. Louis, Missouri. Each is best at comedy and each was always uneasy when not so innocently abroad. Tennessee loved to sprinkle foreign phrases throughout his work, and they are *always* wrong.

• • •

Tennessee worked every morning on whatever was at hand. If there was no play to be finished or new dialogue to be sent round to the theater, he would open a drawer and take out the draft of a story already written and begin to rewrite it. I once found him revising a short story that had just been published. "Why," I asked, "rewrite what's already in print?" He looked at me, vaguely; then he said, "Well, obviously it's not finished." And went back to his typing.

In Paris, he gave me the story "Rubio y Morena" to read. I didn't like it. So fix it, he said. He knew, of course, that there is no fixing someone else's story (or life) but he was curious to see what I would do. So I reversed backward-running sentences, removed repetitions, eliminated half those adjectives and adverbs that he always insisted do their work in pairs. I was proud of the result. He was deeply irritated. "What you have done is remove my *style*, which is all that I have."

Tennessee could not possess his own life until he had written about it. This is common. To start with, there would be, let us say, a sexual desire for someone. Consummated or not, the desire ("something that is made to occupy a larger space than that which is afforded by the individual being") would produce reveries. In turn, the reveries would be written down as a story. But should the desire still remain unfulfilled, he would make a play of the story and then—and this is why he was so compulsive a working playwright—he would have the play produced so that he could, at relative leisure, like God, rearrange his original experience into something that was no longer God's and unpossessable but *his*. The Bird's frantic lifelong pursuit of—and involvement in—play productions was not just ambition or a need to be busy; it was the only way that he ever had of being entirely alive. The sandy encounters with his first real love, a dancer, on the beach at Provincetown and the dancer's later death ("an awful flower grew in his brain") instead of being forever lost were forever his once they had been translated to the stage where living men and women could act out his text and with their immediate flesh close at last the circle of desire. "For love I make characters in plays," he wrote; and did.

I had long since forgotten why I called him the Glorious Bird until I reread the stories. The image of the bird is everywhere in his work. The bird is flight, poetry, life. The bird is time, death: "Have you ever seen the skeleton of a bird? If you have you will know how completely they are still flying." In "The Negative" he wrote of a poet who can no longer assemble a poem. "Am I a wingless bird?" he writes; and soars no longer.

Although the Bird accepted our "culture's" two-team theory, he never seriously wanted to play on the good team, as poor Dr. Kubie discovered on prime-time television. He went right on having sex; he also went right on hating the "squares" or, as he put it, in the story "Two on a Party" (1954), where Billy (in life the poet Oliver Evans) and Cora (Marion Black Vaccaro) cruise sailors together:

> It was a rare sort of moral anarchy, doubtless, that held them together, a really fearful shared hatred of everything that was restrictive and which they felt to be false in the society they lived in and against the grain of which they continually operated. They did not dislike what they called "squares." They loathed and despised them, and for the best of reasons. Their existence was a never-ending contest with the squares of the world, the squares who have such a virulent rage at everything not in their book.

The squares had indeed victimized the Bird but by 1965, when he came to write *The Knightly Quest*, he had begun to see that the poor squares' "virulent rage" is deliberately whipped up by the rulers in order to distract them from such real problems as, in the Sixties, the Vietnam War and Watergate and Operation Armageddon then—and now—under way. In this story, Tennessee moves Lyndon Johnson's America into a near future where the world is about to vanish in a shining cloud; and he realizes, at last, that the squares have been every bit as damaged and manipulated as he; and so he now writes an elegy to the true American, Don Quixote, an exile in his own country: "His castles are immaterial and his ways are endless and you do not have to look into many American eyes to suddenly meet somewhere the beautiful grave lunacy of his gaze." Also, Tennessee seems to be trying to bring into focus the outlandish craziness of a society which had so wounded him. Was it possible that he was not the evil creature portrayed by the press? Was it possible that they are wrong about *everything*? A light bulb switches on: "All of which makes me suspect that back of the sun and way deep under our feet, at the earth's center, are not a couple of noble mysteries but a couple of joke books." Right on, Bird! It was a nice coincidence that just as Tennessee was going around the bend (drink, drugs, and a trip to the bin in 1969) the United States was doing the same. Suddenly, the Bird and Uncle Sam met face to face in *The Knightly Quest*. Better too late than never. Anyway, he was, finally, beginning to put the puzzle together.

• • •

"I cannot write any sort of story," said Tennessee to me, "unless there is at least one character in it for whom I have physical desire."

In story after story there are handsome young men, some uncouth like Stanley Kowalski; some couth like the violinist in "The Resemblance Between a Violin Case and a Coffin." Then, when Tennessee produced *A Streetcar Named Desire*, he inadvertently smashed one of our society's most powerful taboos (no wonder Henry Luce loathed him): He showed the male not only as sexually attractive in the flesh but as an object for something never before entirely acknowledged by the good team, the lust of women. In the age of Calvin Klein's steaming hunks, it must be hard for those under forty to realize that there was ever a time when a man was nothing but a suit of clothes, a shirt and tie, shined leather shoes, and a gray, felt hat. If he was thought attractive, it was because he had a nice smile and a twinkle in his eye. In 1947, when Marlon Brando appeared on stage in a torn sweaty T-shirt, there was an earthquake; and the male as sex object is still at our culture's center stage and will so remain until the likes of Boy George redress, as it were, the balance. Yet, ironically, Tennessee's auctorial sympathies were not with Stanley but with his "victim" Blanche.

I have never known anyone to complain as much as the Bird. If he was not dying of some new mysterious illness, he was in mourning for a dead lover, usually discarded long before the cancerous death, or he was suffering from the combination of various cabals, real and imagined, that were out to get him. Toward the end, he had personified the ringleaders. They were a Mr. and Mrs. Gelb, who worked for the *New York Times*. Because they had written a book about Eugene O'Neill, the Bird was convinced that the Gelbs were using the *Times* in order to destroy him so that they could sell more copies of their book about O'Neill, who would then be America's *numero uno* dramatist. Among Crier's numerous errors and inventions is the Eugene O'Neill letter, "the only one he ever wrote to Tennessee," who "read it to me, first explaining that he had received it after the opening of *The Glass Menagerie*.... It was a very moving and a very sad letter, and I don't know what became of it." The letter was written not after *Menagerie* but *Streetcar*, and Tennessee never read it to Crier or to anyone else because neither Tennessee nor I, in Rome 1948, could make head or tail of it. O'Neill was suffering from Parkinson's disease; the handwriting was illegible. The Bird and I had a running gag over the years that would begin, "As Eugene O'Neill wrote you..." Except for O'Neill, the Bird's sharp eye saw no dangerous competition. Once, at a function, where the guests were asked to line up alphabetically, Thornton Wilder approached the Bird and said, "I believe Wilder comes before Williams." To which the Bird responded, "*Only* in the alphabet."

I did not see much of him in the last years. I don't recall when he got into the habit of taking barbiturates (later, speed; and worse). He certainly did his mind and body no good; but he was tough as they come, mind and body. The current chroniclers naturally emphasize the horrors of the last years because the genre requires that they produce A Cautionary Tale. Also, since the last years are the closest to us, they give us no sense at all of what he was like for most of his long life. Obviously, he wasn't drunk or drugged all that much because he lived to write; and he wrote, like no one else.

I remember him best one noon in Key West during the early Fifties (exact date can be determined because on every jukebox "Tennessee Waltz" was being mournfully sung by Patti Page). Each of us had finished work for the day. We met on South Beach, a real beach then. We made our way through sailors on the sand to a terraced restaurant where the Bird sat back in a chair, put his bare feet up on a railing, looked out at the bright blue sea, and, as he drank his first and only martini of the midday, said, with a great smile, "I like my life."

The New York Review of Books
June 13, 1985

Oscar Wilde: On the Skids Again

Must one have a heart of stone to read *The Ballad of Reading Gaol* without laughing? (In life, practically no one ever gets to kill the thing he hates, much less loves.) And did not *De Profundis* plumb for all time the shallows of the most-reported love affair of the past hundred years, rivaling even that of Wallis and David, its every nuance (O Bosie!) known to all, while trembling rosy lips yet form, over and over again, those doom-laden syllables *The Cadogan Hotel?* Oscar Wilde. Yet again. Why?

In *Four Dubliners* (1987), Richard Ellmann published essays on Yeats, Joyce, Wilde, and Beckett. "These four," he admits, "make a strange consortium. Yet resemblances of which they were unaware begin to appear." Certainly no one could detect these resemblances better than the late Professor Ellmann, who devoted much of a distinguished career to Joyce and Yeats. He tells us that at eighteen Yeats heard Wilde lecture, while Joyce, at twenty, met Yeats and called him too old. In 1928 young Beckett met Joyce and they became friends.... So much for the traffic, somewhat more to the point, "Wilde and Yeats reviewed each other's work with mutual regard, and sometimes exploited the same themes. Joyce memorialized Wilde as a heroic victim, and repeatedly quoted or referred to him in his writings later. Beckett was saturated in all their works.... Displaced, witty, complex, savage they companion each other." I wonder.

Since Ellmann had already written magisterial works on two of the four, symmetry and sympathy plainly drew him to a third; hence, this latest biography of Wilde, this last biography of Ellmann, our time's best academic biographer. Although Ellmann was unusually intelligent, a quality seldom found in academe or, indeed, on Parnassus itself, Wilde does not quite suit his schema or his talent. Aside from the fact that the four Dubliners, as he acknowledges, "were chary of acknowledging their connection," I suspect that the controlling adjective here is "academic." To an academic of Ellmann's generation, explication is all.

The problem with Wilde is that he does not need explication or interpretation. He needs only to be read, or listened to. He plays no word games other than that most mechanical of verbal tricks: the paradox. When he rises to the sublime in poetry or prose there is so much purple all over the place that one longs for the clean astringencies of Swinburne.

On those occasions when Wilde is true master, the inventor of a perfect play about nothing and everything, we don't need to have the jokes explained. One simply laughs and wonders why no one else has ever been able to sustain for so long so flawlessly elegant a verbal riff. I would not like to rise in the academic world with a dissertation on Wilde's masterpiece and I suspect (but do not know) that hardly anyone has tried, particularly now that ever-easy Beckett's clamorous silences await, so temptingly, tenure seekers.

All in all, Wilde provides little occasion for Ellmann's formidable critical apparatus. Where Ellmann showed us new ways of looking at Yeats and, above all, at Joyce, he can do nothing more with Wilde than fit him into a historical context and tell, yet again, the profane story so well known to those who read. Is this worthwhile? I am not so sure. Ellmann does straighten out earlier versions of the gospel— or bad news, I suppose one should say. He rises to the essential prurience; and it is interesting to know that at thirty-one, after a lifetime of vigorous heterosexuality which had given him not only two children but syphilis, Wilde was seduced by Robert Ross, then aged seventeen, at Oxford. It is also interesting to know that Wilde, unlike Byron, Charlemagne, and Lassie, was not into buggery, preferring either oral sex or the Dover-sole kiss *cum* intercrural friction. What a one-time warden of All Souls did for Lawrence, Ellmann now does for Wilde. Future generations will be in his—their—debt.

Future generations. Now let us be relevant, the essential task of the irrelevant (O Oscar!): *Will there be future generations?* The British press of the AIDSy eighties thinks not. According to the *Daily Mail*, the last man on earth died in 1986, clutching to his dehydrated bosom a portrait of Margaret Thatcher. According to the *New York Post* (an Australian newspaper whose editors are able to do simple sums), the human race will be dead by century's end due to rabid homos and drug takers (mostly black and Hispanic and viciously opposed to prayer in America's chaste bookless schools). Therefore, it is now necessary to trot out an Oscar Wilde suitable for our anxious plague-ridden times. In the four decades since the Second World War, Wilde has gradually become more and more a victim-hero of a hypocritical society whose most deeply cherished superstitions about sex were to be violently shaken, first, by the war, where the principal secret of the warrior male lodge was experienced by millions on a global scale and, second, by Dr. Alfred C. Kinsey, who reported that more than one third of the triumphant Butch Republic's male population had participated in the tribal mysteries. The revolution in consciousness attributed to the Beatles and other confusions of the 1960s actually took place in the 1940s: war and Kinsey, penicillin and the Pill. As a result, Oscar Wilde ceased to be regarded as a criminal; he had been nothing worse than maladjusted to a society that was not worth adjusting to. Wilde himself became a symbol of mental if not of physical health: Ellmann pinpoints the when and how of the syphilis that killed him when every orifice, suddenly, hugely, voided in a Paris hotel room. The cumulative effect of Ellmann's Wilde may suit altogether too well the AIDSy Eighties.

Currently, our rulers are tightening the screws; too much sexual freedom is bad for production and, even worse, for consumption. Sex is now worse than mere sin; it is murderous. In the selfish pursuit of happiness another may die. One understands those paranoids who think that AIDS was deliberately cooked up in a laboratory, for the idea of plague is endlessly useful, transforming society-persecutor into society-protector: urine samples here, blood tests there.

Although Ellmann certainly did not set out to recast Wilde for our dismal age, he was, like the rest of us, a part of the way we live now, and his Wilde is more cautionary tale than martyr-story. There is the obligatory Freudianism. *Cherchez la mère* is indulged in, legitimately, I suppose. Jane Wilde, self-dubbed Speranza Francesca, was, if not larger than life, a good deal larger than average. A Protestant, Lady Wilde kept a literary salon rather than saloon in Dublin, favored an independent Ireland, wrote thundering verse worthy of her son (anent child-nurture: "Alas! The Fates are cruel. / Behold Speranza making gruel!"). She loved sensation-making and came into her own at a treason trial in Dublin, where she was gaveled down by the judge as she tried to make herself, rather than the defendant, the fount of sedition. Later, she endured the trial for seduction, of her husband, Sir William, an oculist. Trials were, rather ominously, her ice cream. Son deeply admired mother and vice versa. But Ellmann controls himself: "However accommodating it is to see a maternal smothering of masculinity as having contributed to [Oscar's] homosexuality there is reason to be skeptical."

Although Ellmann has not worked out that homosexual is an adjective describing an act not a noun descriptive of a human being, he has been able to assemble data which he then tests against fashionable theory; in this case he finds theory wanting. Oscar was a brilliant creature neither more nor less "masculine" than any other man. What he learned from his mother was not how to be a woman but the importance of being a Show-off and a Poet and a questioner of whatever quo was currently status. He also inherited her talent for bad poetry. In due course, he re-created himself as a celebrity (a terrible word that has been used in our sense since the mid-1800s), and he was well known long before he had actually done anything at all of note. The Anglo-Irish gift of the gab, combined with an actor's timing, made him noticeable at Oxford and unescapable in London's drawing rooms during the 1880s. He invented a brand-new voice for himself (the Irish brogue, no matter how Merrion Squared, was dispensed with), and Beerbohm reports on his "mezzo voice, uttering itself in leisurely fashion, with every variety of tone." He also took to gorgeous costumes that set off his large ungainly figure to splendid disadvantage. With the death of Sir William, he possessed a small inheritance, expensive tastes and no focused ambition other than poetry, a common disease of that day; also, as Yeats put it, "the enjoyment of his own spontaneity."

What is most interesting in Ellmann's account is the intellectual progress of Wilde. He is particularly good on Wilde's French connection, much of it unknown to me, though I once asked André Gide several searching questions about his friend, and Gide answered me at length. That was in 1948. I have now forgotten both questions and answers. But until I read Ellmann I did not know how well and for how long the two had known each other and what an impression Wilde ("Creation began when you were born. It will end on the day you die") had made on Gide's tormented passage through that strait gate that leads the few to life.

As a result of a collection of fairy tales, *The Happy Prince* (a revelation to at least one American child forty years later), Wilde became famous for writing as well as for showing off, and Paris stirred, as it sometimes will, for an Anglo (the Celtic distinction is unknown there). With the publication of the dialogue "The Decay of Lying," Wilde took note of a change of direction in literature, and the French were both startled and delighted that the cultural wind was coming from the wrong side of the channel. Ellmann writes,

> In England decadence had always been tinged with self-mockery. By 1890, symbolism, not decadence, had the cry, as Wilde acknowledged in the preface to *Dorian Gray*. "All art is at once surface and symbol. Those who go beneath the surface do so at their peril. Those who read the symbol do so at their peril." These aphorisms were a bow to Stéphane Mallarmé, whom he had visited in February 1891, when he was writing the preface.

Wilde then proceeded to conquer Parisian literary life in much the same way that he had the drawing rooms of London and the lecture halls of the United States. Incidentally, Ellmann's list of the number of places where Wilde spoke is positively presidential. In hundreds of cities and towns he lectured on the Beautiful, with numerous household hints. In his two chats "The House Beautiful" and "The

Decorative Arts," he foreshadowed today's how-to-do-it books. He was a sensation. My twelve-year-old grandfather (during Reconstruction, southern boys were bred early and often) recalled Wilde's performance (July 15, 1882) at the Opera House in Vicksburg, Mississippi: "He wore," and the old man's voice trembled, "a *girdle*, and he held a flower in his hand." Happily, my grandfather never knew that two weeks later Wilde was received by General Grant. (As I write these lines, I wonder *how* did he know that Wilde was wearing a girdle?)

The siege of Paris was swift, the victory total. Symbolism did not need to lay siege to Wilde; he surrendered to the modernist movement, now the world's oldest *vague*, whose long roar shows no sign of withdrawing. Wilde also appropriated Mallarmé's unfinished *Hérodiade* for his own *Salomé*, written in French for Bernhardt; but the play was admired. It is interesting just how learned the writers of the last century were: The educational system Greeked and Latined them; other languages came easily to them, cultures, too. Today's writers know very little about anything. But then those who teach cannot be taught.

During the enchantment of Paris, Wilde himself was, significantly, overwhelmed by Huysmans's *À Rebours*, still a touchstone as late as the 1940s. The young Proust was impressive to Wilde because of his "enthusiasm for English literature, especially for Ruskin (whom he translated) and George Eliot..." But when Proust invited him to dinner, Wilde arrived before Proust: "I looked at the drawing room and at the end of it were your parents, my courage failed me." Wilde departed, after the thoughtful observation to M. and Mme. Proust: "How ugly your house is."

With the local cat-king, Edmond de Goncourt, Wilde was no less magisterial. In a newspaper piece, Goncourt had got all wrong Wilde's remarks about Swinburne, while Wilde himself was sneered at as "this individual of doubtful sex, with a ham actor's language, and tall stories." Wilde chose to ignore the personal attack in a letter that set straight the gossip: "In Swinburne's work we meet for the first time the cry of flesh tormented by desire and memory, joy and remorse, fecundity and sterility. The English public, as usual hypocritical, prudish, and philistine, has not known how to find the art in the work of art: it has searched for the man in it." *Tiens!* as Henry James liked to write in his notebook. The biographer has license to go a-hunting for the man; the critic not; the reader—why not just read what's written?

Wilde, the playwright, is duly recorded, duly celebrated. Ellmann has some nice greenroom gossip for those who like that sort of thing. It is interesting to know that when Beerbohm Tree addressed a "brilliant lady" on stage he did so with his back to the audience (a Bernhardt trick, too). But then when he had an epigram to launch, he would turn to face the audience, to their ravishment. For those who like such things, there is also a very great deal about Wilde's love affair with a boring boy-beauty called Bosie. At this late date it is no longer a story worth retelling, and if Ellmann has added anything new to it I did not notice. The trial. Prison. Exile. The usual. I suspect that one of the reasons we create fiction is to make sex exciting; the fictional meeting between Vautrin and Lucien de Rubempré at the coach house in Balzac's *Illusions Perdues* is one of the most erotic ever recorded. But details of the real Oscar and Bosie in bed together or in combination with bits and pieces of England's adenoidal trade, more gifted at blackmail than ganymedery, create for the reader neither tumescence nor moistness; rather, one's thoughts turn somberly to laundry and to the brutal horror of life in a world without dry cleaning.

Ellmann's literary criticism is better than his telling of the oft-told tale. He is particularly good on *Dorian Gray*, a book truly subversive of the society that produced it—and its author. He is interesting on Wilde's conversion to a kind of socialism. Of Wilde's essay "The Soul of Man Under Socialism," Ellmann tells us that it "is based on the paradox that we must not waste energy in sympathizing with those who suffer needlessly, and that only socialism can free us to cultivate our personalities. Charity is no use—the poor are...right to steal rather than to take alms." On the other hand, Wilde was wary of authoritarianism, so often socialism's common-law helpmeet. In the end, Wilde veered off into a kind of anarchy; and defined the enemy thus:

> There are three sorts of despots. There is the despot who tyrannizes over the body. There is the despot who tyrannizes over the soul. There is the despot who tyrannizes over the

soul *and* body alike. The first is called the Prince. The second is called the Pope. The third is called the People.

Joyce was impressed by this and borrowed it for *Ulysses*. Inadvertently (I suspect), Richard Ellmann does make it clear that for all the disorder of Wilde's life he was never, in the Wordsworthian sense, "neglectful of the universal heart."

Yeats thought Wilde a man of action, like Byron, who had got waylaid by literature. When this was repeated to Wilde, he made an offhand remark about the boredom of Parliament. But Yeats did sense in Wilde the energy of the actor: of one who acts, rather than of one who simply, bemusedly *is*—the artist. But whatever Wilde might or might not have done and been, he was an extremely good man and his desire to subvert a supremely bad society was virtuous. Cardinal Newman, writing of their common day, said, "The age is so very sluggish that it will not hear you unless you bawl—you must first tread on its toes, and then apologise." But behavior suitable for an ecclesiastical busybody is all wrong for Oscar Wilde, whose only mistake was to apologize for his good work and life.

The Times Literary Supplement (London)
October 2-8, 1987

Maugham's Half & Half

1

Mr. Robert Calder has written a biography of W. Somerset Maugham in order to redress, nicely, I think, some recent studies of the man who was probably our century's most popular novelist as well as the most successful of Edwardian playwrights. Maugham's last biographer, Mr. Ted Morgan, concentrated morbidly on the incontinences and confusions of a mad old age while scanting works and bright days. Doubtless, he was influenced by the young Maugham's remark:

> I cannot understand why a biographer, having undertaken to give the world details of a famous man's life, should hesitate, as so often happens, to give details of his death…Our lives are conditioned by outer circumstances but our death is our own.

Not, as it proves, with Mr. Morgan on the case. But then, as demonstrated by Mr. Morgan and other biographers of known sexual degenerates (or merely suspected—Lennon, Presley, by one A. Goldman, the master of that expanding cottage industry, Bioporn), a contemptuous adversarial style seems to be the current…norm. Despite the degenerate's gifts, he is a Bad Person; worse, he is

Immature; even worse, he is Promiscuous. Finally, he is demonstrably more Successful than his biographer, who is Married, Mature, Monogamous, and Good.

Although Mr. Calder is MMM&G, he does believe that

> Morgan's antipathy to the man is most damaging. Though his treatment of Maugham's homosexuality is more explicit than anything previously published, it always emphasizes the nasty procuring side of his homosexual life.

Yet even a gentle schoolteacher in Saskatchewan like Mr. Calder must know that the men of Maugham's generation paid for sex with men or women or both (the last century was prostitution's Golden Age— for the buyer, of course). Would Mr. Calder think it relevant to note and deplore as immature if Joseph Conrad, say, had visited women prostitutes? I doubt it. Obviously a double standard is at work here. What is sheer high animal spirits in the roaring boy who buys a pre-feminist girl is vileness in the roaring boy who buys another boy.

To Mr. Calder's credit, he does his best to show the amiable side to the formidable Mr. Maugham—the side that Mr. Calder terms "Willie," as he was known to friends. But our schoolteacher also distances himself from "nastiness" in his acknowledgments where he notes "the unqualified encouragement of my parents, and my children—Alison, Kevin, Lorin, and Dani." (Did they pipe "What's rough trade, Daddy?" with *unqualified* encouragement?) No matter. By and large, children, your Daddy has done the old fruitcake proud.

Maugham spent his first twenty-six years in the nineteenth century and for the subsequent sixty-five years he was very much a nineteenth-century novelist and playwright. In many ways he was fortunately placed, though he himself would not have thought so. He was born in Paris where his lawyer father did legal work for the British Embassy, and his mother was a popular figure in Paris society. Maugham's first language was French and although he made himself into the premier English storyteller, his prose has always had a curious flatness to it, as if it wanted to become either Basic English or Esperanto or perhaps go back into French.

Maugham's self-pity, which was to come to a full rather ghastly flowering in *Of Human Bondage*, is mysterious in origin. On the demerit side, he lost a beloved mother at eight; lost three older brothers to boarding school (all became lawyers and one Lord Chancellor); lost, at eleven, a not-so-well-loved father. He was then sent off to a clergyman uncle in Whitstable—home of the oyster—and then to the standard dire school of the day. On the credit side, under his father's will, he got £150 a year for life, enough to live on. He was well-connected in the professional upper middle class. He had the run of his uncle's considerable library—the writer's best education. When he proved to be sickly, he was sent to the south of France; when, at seventeen, he could endure his school no more, he was sent to Heidelberg and a merry time.

On balance, the tragic wound to which he was to advert throughout a long life strikes me as no more than a scratch or two. Yes, he wanted to be taller than five foot seven; yes, he had an underslung jaw that might have been corrected; yes, he stammered. But...*tant pis,* as he might have observed coldly of another (used in a novel, the phrase would be helpfully translated).

Yet something *was* gnawing at him. As he once observed, sardonically, to his nephew Robin Maugham, "Jesus Christ could cope with all the miseries I have had to contend with in life. But then, Jesus Christ had advantages I don't possess." Presumably, Jesus was a six-foot-tall blond blue-eyed body-builder whereas Maugham was slight and dark with eyes like "brown velvet," and, of course, Jesus' father owned the shop. On the other hand, Maugham was not obliged to contend with the sadomasochistic excitement of the Crucifixion, much less the head-turning rapture of the Resurrection. It is the common view of Maugham biographers that the true tragic flaw was homosexuality, disguised as a club foot in *Of Human Bondage*—or was that the stammer? Whatever it was, Maugham was very sorry for himself. Admittedly, a liking for boys at the time of Oscar Wilde's misadventures was dangerous but Maugham was adept at passing for MMM&G: he *appeared* to have affairs with women, not men, and he married and fathered a daughter. There need not have been an either/or for him.

Maugham's career as a writer was singularly long and singularly successful. The cover of each book was adorned with a Moorish device to ward off the evil eye: the author knew that too much success over-excites one's contemporaries, not to mention the gods. Also much of his complaining may have been prophylactic: to avert the Furies if not the book-chatterers, and so he was able to live just as he wanted for two thirds of his life, something not many writers—or indeed anyone else—ever manage to do.

At eighteen, Maugham became a medical student at St. Thomas's Hospital, London. This London was still Dickens's great monstrous invention where "The messenger led you through the dark and silent streets of Lambeth, up stinking alleys and into sinister courts where the police hesitated to penetrate, but where your black bag protected you from harm." For five years Maugham was immersed in the real world, while, simultaneously, he was trying to become a writer. "Few authors," Mr. Calder tells us, "read as widely as Maugham and his works are peppered with references to other literature." So they are— peppered indeed—but not always seasoned. The bilingual Maugham knew best the French writers of the day. He tells us that he modeled his short stories on Maupassant. He also tells us that he was much influenced by Ibsen, but there is no sign of that master in his own school of Wilde comedies. Later, he was awed by Chekhov's stories but, again, he could never "use" that master because something gelled very early in Maugham the writer, and once his own famous tone was set it would remain perfectly pitched to the end.

In his first published novel, *Liza of Lambeth* (1897), Maugham raised the banner of Maupassant and the French realists but the true influence on the book and its method was one Arthur Morrison, who had made a success three years earlier with *Tales of Mean Streets*. Mr. Calder notes that Morrison,

> writing with austerity and frankness...refused to express sympathy on behalf of his readers so that they could then avoid coming to terms with the implications of social and economic inequality. Maugham adopted this point of view in his first novel, and was therefore, like Morrison, accused of a lack of conviction.

In general, realists have always been open to the charge of cold-
ness, particularly by romantics who believe that a novel is essentially
a sermon, emotional and compassionate and so inspiring that after
the peroration, the reader, wiser, kinder, *bushier* indeed, will dry his
eyes and go forth to right wrong. This critical mindset has encouraged a great deal of bad writing. The unemotional telling of a terrible
story is usually more effective than the oh, by the wind-grieved school
of romantic (that is, self-loving) prose. On the other hand, the plain
style can help the dishonest, pusillanimous writer get himself off every
kind of ideological or ethical hook. Just the facts, ma'am. In this
regard, Hemingway, a literary shadow-self to Maugham, was our
time's most artful dodger, all busy advancing verbs and stony nouns.
Surfaces coldly rendered. Interiors unexplored. Manner all.

For someone of Maugham's shy, highly self-conscious nature
(with a secret, too) the adoption of classic realism, Flaubert with bit-
ters, was inevitable. Certainly, he was lucky to have got the tone
absolutely right in his first book, and he was never to stray far from
the appearance of plain story-telling. Although he was not much of
one for making up things, he could always worry an anecdote or bit
of gossip into an agreeable narrative. Later, as the years passed, he
put more and more effort—even genius—into his one triumphant creation, W. Somerset Maugham, world-weary world-traveller, whose
narrative first person became the best-known and least wearisome in
the world. At first he called the narrator "Ashenden" (a name carefully chosen so that the writer would not stammer when saying it,
unlike that obstacle course for stammerers, "Maugham"); then he
dropped Ashenden for Mr. Maugham himself in *The Razor's Edge*
(1944). Then he began to appear, as narrator, in film and television
dramatisations of his work. Thus, one of the most-read novelists of
our time became widely known to those who do not read.

Shaw and Wells invented public selves for polemical reasons,
while Mark Twain and Dickens did so to satisfy a theatrical need, but
Maugham contrived a voice and a manner that not only charm and
surprise in a way that the others did not, but where they were men-
acingly larger than life, he is just a bit smaller (5' 7"), for which he
compensates by sharing with us something that the four histrionic
masters would not have dreamed of doing: inside gossip. It is these

confidences that made Maugham so agreeable to read: *nothing*, he tells us with a smile, *is what it seems*. That was his one trick, and it seldom failed. Also, before D. H. Lawrence, Dr. Maugham (obstetrician) knew that women, given a fraction of a chance, liked sex as much as men did. When he said so, he was called a misogynist.

In October 1907, at thirty-three, Maugham became famous with the triumphant production of *Lady Frederick* (one of six unproduced plays that he had written). Maugham ravished his audience with the daring trick of having the star—middle-aged with ardent unsuitable youthful admirer—save the boy from his infatuation by allowing him to see her un-made-up at her dressing-table. So stunned is the lad by the difference between the beauty of the *maquillage* and the crone in the mirror that he is saved by her nobleness, and right before our eyes we see "nothing is what it seems" in spades, raw stuff for the theatre of those days.

By 1908 Maugham had achieved the dream of so many novelists: he had four plays running in the West End and he was financially set for life. In that same year, the sixty-five-year-old impecunious Henry James was having one last desperate go at the theatre. To Edith Wharton he wrote that he was

> working under a sudden sharp solicitation (heaven forgive me!) for the Theatre that I had, as a matter of life or death, to push through with my play, or rather with my two plays (for I'm doing two), the more important of which (though an abject little cochonnerie even *it*, no doubt!) is to be produced...I have been governed by the one sordid & urgent consideration of the possibility of making some money...Forgive so vulgar a tale—but I am utterly brazen about it; for my base motive is all of that brassy complexion—till sicklied o'er with the reflection of another metal.

But it was to Maugham, not the Master, that the other metal came.

Maugham enjoyed his celebrity; he was a popular diner-out; he was, when he could get the words out, something of a wit. He was eminently marriageable in Edwardian eyes. So which will it be—the lady or the tiger/man? Mr. Calder cannot get enough of Maugham the faggot in conflict with Maugham the potential MMM&G. Will good drive out evil? Maturity immaturity?

Unhappily, the witch-doctor approach to human behaviour still enjoys a vogue in academe and Mr. Calder likes to put his subject on the couch, while murmuring such Freudian incantations as "loss of a beloved mother, the lack of a father with whom to identify...followed a common pattern in the development of homosexuality." That none of this makes any sense does not alter belief: in matters of faith, inconvenient evidence is always suppressed while contradictions go unnoticed. Nevertheless, witch-doctors to one side, witches did—and do—get burned, as Oscar Wilde discovered in 1895, and an entire generation of same-sexers were obliged to go underground or marry or settle in the south of France. I suspect that Maugham's experiences with women were not only few but essentially hydraulic. Writers, whether same-sexers or other-sexers, tend to have obsessive natures; in consequence, they cross the sexual borders rather less often than the less imaginative who want, simply, to get laid or even loved. But whereas a same-sexer like Noël Coward never in his life committed an other-sexual act ("Not even with Gertrude Lawrence?" I asked. "Particularly not with Miss Lawrence" was the staccato response), Dr. Maugham had no fear of vaginal teeth—he simply shut his eyes and thought of Capri.

At twenty-one Maugham was well and truly launched by one John Ellingham Brooks, a littérateur who lived on Capri, then known for the easy charm of its boys. "The nasty procuring side" of Maugham started in Capri and he kept coming back year after year. At ninety, he told a reporter, "I want to go to Capri because I started life there." In old age, he told Glenway Wescott that Brooks was his first lover. This is doubtful. Maugham told different people different things about his private life, wanting always to confuse. Certainly, for sheer energetic promiscuity he was as athletic as Byron; with a club foot, what might he not have done! Even so, "He was the most sexually voracious man I've ever known," said Beverley Nichols, the journalist and one-time Maugham secretary, who knew at first hand. Robin Maugham and the last companion, Alan Searle, agreed.

Ironically, within a dozen years of Wilde's imprisonment,

Maugham was the most popular English playwright. Unlike the reckless Oscar, Maugham showed no sign of ever wanting to book so much as a room at the Cadogan Hotel. Marriage it would be. With Syrie Barnardo Wellcome, an interior decorator much liked in London's high bohemia. Fashionable wife for fashionable playwright. A daring woman of the world—an Iris March with a green hat *pour le sport*—Syrie wanted a child by Maugham without wedlock. Got it. As luck—hers and his—would have it, Maugham then went to war and promptly met the great love of his life, Gerald Haxton.

For a time Maugham was a wound dresser. Gerald was in the Ambulance Corps. They were to be together until Gerald's death twenty-nine years later, "longer than many marriages," observes the awed Mr. Calder. But there was a good deal of mess to be cleaned up along the way. Haxton could not go to England: he had been caught by the police in bed with another man. Maugham himself did not want, finally, to be even remotely MMM&G. Syrie suffered. They separated. Toward the end of his life, Maugham tried to disinherit his daughter on the ground that she was not his but, ironically, he had got a door prize for at least one dutiful attendance and she was very much his as anyone who has ever seen her or her descendants can attest: the saturnine Maugham face still gazes by proxy upon a world where nothing else is ever what it seems.

During the war, Maugham was hired by the British secret service to go to Moscow and shore up the Kerensky government. He has written of all this in both fiction (*Ashenden*—literary ancestor to Eric Ambler, Ian Fleming, John le Carré) and two books of memoirs. Unfortunately, the mission to Moscow was aborted by the overthrow of Kerensky.

Maugham developed tuberculosis. During twenty months in a Scottish sanatorium he wrote four of his most popular plays, including *The Circle* and the highly successful novel *The Moon and Sixpence*, where a Gauguin-like English painter is observed by the world-weary Ashenden amongst Pacific palms. Maugham wrote his plays rather the way television writers (or Shakespeare) write their serials—at great speed. One week for each act and a final week to put it all together. Since Mr. Calder is over-excited by poor Willie's rather unremarkable (stamina to one side) sex life, we get far too little analysis of Maugham's writing and of the way that he worked, particularly in the theatre. From what little Mr. Calder tells us, Maugham stayed away from rehearsals but, when needed, would cut almost anything an actor wanted. This doesn't sound right to me but then when one has had twenty play productions in England alone, there is probably not that much time or inclination to perfect the product. In any case, Mr. Calder is, as he would put it, "disinterested" in the subject.

In 1915, while Maugham was spying for England, *Of Human Bondage* was published. Maugham now was seen to be not only a serious but a solemn novelist—in the ponderous American manner. The best that can be said of this masterpiece is that it made a good movie and launched Bette Davis's career. I remember that on all the pre-Second War editions, there was a quotation from Theodore Dreiser to the effect that the book "has rapture, it sings." Mr. Calder does not mention Dreiser but Mr. Frederic Raphael does, in his agreeable picture book with twee twinkly text, *Somerset Maugham and His World* (1977). Mr. Raphael quotes from Dreiser, whom he characterises as "an earnest thunderer in the cause of naturalism and himself a Zolaesque writer of constipated power." Admittedly, Dreiser was not in a class with Margaret Drabble but—constipated?*

The Maugham persona was now perfected in life and work. Maugham's wit was taken for true evil as he himself was well known, despite all subterfuge, to be non-MMM&G. Mr. Calder is disturbed by Maugham's attempts at epigrams in conversation. Sternly, Mr. Calder notes: "Calculated flippancy was nonetheless a poor substitute for natural and easy insouciance." But despite a near-total absence of easy insouciance, Maugham fascinated everyone. By 1929 he had settled into his villa at Cap Ferrat; he was much sought after socially even though the Windsors, the Churchills, the Beaverbrooks all knew that Haxton was more than a secretary. But the very rich and the very famous are indeed different from really real folks. For one thing, they often find funny the MMM&Gs. For another, they can create their own world and never leave it if they choose.

---

*Mr. Raphael has many opinions about books that he has not actually read. You will see him at his glittering best in the *Times*, in his obituary of Gore Vidal (date to come).

It is a sign of Maugham's great curiosity and continuing sense of life (even maturity) that he never stopped traveling, ostensibly to gather gossip and landscape for stories, but actually to come alive and indulge his twin passions, boys and bridge, two activities far less damaging to the environment than marriages, children, and big-game hunting. Haxton was a splendid organiser with similar tastes. Mr. Calder doesn't quite get all this but then his informants, chiefly nephew Robin Maugham and the last companion, Alan Searle, would have been discreet.

During the Second War, Maugham was obliged to flee France for America. In Hollywood he distinguished himself on the set of *Dr. Jekyll and Mr. Hyde.* George Cukor had explained to Willie how, in this version of the Stevenson story, there would be no horrendous make-up change for the star, Spencer Tracy, when he turned from good Dr. Jekyll into evil Mr. Hyde. Instead, a great actor, Tracy, would bring forth both evil and good from within. Action! Tracy menaces the heroine. Ingrid Bergman cowers on a bed. Tracy simpers, drools, leers. Then Maugham's souciant voice is heard, loud and clear and stammerless. "And which one is he supposed to be now?"

During this time, the movie of *The Moon and Sixpence* was released—the twenty-third Maugham story to be filmed. Maugham himself travelled restlessly about the East coast, playing bridge. He also had a refuge in North Carolina where, while Maugham was writing *The Razor's Edge,* Haxton died. For a time Maugham was inconsolable. Then he took on an amiable young Englishman, Alan Searle, as secretary-companion, and together they returned to the Riviera where Maugham restored the war-wrecked villa and resumed his life.

One reason, prurience aside, why Mr. Calder tells us so much about Maugham's private life (many kindnesses and charities are duly noted) is that Maugham has no reputation at all in North American academe where Mr. Calder is a spear-carrier. The result is a lot of less than half-praise: "His career had been largely a triumph of determination and will, the success in three genres of a man not naturally gifted as a writer." Only a schoolteacher innocent of how literature is made could have written such a line. Demonstrably, Maugham was very talented at doing what he did. Now, this is for your final grade, *what* did he do? Describe, please. Unfortunately, there aren't many good describers (critics) in any generation. But I shall give it a try, presently.

At seventy-two, Maugham went to Vevey, in Switzerland, where a Dr. Niehans injected ageing human organisms with the cells of unborn sheep, and restored youth. All the great came to Niehans, including Pius XII—in a business suit and dark glasses, it was said—an old man in no hurry to meet his Jewish employer. Thanks perhaps to Niehans, Maugham survived for nearly fifteen years in rude bodily health. But body outlived mind and so it was that the senile Maugham proceeded to destroy his own great invention, W. Somerset Maugham, the teller of tales, the man inclined to the good and to right action and, above all, to common sense. By the time that old Maugham had finished with himself, absolutely nothing was what it seemed and the double self-portrait that he had given the world in *The Summing Up* and *A Writer's Notebook* was totally undone by this raging Lear upon the Riviera, who tried to disinherit his daughter while adopting Searle as well as producing *Looking Back*, a final set of memoirs not quite as mad as Hemingway's but every bit as malicious. With astonishing ingenuity, the ancient Maugham mined his own monument; and blew it up.

For seven decades Maugham had rigorously controlled his personal and his artistic life. He would write so many plays, and stop; and did. So many short stories…He rounded off everything neatly, and lay back to die, with a quiet world-weary smile on those ancient lizard lips. But then, to his horror, he kept on living, and having sex, and lunching with Churchill and Beaverbrook. Friends thought that Beaverbrook put him up to the final memoir, but I suspect that Maugham had grown very bored with a lifetime of playing it so superbly safe.

2

It is very difficult for a writer of my generation, if he is honest, to pretend indifference to the work of Somerset Maugham. He was always so entirely *there*. By seventeen I had read all of Shakespeare; all of Maugham. Perhaps more to the point, he dominated the movies at a time when movies were the lingua franca of the world. Although the French have told us that the movie is the creation of the director, no one in the Twenties, Thirties, Forties paid the slightest attention to who had directed *Of Human Bondage, Rain, The Moon and Sixpence, The Razor's Edge, The Painted Veil, The Letter.* Their true creator was W. Somerset Maugham, and a generation was in thrall to his sensuous, exotic imaginings of a duplicitous world.

Although Maugham received a good deal of dutiful praise in his lifetime, he was never to be taken very seriously in his own country or the United States, as opposed to Japan where he has been for two thirds of a century the most read and admired Western writer. Christopher Isherwood tells us that he met Maugham at a Bloomsbury party where Maugham looked most ill-at-ease with the likes of Virginia Woolf. Later Isherwood learned from a friend of Maugham's that before the party, in an agony of indecision, as the old cliché master might have put it, he had paced his hotel sitting room, saying, "I'm just as good as they are."

I suspect that he thought he was probably rather better *for what he was* which was not at all what they were. Bloomsbury disdained action and commitment other than to Art and to Friendship (which meant going to bed with one another's husbands and wives). Maugham liked action. He risked his life in floods, monsoons, the collapse of holy Russia. He was worldly like Hemingway, who also stalked the big game of wild places, looking for stories, self. As for what he thought of himself, Mr. Calder quotes Maugham to the head-master of his old school: "I think I ought to have the OM [Order of Merit]...They gave Hardy the OM and I think I am the greatest living writer of English, and they ought to give it to me." When he did get a lesser order, Companion of Honour, he was sardonic: "It means very well done...but."

But. There is a definite but. I have just reread for the first time in forty years *The Narrow Corner,* a book I much admired; *The Razor's Edge,* the novel on which the film that I found the ultimate in worldly glamour was based; *A Writer's Notebook,* which I recalled as being very wise; and, yet again, *Cakes and Ale.* Edmund Wilson's famous explosion at the success of Maugham in general and *The Razor's Edge* in particular is not so far off the mark.

The language is such a tissue of clichés that one's wonder is finally aroused at the writer's ability to assemble so many and at his unfailing inability to put anything in an individual way.

Maugham's reliance on the banal, particularly in dialogue, derived from his long experience in the theatre, a popular art form in those days. One could no more represent the people on stage without clichés than one could produce an episode of *Dynasty*: Maugham's dialogue is a slightly sharpened version of that of his audience.

Both Wilde and Shaw dealt in this same sort of realistic speech but Shaw was a master of the higher polemic (as well as of the baleful clichés of the quaint working-man, rendered phonetically to no one's great delight) while Wilde made high verbal art of clichés so slyly crossed as to yield incongruent wit. But for any playwright of that era (now, too), the *mot juste* was apt to be the correctly deployed *mot banal*. Maugham's plays worked very well. But when Maugham transferred the tricks of the theatre to novel writing, he was inclined not only to write the same sort of dialogue that the stage required but in his dramatic effects he often set his scene with stage directions, ignoring the possibilities that prose *with* dialogue can yield. The economy won him many readers, but there is no rapture, song. Wilson, finally, puts him in the relation of Bulwer-Lytton to Dickens: "a half-trashy novelist who writes badly, but is patronized by half-serious readers who do not care much about writing." What ever happened to those readers? How can we get them back?

Wilson took the proud modernist view that, with sufficient education, everyone would want to move into Axel's Castle. Alas, the half-serious readers stopped reading novels long ago, while the "serious" read literary theory, and the castle's ruins are the domain of literary archaeologists. But Wilson makes a point, inadvertently: if Maugham is half-trashy (and at times his most devoted admirers would probably grant that) what, then, is the other half, that is not trash? Also, why is it that just as one places, with the right hand, the laurel wreath upon his brow, one's left hand starts to defoliate the victor's crown?

A Writer's Notebook (kept over fifty years) is filled with descriptions of sunsets and people glimpsed on the run. These descriptions are every bit as bad as Wilson's (in *The Twenties*) and I don't see why either thought that writing down a fancy description of a landscape could—or should—be later glued to the page of a novel in progress. Maugham's descriptions, like Wilson's, are disagreeably purple while the physical descriptions of people are more elaborate than what we now put up with. But Maugham was simply following the custom of nineteenth-century novelists in telling us whether or not eyebrows grow together while noting the exact placement of a wen. Also, Dr. Maugham's checklist is necessary for diagnosis. Yet he does brood on style; attempts to make epigrams. "Anyone can tell the truth, but only very few of us can make epigrams." Thus, young Maugham, to which the old Maugham retorts, "In the nineties, however, we all tried to."

In the preface, Maugham expatiates on Jules Renard's notebooks, one of the great delights of world literature and, as far as I can tell, unknown to Anglo-Americans, like so much else. Renard wrote one small masterpiece, *Poil de Carotte*, about his unhappy childhood— inhuman bondage to an evil mother rather than waitress.

Renard appeals to Maugham, though "I am always suspicious of a novelist's theories, I have never known them to be anything other than a justification of his own shortcomings." Well, that is common-sensical. In any case, Maugham, heartened by Renard's marvelous notebook, decided to publish his own. The tone is world-weary, modest. "I have retired from the hurly-burly and ensconced myself not uncomfortably on the shelf." Thus, he will share his final musings.

There is a good deal about writing. High praise for Jeremy Taylor:

> He seems to use the words that come most naturally to the mouth, and his phrases, however nicely turned, have a collo-quial air...The long clauses, tacked on to one another in a string that appears interminable, make you feel that the thing has been written without effort.

Here, at twenty-eight, he is making the case for the plain and the flat and the natural sounding:

> There are a thousand epithets with which you may describe the sea. The only one which, if you fancy yourself a stylist, you will scrupulously avoid is *blue*; yet it is that which most satisfies Jeremy Taylor...He never surprises. His imagination is without violence or daring.

Of Matthew Arnold's style, "so well suited to irony and wit, to expo-

sition...It is a method rather than an art, no one more than I can realize what enormous labour it must have needed to acquire that mel-
lifluous cold brilliance. It is a platitude that simplicity is the latest
acquired of all qualities..." The interesting giveaway here is
Maugham's assumption that Arnold's style must have been the work
of great labour. But suppose, like most good writers, the style was
absolutely natural to Arnold and without strain? Here one sees the
hard worker sternly shaping himself rather than the natural writer
easily expressing himself as temperament requires:

> My native gifts are not remarkable, but I have a certain force
> of character which has enabled me in a measure to supple-
> ment my deficiencies. I have common sense...For many years
> I have been described as a cynic; I told the truth. I wish no
> one to take me for other than I am, and on the other hand I
> see no need to accept others' pretences.

One often encounters the ultimate accolade "common sense" in these
musings. Also, the conceit that he is what you see, when, in fact, he
is not. For instance, his native gifts for narrative were of a very high
order. While, up to a point, he could tell the truth and so be thought
cynical, it was always "common sense," a.k.a. careerism, that kept
him from ever saying all that he knew. Like most people, he wanted
to be taken for what he was not; hence, the great invention W.
Somerset Maugham.

Maugham uses his Moscow experience to good literary advan-
tage. He reads the Russians. Marvels at their small cast of characters.
Notes that no one in a Russian book ever goes to an art gallery. Later,
he travels through America, wondering what the people on the trains
are really like. Then he reads, with admiration, *Main Street*, where he
detects the emergence of a complex caste system: "The lip service
which is given to equality occasions a sort of outward familiarity, but
this only makes those below more conscious of the lack of inward
familiarity; and so nowhere is class-hatred likely to give rise in the
long run to more bitter enmity."

Maugham was alert to the persisting problem of how to be a
writer at all: certainly the writer "must never entirely grow up...It

needs a peculiar turn of mind in a man of fifty to treat with great seriousness the passion of Edwin for Angelina." Or Edmund for Daisy. "The novelist is dead in the man who has become aware of the triviality of human affairs. You can often discern in writers the dismay with which they have recognized this situation in themselves." He notes how Flaubert turned from *Madame Bovary* to *Bouvard et Pécuchet*, George Eliot and H. G. Wells to "sociology," Hardy to *The Dynasts*—a step farther up Parnassus but no one thought so then.

Maugham's great enthusiasm is for Chekhov, a fellow doctor, playwright, and short-story writer:

> He has been compared with Guy de Maupassant, but one would presume only by persons who have read neither. Guy de Maupassant is a clever story-teller, effective at his best— by which, of course, every writer has the right to be judged— but without much real relation to life...But with Chekhov you do not seem to be reading stories at all. There is no obvious cleverness in them and you might think that anyone could write them, but for the fact that nobody does. The author has had an emotion and he is able so to put it in words that you receive it in your turn. You become his collaborator. You cannot use of Chekhov's stories the hackneyed expression of the slice of life, for a slice is a piece cut off and that is exactly the impression you do not get when you read them; it is a scene seen through the fingers which you know continues this way and that though you only see a part of it.

Mr. Maugham knows very well what literature is, and how great effects are, if not made, received.

Finally, he makes a bit of literature in one of the notebook entries. A popular writer of the day, Haddon Chambers, is dead. He is known for one phrase, "the long arm of coincidence." Maugham does a short amusing sketch of Chambers, the man and the writer; then he concludes: "I seek for a characteristic impression with which to leave him. I see him lounging at a bar, a dapper little man, chatting good-humouredly with a casual acquaintance of women, horses and Covent Garden opera, but with an air as though he were looking for someone who might at any moment come in at the door." That is very fine indeed, and Mr. Chambers still has a small corner of life in that bar, in that paragraph.

My only memory of *The Razor's Edge* (1944) was that of an American lady who threw a plate at the narrator, our own Mr. Maugham, with the cry, "And you can call yourself an English gentleman," to which Mr. Maugham, played urbanely in the movie by Herbert Marshall, responded niftily, "No, that's a thing I've never done in all my life." The scene has remained in my memory all these years because it is almost the only one in the book that has been dramatised. Everything else is relentlessly told. The first-person narrator, so entirely seductive in the short stories, is now heavy, garrulous, and awkward, while the clichés are not only "tissued" but Maugham even cocks, yes, a snook at his critics by recording every one of an American businessman's relentless banalities. Of course, the author is sixty-nine. Maugham's view of the world was consistent throughout his life. Intrigued by religion, he remained an atheist. Vedanta was attractive, but reincarnation was simply not common sense. If you had no recollection of any previous incarnations, what was the point? For all practical purposes the first carnation was extinct when it died, and all the others random. But during the Second War there was a lot of musing about the meaning of it all, and out of that age's anxiety did come Thomas Mann's masterpiece, *Dr. Faustus*.

Maugham stalks similar game. Again, the narrator is our Mr. Maugham, the all-wise, all-tolerant Old Party who knows a thing or two. Nearby, on the Riviera, lives Elliot Templeton, an elegant snobbish old queen whose identity was revealed for the first time in the pages of *The New York Review of Books* (September 29, 1983) as Henry de Courcey May. (Mr. Calder thinks that the character is, in part, Chips Channon, but Chips is separately present as Paul Barton, another American social climber.) Elliott is an amusing character (Mr. Calder finds him "brilliant") but Maugham can't do very much with him other than give him a Chicago niece. And money, Paris. Love. The niece is in love with Larry Darrell—why a name so close to real life Larry Durrell? Maugham's names for characters (like Hemingway's) are standard for the time—highly forgettable Anglo-Saxon names.

Why? Because novels were read by a very large public in those days and any but the most common names could bring on a suit for libel.

Larry does not want to go to work, he wants to "loaf." This means that he has spiritual longings: what does it all mean? He wants to know. He loses the girl to a wealthy young man who doesn't care what it may or may not mean. In pursuit of *it*, Larry becomes very learned in Germany; he works in a coal mine; he goes to India and discovers Vedanta. He returns to the world perhaps with *it* or perhaps not since *it* is an illusion like all else.

Maugham and Larry sit up all night in a bistro while Larry tells him the entire story of his life, much of which Maugham has already told us: it is very dangerous to be your own narrator in a book. Finally, as the dawn like a frightened Scottish scone peeps through the bistro window, Larry tells and tells about India. And Vedanta.

Larry wants nothing less than Enlightenment. Does he achieve it? Maugham teases us. Yes, no, it's all the same, isn't it? There are several short stories intercut with Larry's passion play: a brilliant poetic girl becomes a drunken drug-ridden hag and ends up on the Riviera and in the Mediterranean, murdered by a piece of trade. Proof to Mr. Calder and his Freudian friends that because Maugham liked males he (what else?) hated females. This is one of the rocks on which the whole Freudian structure has been, well...erected. For the witch-doctors, Maugham's invention of such a woman is *prima facie* evidence of his hatred of the opposite sex, which vitiated his work and made it impossible for him to be truly great and married. Yet in real life it is the other-sexers (Hemingway) who hate women, and the same-sexers (Maugham) who see them not as women but, as someone observed of Henry James's response to the ladies, as people. Finally, even the most confused witch-doctor must have stumbled upon that essential law of human behaviour: one cannot hate what one cannot love. Nevertheless, as members of chemistry departments still search for cold fusion, so dedicated English teachers still seek to crack the fairy code.

Depressed, I move on to *The Narrow Corner*. On the first page, the energy is switched on. First chapter: "All this happened a good many years ago." That's it. One settles in. Second chapter begins. "Dr. Saunders yawned. It was nine o'clock in the morning." An

English doctor (under a cloud in England—abortion? We are not told). He practices medicine in the Chinese port of Fu-chou. There is no Mrs. Saunders. There is a beautiful Chinese boy who prepares his opium pipes. Sentences are short. Descriptions of people are never tedious. We inhabit Dr. Saunders's mind for most of the book though, as always, Maugham will shift the point of view to someone else if for some reason Dr. Saunders is not witness to a necessary scene. This is lazy but a lot better than having someone sit down and tell you the story of his life, in quotation marks, page after page.

Dr. Saunders is offered a great deal of money to operate on a rich Chinese opium trafficker, domiciled on the island of Takana in the distant Malay archipelago (a trip as momentous and hazardous in those days as one from Ann Arbor to East Anglia today). By page seven the trip has been made and a successful operation for cataract has been performed. Now Dr. Saunders and beautiful Chinese boy are looking for a ship to get them home again. Enter Captain Nichols, a man under numerous clouds, but a first-class English skipper. Dr. Saunders is amused by the rogue who has arrived aboard a tugger out of Sydney, destination vague. They spar. Each notes the other's cloud. Will Dr. Saunders leave the island aboard Nichols's boat?

> Dr. Saunders was not a great reader. He seldom opened a novel. Interested in character, he liked books that displayed the oddities of human nature, and he had read over and over again Pepys and Boswell's Johnson, Florio's Montaigne and Hazlitt's essays...He read neither for information nor to improve his mind, but sought in books occasion for reverie.

In 1938, George Santayana dismissed Maugham's stories; "They are not pleasing, they are not pertinent to one's real interests, they are not true; they are simply plausible, like a bit of a dream that one might drop into in an afternoon nap." Yet, perhaps, that is a necessary condition of narrative fiction, a plausible daydreaming. Although Maugham could never have read Santayana's letter to a friend, he returns the compliment in *A Writer's Notebook*:

> I think Santayana has acquired his reputation in America

owing to the pathetically diffident persuasion of Americans that what is foreign must have greater value than what is native...To my mind Santayana is a man who took the wrong turning. With his irony, his sharp tongue, commonsense and worldly wisdom, his sensitive understanding, I have a notion that he could have written semi-philosophical romances after the manner of Anatole France which it would have been an enduring delight to read...It was a loss to American literature when Santayana decided to become a philosopher rather than a novelist.

Kindly vocational guidance from Uncle Willie; or it takes one to...

The plot: aboard the tugger is an edgy young Australian beauty (this was Maugham's one and only crypto-fag novel). Fred Blake is also under a cloud but where Doctor and Skipper each wears his cloud *pour le sport,* Fred seems ready to jump, as they say, out of his skin. It is finally agreed that the Doctor accompany them to one of the Dutch islands where he can find a ship for home. They embark. There is a storm at sea, not quite as well rendered as that in *Williwaw,* but Maugham's influence permeates those chaste pages, even down to the annoying use of *i* and *ii* as chapter heads. Plainly, the book had a large effect on the youthful war writer.

Finally, they arrive at the Dutch island of Banda Neira. There are substantial Dutch houses with marble floors, relics of a former prosperity, as well as nutmeg trees, all the props. They encounter a noble Danish youth, Eric Christessen, who in turn introduces them to a one-time English school teacher, Frith, and his daughter, Louise. The saintly Eric is in love with beautiful Louise, who is enigmatic. Dr. Saunders sees the coming tragedy but the others are unaware, particularly the trusting Eric, who says, early on, how much he likes the East. "Everyone is so nice. Nothing is too much trouble. You cannot imagine the kindness I've received at the hands of perfect strangers." I was not the only American writer to be influenced by this book.

In 1948, after Tennessee Williams had read my "bold" novel, *The City and the Pillar,* we tried to remember what books we had read that dealt, overtly or covertly, with same-sexuality. Each had a vivid memory of *The Narrow Corner.* According to Mr. Calder, Maugham himself was somewhat nervous of his romantic indiscretion. "Thank heavens nobody's seen it," he said to his nephew Robin at about the same time that Tennessee and I were recalling a novel each had intensely "seen." Another novel that each had read was James M. Cain's *Serenade* (1937), where bisexual singer loses voice whenever he indulges in same-sex but gets it back when he commits other-sex, which he does, triumphantly, in Mexico one magical night in the presence of—get cracking, Williams scholars—an iguana.

Fred and Louise couple for a night. Eric finds out and kills himself. Louise is sad but confesses to the doctor that she really did not love Eric, who had been enamoured not so much of her as of her late mother. She is, in her quiet way, a startling character. The lugger sails away. Then Fred's cloud is revealed: by accident, he murdered the husband of an older woman who had been hounding him. Fred's lawyer father is a great power in the corrupt government of New South Wales (*tout ça change*, as we say in Egypt), Fred is whisked away by Captain Nichols. In due course, it is learned that Fred is supposed to have died in a flu epidemic. So he is now a nonperson under two clouds. Dr. Saunders leaves them. Some time later, Dr. Saunders is daydreaming in Singapore when Nichols reappears. Fred fell overboard and drowned. Apparently all his money was in his belt which so weighed him down...Worse, he had won all of Nichols's money at cribbage. Plainly, the doomed boy had been killed for his money which, unknown to Nichols, he took with him to Davy Jones's locker. Nothing is...

The novel still has all of its old magic. There is not a flaw in the manner except toward the end where Maugham succumbs to sentiment. Fred:

'Eric was worth ten of her. He meant all the world to me. I loathe the thought of her. I only want to get away. I want to forget. How could she trample on that lone noble heart!' Dr. Saunders raised his eyebrows. Language of that sort chilled his sympathy. 'Perhaps she's very unhappy,' he suggested mildly. 'I thought you were a cynic. You're a sentimentalist.' 'Have you only just discovered it?'

Sincerity in a work of art is always dangerous and Maugham, uncharacteristically, lets it mar a key scene because, by showing that boy cared more for boy than girl, he almost gives away at least one game. But recovery was swift and he was never to make that mistake again. As he observed in *Cakes and Ale*:

> I have noticed that when I am most serious people are apt to laugh at me, and indeed when after a lapse of time I have read passages that I wrote from the fullness of my heart I have been tempted to laugh at myself. It must be that there is something naturally absurd in a sincere emotion, though why there should be I cannot imagine, unless it is that man, the ephemeral inhabitant of an insignificant planet, with all his pain and all his striving is a jest in an eternal mind.

What then of *Cakes and Ale*? The story is told in the first person by the sardonic Ashenden, a middle-aged novelist (Maugham was fifty-six when the book was published in 1930). The manner fits the story, which is not told but acted out. What telling we are told is simply Maugham the master essayist, heir of Hazlitt, commenting on the literary world of his day—life, too. In this short novel he combines his strengths—the discursive essay "peppered" this time with apposite literary allusions to which is added the high craftsmanship of the plays. The dialogue scenes are better than those of any of his contemporaries while the amused comments on literary ambition and reputation make altogether enjoyable that small, now exotic, world.

Plot: a great man of letters, Edward Driffield (modelled on Thomas Hardy), is dead and the second wife wants someone to write a hagiography of this enigmatic rustic figure whose first wife had been a barmaid; she had also been a "nymphomaniac" and she had left the great man for an old lover. The literary operator of the day, Alroy Kear (Maugham's portrait spoiled the rest of poor Hugh Walpole's life), takes on the job. Then Kear realises that Ashenden knew Driffield and his first wife, Rosie. When Ashenden was a boy, they had all lived at the Kentish port, Blackstable. The first line of the book:

> I have noticed that when someone asks for you on the telephone and, finding you out, leaves a message...as it's impor-

tant, the matter is more often important to him than to you. When it comes to making you a present or doing you a favour most people are able to hold their impatience within reasonable bounds.

Maugham is on a roll, and the roll continues with great wit and energy to the last page. He has fun with Kear, with Driffield, with himself, with Literature. Ashenden purrs his admiration for Kear: "I could think of no one of my contemporaries who had achieved so considerable a position on so little talent." He commends Kear's largeness of character. On the difficult business of how to treat those who were once equals but are now failed and of no further use at all, Kear "when he had got all he could from people...dropped them." But Maugham is not finished:

> Most of us when we do a caddish thing harbour resentment against the person we have done it to, but Roy's heart, always in the right place, never permitted him such pettiness. He could use a man very shabbily without afterward bearing him the slightest ill-will.

This is as good as Jane Austen.

Will Ashenden help out even though it is clear that second wife and Kear are out to demonise the first wife, Rosie, and that nothing that Ashenden can tell them about her will change the game plan? Amused, Ashenden agrees to help out. He records his memories of growing up in Blackstable, of the Driffields who are considered very low class indeed: Ashenden's clergyman uncle forbids the boy to see them, but he does. Rosie is a creature of air and fire. She is easy, and loving, and unquestioning. Does she or does she not go to bed with her numerous admirers in the village and later in London where Ashenden, a medical student, sees them again (they had fled Blackstable without paying their bills)?

In London Driffield's fame slowly grows until he becomes the Grand Old Man of Literature. Ashenden's secret—for the purposes of the narrative—is that he, too, had an affair in London with Rosie and when he taxed her with all the others, she was serene and said that

that was the way she was and that was that. As writer and moralist Maugham has now travelled from the youthful blurter-out of the truth about woman's potential passion for sex to an acceptance that it is a very good thing indeed and what is wrong with promiscuity if, as they say, no one is hurt? In the end Rosie leaves Driffield for an old love; goes to New York, where, presumably, she and old love are long since dead.

As the narrative proceeds, Maugham has a good deal of fun with the literary world of the day, where, let us note, not one academic can be found (hence its irrelevance?). On the subject of "longevity is genius," he thinks old extinct volcanoes are apt to be praised as reviewers need fear their competition no longer:

> But this is to take a low view of human nature and I would not for the world lay myself open to a charge of cheap cynicism. After mature consideration I have come to the conclusion that the real reason for the applause that comforts the declining years of the author who exceeds the common span is that intelligent people after thirty read nothing at all.

This auctorial self-consciousness now hurls old Maugham into the mainstream of our *fin-de-siècle* writing where texts gaze upon themselves with dark rapture. "As they grow older the books they read in their youth are lit with its glamour and with every year that passes they ascribe greater merit to the author that wrote them." Well, that was then; now most intelligent readers under thirty read nothing at all that's not assigned.

"I read in the *Evening Standard* an article by Mr. Evelyn Waugh in the course of which he remarked that to write novels in the first person was a contemptible practice...I wish he had explained why..." Maugham makes the modest point that with "advancing years the novelist grows less and less inclined to describe more than what his own experience has given him. The first-person singular is a very useful device for this limited purpose."

In *Looking Back*, Maugham "explains" his uncharacteristic portrait of a good and loving woman who gave of herself (sympathy, please, no tea) as being based on an actual woman/affair. Plainly, it is not. But this charade is harmless. What he has done is far better: he makes a brand-new character, Rosie, who appears to be a bad woman, but her "badness" is really goodness. Once again, nothing is what it seems. To the end this half-English, half-French writer was a dutiful and often worthy heir to his great forebears Hazlitt and Montaigne.

Posterity? That oubliette from which no reputation returns. Maugham:

> I think that one or two of my comedies may retain for some time a kind of pale life, for they are written in the tradition of English comedy...that began with the Restoration drama-tists...I think a few of my best short stories will find their way into anthologies for a good many years to come if only because some of them deal with circumstances and places to which the passage of time and the growth of civilization will give a romantic glamour. This is slender baggage, two or three plays and a dozen short stories...

But then it is no more than Hemingway, say, will be able to place in the overhead rack of the economy section of that chartered flight to nowhere, Twentieth Century Fiction.

I would salvage the short stories and some of the travel pieces, but I'd throw out the now-too-etiolated plays and add to Maugham's luggage *Cakes and Ale*, a small perfect novel, and, sentimentally, *The Narrow Corner*. Finally, Maugham will be remembered not so much for his own work as for his influence on movies and television. There are now hundreds of versions of Maugham's plays, movies, short sto-ries available on cassettes, presumably forever. If he is indeed half-trashy, then one must acknowledge that the other half is of value; that is, *classicus*, "belonging to the highest class of citizens," or indeed of any category; hence, our word "classic"—as in Classics *and* Commercials. Emphasis added.

The New York Review of Books
February 1, 1990

The Birds and the Bees

Recently, while assembling forty years of bookchat, I noted with some alarm—even guilt—that I had never really explained sex. True, I have demonstrated that sex is politics and I have noted that the dumb neologisms, homo-sexual and hetero-sexual, are adjectives that describe acts but never people. Even so, I haven't spelled the whole thing out. So now, before reading skills further atrophy, let me set the record straight, as it were.

First, the bad news: Men and women are *not* alike. They have different sexual roles to perform. Despite the best efforts of theologians and philosophers to disguise our condition, there is no point to us, or to any species, except proliferation and survival. This is hardly glamorous, and so to give Meaning to Life, we have invented some of the most bizarre religions that...alas, we have nothing to compare ourselves to. We are biped mammals filled with red sea water (reminder of our oceanic origin), and we exist to reproduce until we are eventually done in by the planet's changing weather or a stray meteor.

Men and women are dispensable carriers, respectively, of seeds and eggs; programmed to mate and die, mate and die, mate and die. One can see why "love" was invented by some artist who found depressing the dull mechanics of our mindless mission to be fruitful and multiply.

Apparently, the first human societies were tribal—extended families. Then the prenuclear family was invented. Skygods were put in place—jealous ones, too. The monotheistic religions from which we continue to suffer are fiercely grounded on the only fact that we can be certain of: Man plus Woman equals Baby. This, for many, is *the* Natural Law. Inevitably, if unnaturally, natural lawyers thought up marriage and monogamy and then, faced with the actual nature of the male and the female, they created numerous sexual taboos in order to keep the population in line so that the senior partners in the earthly firm could keep the rest of us busy building expensive pyramids to the glory of the Great Lawyer in the Sky.

But as a certain Viennese novelist and classics buff, Sigmund ("It's all in the vagina, dear") Freud, noted, all those fierce do's and don'ts have created discontents, not to mention asthma and date rape. In fact, everything that the Book (from which come Judaism, Christianity, Islam) has to say about sex is wrong. Of course, practically everything the Book has to say about everything else, including real estate, is wrong too, but today's lesson is sex.

The male's function is to shoot semen as often as possible into as many women (or attractive surrogates) as possible, while the female's function is to be shot briefly by a male in order to fertilize an egg, which she will lay nine months later. Although there is nothing anywhere in the male psyche that finds monogamy natural or normal (the scientific search for monogamous, exclusively heterosexual mammals has been sadly given up, while our feathery friends—those loving doves, too—have let the natural lawyers down), the monogamous concept is drilled into the male's head from birth because, in the absence of those original tribal support systems that we discarded for the Book, someone must help the woman during gravidity and the early years of baby rearing.

If one starts with the anatomical difference, which even a patriarchal Viennese novelist was able to see was destiny, then one begins to understand why men and women don't get on very well within marriage, or indeed in any exclusive sort of long-range sexual relationship. *He* is designed to make as many babies as possible with as many different women as he can get his hands on, while *she* is designed to take time off from her busy schedule as astronaut and role model to lay an egg and bring up the result. Male and female are on different sexual tracks, and that cannot be changed by the Book or any book. Since all our natural instincts are carefully perverted from birth, it is no wonder that we tend to be, if not all of us serial killers, killers of our own true nature.

It is a fact that, like any species, our only function is replication. It is a fact that even the dullest and most superstitious of us now suspects that we may have overdone the replicating. Five and a half billion people now clutter a small planet built for two. Simply to maintain the breeders in the United States we have managed to poison all our water. Yes, *all* of it. When I was told this by a member of the Sierra Club, I asked, so what do we drink? And he said, well, some of it's less poisoned than the rest. Despite the fulminations of the Sky Lawyer's earthly representatives, some effort is being made to limit population. But the true damage is already done, and I would not bet the farm on our species continuing in rude health too far into the next century. Those who would outlaw abortion, contraception and same-sex while extolling the family and breeding are themselves the active agents of the destruction of our species. I would be angrier if I had a high opinion of the species, but I don't, and so I regard with serenity Pope and Ayatollah as the somehow preprogrammed agents of our demise, the fate of every species. Hordes of furious lemmings are loose among us; and who would stay them, particularly if they have the Book to throw?

But while we are still here, I suggest a change in attitude among those few capable of rational thought. Let us accept the demonstrable fact that the male has no exclusive object in his desire to shoot. Instead of hysteria, when he wants to shoot with another shootist, he should be encouraged in an activity that will not add another consumer to the population. The woman who decides not to lay that egg should be encouraged, if so minded, to mate with another woman. As it is, a considerable portion of the population, despite horrendous persecution, does just that, and they should be considered benefactors by everyone, while the breeders must be discouraged though, of course, not persecuted.

The Day America Told the Truth is a recent book in which a cross section of the population expressed its ignorance on many issues and confessed to some of its most dreadful deeds and reveries. Since 91 percent of the population admit to telling lies habitually, I can't think why the authors should take too seriously the lies new-minted for them; but then lies often illustrate inadvertent truths. A majority of men and women like oral sex (as the passive partner, presumably). Next in popularity was sex with a famous person. Plainly being blown by George or Barbara Bush would be the ultimate trip for our huddled masses.

Although the authors list twenty-three sexual fantasies (such as sex in a public—pubic?—place), they do not ask about same-sex fantasies, which tells us where they are, as we say in pollster land, coming from. But in what people do do, they report that 17 percent of the men and 11 percent of the women practice same-sex. This strikes me as low—even mendacious. It is true that in the age of AIDS both sexes are very nervous about same-sex or even other-sex, but not, surely, in experimental youth. In the prewar Southern town of Washington, D.C., it was common for boys to have sex with one another. It was called "messing around," and it was no big deal. If the boy became a man who kept on messing around, it was thought a bit queer—sexual exclusivity *is* odd and suggests obsession—but no big deal as long as he kept it quiet. If he didn't, our natural lawyers would do their best to deprive him of his inalienable rights. In any case, I don't think the folks have changed all that much since 1948, when 37 percent of the men told Dr. Kinsey that they had messed around in those years.

Certainly, women today are more candid about their preference for other women. Although this "preference" has been noted for millenniums, it was thought by shootists to be simply a coming together of two unhappy wives for mutual solace. Instead, there seems to have been a strong sexual element all along. But then a pair of egg-layers will have more in common (including a common genetic programming for nurturing) than they will ever have with a shootist, who wants to move on the second he's done his planting—no nurturing for him, no warm, mature, caring relationship. He isn't built for it. His teats may have a perky charm but they are not connected to a dairy. He can fake a caring relationship, of course, but at great cost to his own nature, not to mention battered wife and abused little ones. The fact that couples may live together harmoniously for decades is indeed a fact, but such relationships are demonstrations not of sexuality but of human comity—I dare not use the word "love," because the 91 percent who habitually lie do so about love.

Unfortunately, the propaganda to conform is unrelenting. In a charming fable of a movie, *Moonstruck*, a middle-aged woman discovers that her husband is having an affair with another woman. As the wife is a loving, caring, warm, mature person in love with her husband, why on earth would he stray from her ancient body, which is ever-ready to receive his even greater wreck of a biped? Why do men chase women? Why do they want more than one woman? She asks everyone in sight and no one can think of an answer until she herself does: *Men fear death*, she says—something that, apparently, women never do. Confronted with this profound insight, the husband stops seeing the other woman. Whether or not he loses the fear of death is unclear. This is really loony. It is true that sex/death are complementary: No sex, no birth for the unlucky nonamoeba; once born, death—that's our ticket. Meanwhile, fire at will.

When people were few and the environment was hostile, it is understandable that we should have put together a Book about a Skygod that we had created in our own image—a breathtaking bit of solipsism, but why not? The notion is comforting, and there were no Book reviewers at the time of publication, while later ones, if they wrote bad Book reviews, were regularly condemned to death by natural lawyers employing earthly hit men, as Salman Rushdie can testify. Then our Skygod told us to multiply in a world that he had put together just for us, with dominion over every living thing. Hence the solemn wrecking of a planet that, in time, will do to us what we have done to it.

Meanwhile, "the heterosexual dictatorship," to use Isherwood's irritable phrase, goes on its merry way, adding unwanted children to a dusty planet while persecuting the virtuous nonbreeders. Actually, the percentage of the population that is deeply enthusiastic about other-sex is probably not much larger than those exclusively devoted to same-sex—something like 10 percent in either case. The remaining 80 percent does this, does that, does nothing; settles into an acceptable if dull social role where the husband dreams of Barbara Bush while pounding the old wife, who lies there, eyes shut, dreaming of

Barbara too. Yes, the whole thing is a perfect mess, but my conscience is clear. I have just done something more rare than people suspect—stated the obvious.

The Nation
October 28, 1991

J'accuse!

A political decision was made some 20 years ago by a right-wing money-raiser and political operator, Richard Viguerie, that henceforth the far right would not only raise vast sums of money, which they had been doing from tax-free "church" donations and foundations, but they must now use that money effectively to defeat any politician who might not sufficiently worship flag and fetus, in whose sign they mean to conquer.

Despite millions of dollars raised and spent, these subversives failed to capture the House of Representatives until 1994, when, thanks to President Clinton's political ineptitude, they were able to shift enough of the flat rocks of the republic to provide the Republican Party with a truly weird, squirming majority of nonrepresentative (let us hope) representatives. Meanwhile, according to the Viguerie blueprint of 1979, they are careful to avoid actual politics (there is, as yet, no foreseeable majority to repeal the 13th Amendment) in favor of what they call "hot buttons," which means sex and drugs or both. Just press the hot button, and you can destroy your opponent by revealing his sex life, real or imagined—it makes no difference if you have the hard-soft cash to buy time for a TV ad or to finance something like Gary Bauer's Family Research Council, where gays are compassionately demonized for having made a "a bad choice" in the cafeteria of sexual delights when, with a bit of therapy or prayer, they could change and become as wretched as those sad straights, half of whom are doomed to undergo divorce, battles over child custody, and charges of overpopulating the planet (if only from me) while glumly submitting, if in office—if oval-shaped—to the eager, if incompetent (the navy blue dress!), blowjobs from crazed fans.

This year's hot button, impeachment, is now too hot for even Newt G. to press, at least preelection. That leaves the children of mud only the fag villain, a permanent fixture in the America psyche, where every eve is Halloween.

The tragedy in Wyoming has now cast a bright light on the Christian right. Predictably, liberals have wrung their hands. But easily the most chilling sight in years on TV was Wyoming's hard-eyed governor, Jim Geringer, saying that he hoped "we would not use Matt to further our agenda [sic]." But we must further one if good is ever to come from the ooze and the slime where Matt's death came from.

I propose a class action of interested and concerned organizations and individuals. Since it is bad law that has made our republic so safe a place for hate to fester in, I suggest that only at law can there be the war *they* want and a victory that a sane society must win. Sen. Trent Lott recently denounced homosexuality as an illness akin to "alcoholism and kleptomania" (two popular pastimes of Congress). Simultaneously Bauer's Family Research Council began its hate-campaign ads on TV, condemning those men and women who made "bad choices" sexually, as if choice were any more involved than the color of one's eyes or the degree of mental sickness—or crass opportunism—as expressed by Lott and Bauer.

I believe that as the highest-ranking member of the U.S. Senate, Mr. Lott should be charged with incitement to violence and to murder, specifically in the case of Matthew Shepard, and that Mr. Bauer and others who have indulged in the same reckless demonizing of millions of Americans be equally charged.

Amnesty International recently reported that the United States is the most barbarous of first-world countries in the treatment of its citizens by its government. If so, then the Tree of Liberty ... I trust that all of you know the rest of Mr. Jefferson's sentence.

The Advocate
November 24, 1998

INTERVIEWS

Introduction

by Donald Weise

When *New York Times* journalist Andrew Solomon met Gore Vidal in 1995 for what was expected to be the author's final print interview in English—at least to appear in the *New York Times*—Mr. Solomon depicted his host's Italian home in impressive detail. "Vidal's villa in Ravello, though not particularly big or grand, is as enchanting as he makes it sound: white stucco anchored miraculously into the sheer face of the cliff, twelve acres of vertical stone and terraced gardens, a pool that commands the same panorama as the house, an extra balcony for cocktails just along the rock face." *Palimpsest*, Mr. Vidal's memoir, had just been published, and in the words of the *Times* reporter, "Vidal is on stage for the moment not for his accomplishments, but for who and how he was."

Like Mr. Solomon before me, I was received at the author's much-praised residence. While Mr. Solomon successfully evoked the setting of my visit, we part company on our interpretations. For Gore Vidal's life—"who and how he was"—must rank as one among many distinguished accomplishments in a career full of distinguished accomplishments, particularly where topics of sexuality and gender are involved. Indeed, he has been "on stage" for over half a century, and it is precisely the voice of "who and how he was" that resonates most clearly on matters of sex.

Whether in public or private life, Mr. Vidal has attempted to rede-fine even our most basic assumptions about sexuality. Admittedly, he has not been entirely successful. His insistence that there is no such thing as a "gay person," for example, continues to perplex and ran-kle the pride of "same-sexualists" everywhere. "The only fact is that each of us is a human being capable of all sorts of things, good and bad." His arguments on behalf of prostitution ("an art as legitimate as any other") are no less controversial. Even his often repeated remark, attributing the longevity of a fifty-year partnership with Howard Austen to the absence of sex between them ("I wouldn't dream of it"), remains a source of confusion to many, if not an inspi-ration to as many more. "I think when it comes to writing about sub-jects like sex," Mr. Vidal explained to me, "people want reassurance. I'm not terribly reassuring."

When the topic of conversation turns to the private sex lives of famous Americans, reassurance becomes a relative term. On Eleanor Roosevelt: "When she said 'sex', she meant hetero sex. She didn't like anything about it. When I finally read the unauthorized letters between her and Lorena Hickcock, it became perfectly clear that they were having sex. The writing is full of tactile images which are erot-ic." On President Kennedy: "He was relaxed on the subject of homo-sexuality, as he was about anything related to sex." On Jack Kerouac: "His psychic balance was more homo then heteroerotic; he was far more attracted to boys than to girls." On Dr. Alfred C. Kinsey: "He himself had gone through sexual stages with males, females, and groups while writing The Kinsey Report."

Among his most provocative observations, however, is the simple fact that sex is politics. At the time of our meeting in Ravello, the U.S. Senate was nearing a vote on whether to impeach President Clinton on grounds of perjury and obstruction of justice relating to a sexual harassment investigation. The House of Representatives had already voted to remove the President from office, and his eventual acquittal on both charges was by no means certain even at that late date. Mr. Vidal was of course following the events closely. "Do you mind if I turn on the trial?" he asked, moving toward the television on the other side of the room.

The trial brought to mind a scene from *The Best Man*, Mr. Vidal's popular play about sex in politics. Set against the background of a Democratic National Convention, candidate William Russell, one of two top contenders for the presidential nomination, meets privately with the incumbent to discuss the likelihood of an endorsement. The President, however, is evasive, but it is unclear whether his lack of enthusiasm reflects his opinion of the candidate's politics or his rather open extramarital relations. "These rumors about you and your lady friends," the President remarks, at last broaching the subject as he prepares to leave, "...won't do you a bit of harm." That was written in 1960. I repeated this line to its author, who now sat opposite me engrossed in a very different presidential drama almost forty years later. Without looking away from the television, he replied, "Today politics is nothing but sex."

Politics is sex and sex is politics. And depending on how the two are interpreted, particularly when interpreted together, the consequences are not always pleasant, and sometimes, they are plainly unjust. When a writer has been at work "in the field," to borrow Dr. Kinsey's expression, the consequences are understandably even more pronounced. "What is written about me is 'Clintonian.' In fifty years I've had the Kennedys attack, the Jesus Christers attack, the neo-conservatives attack. And not just an occasional group of bad notices but all-out war."

In concluding our meeting, I assured Mr. Vidal that he would have an opportunity to review this book's manuscript before going to press. "Dates are important," he said, referring to his request that each essay appear with the date of publication. "Sometimes you're ahead of the pack and sometimes you're going against it. Sometimes you're saying what was then the unsayable and now it's said by everybody. When things are said is all-important." Would that the sexual politics advocated by Mr. Vidal in the following interviews be at last "sayable" by everybody.

Donald Weise, Cleis Press
San Francisco
March 1999

The Fag Rag Interview

by John Mitzel and Steven Abbott

1974

FAG RAG: Have allegations of homosexuality ever been used to ruin anyone in politics in your lifetime as far as you know?

GORE VIDAL: The senator from Massachusetts, David Ignatius Walsh, tried to make my father when my father was a West Point cadet. Chased my father and his roommate, who had been down for the inauguration of Woodrow Wilson. Senator Walsh picked them up. They were both very innocent West Pointers. My father said it was just appalling. He chased them around the room. West Point was very innocent in those days. When my father joined Roosevelt's administration, he went absolutely to pieces when he had to go before a Senate committee. I always told him that way in the back of his mind there was the memory of his bad experience of Senator Walsh. So he regarded all senators as potential rapists and pederasts. Walsh was caught during the war in a boy whorehouse, supposedly frequented by Nazi sympathizers, in Brooklyn, with a man who will be nameless—Virgil Thomson. Not together, but Virgil was also caught. One newspaper started to break the story. Walsh was chairman of naval affairs, as well as the master of Massachusetts, and he was the Cardinal's business man. Roosevelt, under his wartime powers, said that any newspaper that printed this would be prosecuted and shut down. The *New York Post* printed it in the first edition, then got the word. Nothing ever appeared. And Walsh? Nothing ever happened to him. He was re-elected in due course. There wasn't anybody in Massachusetts from the little birds on the Common who didn't know what David Walsh was up to.

FAG RAG: The Jenkins thing made such an enormous scandal. At the same time you apparently have no problem.

GV: I stay away from YMCA men's rooms, for one thing.

FAG RAG: We understand that J. Edgar Hoover actually sent him a bouquet of flowers. He was the only one in Washington who showed Jenkins any sympathy.

GV: Hoover cared.

FAG RAG: He was helping to give Hoover work.

GV: After all, I dedicated *An Evening with Richard Nixon* to "J. Edgar Hoover and..."

FAG RAG: Clyde Tolson...

GV: With appreciation."

FAG RAG: You've said that you didn't think that anyone was a homosexual.

GV: I've always said it was just an adjective. It's not a noun, though it's always used as a noun. Put it the other way. What is a heterosexual person? I've never met one. When you say Lyndon Johnson and Adlai Stevenson behaved like two typical heterosexuals over the weekend, in their response, well, I don't know what they had in common. To me, it's just descriptive of an act.

FAG RAG: What about faggot or fag, the way we use it today? For example, in the title of the paper *Fag Rag?*

GV: I prefer the word faggot which I tend to use myself. I have never allowed actively in my life the word "gay" to pass my lips. I don't know why I hate that word.

FAG RAG: I think it's because *The Advocate* and the bourgeois press have picked up on it and made it into a noun.

GV: Also, I mean, historically it meant a girl of easy virtue in the seventeenth century. They'd say: "Is she gay?" Which meant: "Is she available?" And this, I don't think, is highly descriptive of anybody. It's just a bad word. You see, I don't think you need a word for it. This is what you have to evolve. These words have got to wither away in a true Hegelian cycle.

FAG RAG: A lot of homosexuals seem to be very concerned about whether they are called gays, faggots, fairies, or homosexuals.

GV: I would give it as a general warning: it may not apply to anybody in your generation, but certainly in the case of mine that I could have been, from 1948 on, The Official Spokesman. But I have no plans to be so limited. I'm a generalist, and I'm interested in a great many other things. Knowing the mania of the media, they want everybody to be in a pigeonhole. Oh, yes. He's The Official Fag. Oh, yes. He's The Official Marxist. And I have never allowed myself to be pigeonholed like that. Also I don't regard myself as one thing over another. The point is, why not discard all the words? Say that all sexual acts have parity. Which is my line.

FAG RAG: In *Fag Rag 5* we reprinted an article by Robert Duncan, "The Homosexual in Society," from Dwight Macdonald's old magazine *Politics*. Duncan used the word "jam" and I had never heard it.

GV: " Jam" was a much-used word. Kind of trade, but not really trade. Pretty hard to get. Perhaps when the fact was removed the word withered away too. No one seemed to be impossible. "Jam" only referred to boys. You'll find "jam" in *The City and the Pillar,* I think. I did a little glossary in there in my World Almanac way. "Dirt" was a word; that was for a bad piece of trade. I'm supposed to have coined the phrase "Last year's trade is this year's competition." That's in *The City and the Pillar.* I noticed it was quoted in *Fag Rag* 6. I don't think it was original with me, but I get the credit because I was the first to write it.

FAG RAG: Something that strikes me in the *Gay Sunshine* interviews is that at some point or other, the interviewees deal with the issue of their own homosexuality and their writing. They act as though homosexuality, the desire for sex, particularly sex with youth—which may not be at all an issue with you—is an obstacle to writing. During the period of sexual activity there is a great deal less writing.

GV: I don't understand that at all. But Hemingway said something very much like that. He always liked to maintain sexual continence when he was writing seriously.

FAG RAG: Are you sexually active when you write?

GV: The more active I am the better I write. I'm much more interested in economics and class than sex. All this is part of the middle class, part of the Puritan work ethic. You keep your seed in your bank and it collects interest; you have too many drafts on it you weaken it. This is a Protestant, work ethic, middle-class thing. It was my very good fortune not to be born middle class. So I'm at a completely different vantage point.

FAG RAG: Do you think you're similar to the working class, in this respect?

GV: Well, that's what's always been claimed by the British, and I think so. The fact is that for us there was really no fuss about sex. You did as much as you could. I'm fascinated by this book about Vita Sackville-West and Harold Nicolson, *Portrait of a Marriage.* That's really mind-blowing to middle-class Americans. Harold Nicolson was a relentless chaser of Guardsmen and Vita Sackville-West of cunt. This is the condition of people who are not trapped into that economic middle-class tightness, and the worry of always keeping up appearances, the worry that they're always going to be "done in" by somebody. The working class, God knows, they're filled with terrible passion and prejudice, but give them a sexual act to perform that seems amusing... In Texas—that relentless Bible belt—there's nobody who's not available. It's like Italy.

FAG RAG: How do you contrast the sort of decadent Puritanism with sensuality—of which you've always been an advocate—in Italy?

GV: The Italians are naturally sensual and opportunistic about sex. They don't fuss. That's one of the reasons why there are really no queer bars.

FAG RAG: The interviews that writers give to *Gay Sunshine* seem to dwell on promiscuity. Your life seems to be very different.

GV: As promiscuous as I can make it.

FAG RAG: Yeah, but you have more style than almost any other writer. I loved that story in one of your essays about your going to bed with Kerouac.

GV: [*Laughs.*]

FAG RAG: So much for the "Tell—

GV: "Tell It Like It Is" school.

FAG RAG: You have been very open in your life in dealing with taboo. First in *The City and the Pillar*, in many of your essays, and then with *Myra Breckinridge*. Where do you draw the line? Is the line constantly shifting? In the interview you gave to *Viva* you were asked: "Was your first sexual experience with a man or a woman?"

GV: I think I had a very funny answer. I don't think she got it right. I said: "I was much too polite to ask."

FAG RAG: Were you younger than eighteen when you had your first experience?

GV: Oh my God! I was eleven! And I was brought up in the South.

FAG RAG: You loved your father very much, didn't you?

GV: I adored him, yes.

FAG RAG: And Hugh D. Auchincloss was your stepfather?

GV: Yeah. I liked Hughdie. But he's a magnum of chloroform.

FAG RAG: Do you still see the Auchinclosses much?

GV: I see my sister. There are so many Auchinclosses around you are bound to see some. They're always around.

FAG RAG: Were you an only child?

GV: I was an only child until I was about thirteen.

FAG RAG: Even though you were not middle class, was there ever a time in that whole period that you felt you worried about your sexuality?

GV: Never. Absolutely never.

FAG RAG: No identity crisis? No breakdown?

GV: I did exactly what I wanted to do all the time.

FAG RAG: You were very beautiful when you were young. You're good-looking now, too, but pretty in your youth.

GV: So I read in all these memoirs of my great beauty.

FAG RAG: Yes. Truman Capote said you took him to the Everard Baths.

GV: I did take Truman to the Everard. Couldn't have been funnier. "I just don't like it." [*Mimics Truman Capote.*]

FAG RAG: Does Truman go to the trucks? What does he do?

GV: He falls in love passionately with air-conditioning repair men. He had a tragic affair recently with an air-conditioning repair man.

FAG RAG: There's one thing you said about Capote's writing: "So like Faith Baldwin." If that's true about his life, he's got the inspiration.

GV: I can't read him because I'm diabetic.

FAG RAG: Regarding youth, are you never attracted by younger people?

GV: Oh, yes. I said I don't flatter the young, either as a writer or as a performer. And I don't flatter them sexually. That doesn't mean I don't like them.

FAG RAG: Do you enjoy being seduced as much as seducing?

GV: No. I hate it.

FAG RAG: Getting back to the right-wing, closet, repressed mentality—*Point of Order* has been playing here in theatres. The David Schine-Roy Cohn thing is intriguing. We've heard stories of them naked snapping towels in hotels. Did that come out at the time?

GV: We used to sing "Come Cohn or Come Schine." Sure. [*Laughter*]. Senator Flanders of Vermont, noble old boy, tried to not only knock them off with it but McCarthy himself.

FAG RAG: The whole Army-McCarthy hearings were meant as a cover-up for this homosexual relationship?

GV: Yeah. McCarthy himself was homosexual. This sort of wing of "preverts."

FAG RAG: Do you have a conscious feeling about your writing and politics? Do you feel you've got a political role?

GV: No.

FAG RAG: Even though you're not in politics per se, you have a base. When I saw you on *The Dick Cavett Show* the other night, after you destroyed that poor Jesuit [John McLaughlin, a speech writer and deputy special assistant to Nixon], I remarked that what's so refreshing about seeing you compared to others on the tube is that you come out with the truth very casually.

GV: I'm not running for office. I don't have to worry about the unpleasant mail. I made the decision in '64 that I was not going to go to Congress. It was very plain that I would have been elected if I had run. And, I turned down, in the beginning of '68, the nomination and support for the Senate.

FAG RAG: You were thinking of running in '68?

GV: As late as '68. This was before *Myra Breckinridge* came out. I finally told them. I said: "Look kids, I think without this book we might do it, but with this book, we won't be able to get through."

FAG RAG: Have you thought much about the Bicentennial and the country remembering its beginning—I know your essays in *Homage to Daniel Shays*.

GV: Bicentennial? I wrote *Burr* as my meditation on the political process.

FAG RAG: Politically, do you see any opportunity for using the whole remembrance of the origins of the country in a political way?

GV: One tactic which is useful: you can always promote radical causes under the guise of Going Back to the Constitution. And sometimes quite legitimately. The Bill of Rights is still a radical document. I find sometimes when I'm trying to be an advocate, trying to convince a really difficult audience, you can always refer back to the origins and tell them that this is the way it was meant to be.

FAG RAG: When you've got Daniel Shays, Tom Paine, and all the rest of them, you've got some rich potential.

GV: Yes.

FAG RAG: What do you think of the talk show circuit?

GV: There's a whole technique to it. You just have to study how to do it. Use it to your own purposes.

FAG RAG: How do you get through mass media with what is essentially an anti-mass message?

GV: You have to become an explainer. You have to make up your mind before you go on that you are going to make the following points. Don't make too many because they can't remember them. You are going to say: if I want to get the sex laws changed, I will then have thought it out in my head how I'll lead the conversation. It doesn't make any difference what they ask; you just go right on. "Yes, that's interesting," and go right on to the point you were going to make. It's like any other kind of skill. You have to learn how to do it. It's very useful.

FAG RAG: But the media itself. It's a sort of reverse from McLuhan.

GV: It's better than nothing. People don't listen. All day yesterday and the day before in Chicago, little old ladies, cabdrivers who I know hate my guts, all came up and wanted to talk about the exchange with the priest on Cavett's show. They were all very pleased by it.

FAG RAG: Did you talk with the Jesuit after the show?

GV: He told me that Walter Cronkite is a notorious left-winger.

FAG RAG: The nature of the bourgeois press, the very fact that they teamed you with someone like that, does this make you feel compromised having to deal with slime? That you're on a par with slime?

GV: No! I'm the detergent!

FAG RAG: I think you did an "Inouye." [Senator Daniel K. Inouye] You said: "Lies. Lies. Priest."

GV: No, no. I said: "You are lying, priest. Think to your immortal soul." The Brother gulped on that.

FAG RAG: The thing that bothers me is that every other elite—you come out of the liberal elite—in Germany, France, etc., produces leaders, phenomenal people.

GV: No revolution ever came from the bottom.

FAG RAG: Exactly. But the United States, just in the last ten years, has had an attempt on the part of many people who come out of the elite—

GV: An attempt to do what? Change things?

FAG RAG: Yes. From the left. We have no leadership. The media have taken every figure in the movement, just to take one example.

GV: And used them up. I watched Abbie Hoffman from the beginning since the first time he appeared on the scene—at a debate between Tom Hayden and me. Abbie was in the audience. He got up and harangued. I could see they loved him on television. "Freako!" "Wild man!" I said to myself: If that man is around in three years I'll be surprised. They'll use him up. And then there will be another wild man, and he will be on a different kick.

FAG RAG: David Bowie now.

GV: Yeah. Survival in the United States is not easy whether it is for a writer or a singer or anyone else. Certainly is a critical society. It's not easy at all.

FAG RAG: You didn't make the "Enemies List."

GV: That's not true! I was number 212. I can't remember. I wasn't in the top twenty, which was one of their ways of destroying me.

FAG RAG: Have you ever had IRS, passport, or FBI trouble?

GV: I've been broken into twice by the FBI when I was with the People's Party. As was Spock. You can always tell because they never take anything. They should at least take the TV set, but they're so damn lazy and it's heavy.

FAG RAG: These are agents?

GV: Yeah. Then they would go through papers, papers, papers.

FAG RAG: Was this under Johnson or Nixon?

GV: Nixon.

FAG RAG: Have they ever tried to talk with you?

GV: No. I am on the FBI list of people never to talk to about anything, because I went after Hoover about twelve years ago.

FAG RAG: Before it was fashionable.

GV: Yeah. And really let him have it.

FAG RAG: Did you ever meet the man?

GV: Yes.

FAG RAG: Did he look you in the eye? My brother always told me you can always tell a queer because he'll never look you in the eye.

GV: Somebody was asking me. Said he thought Richard Nixon was obviously homosexual. I said: "Why do you think that?" He said: "You know, that funny, uncoordinated way he moves." I said: "Yeah. Like Nureyev."

FAG RAG: What was your motivation behind the People's Party with Spock?

GV: I didn't have any. I was just sort of riding along with it. We started the New Party in '68. The idea was simply to try and make a representative party. It wasn't worth doing. It was nothing but young group therapists who believe in "elitism" or "structure." It was pointless.

FAG RAG: *Fag Rag* tries to see homosexuality in America at this point as being a vehicle for radical expression.

GV: Yet when you get with any radical blacks or any radical anything, forget it.

FAG RAG: Remember the quote: "The place for a woman in the movement is on her back?" One wonders if there isn't room now for what Hofstadter did with paranoia in American politics, something to do with sexual repression. I think *Myra B.* is the tip of the iceberg.

GV: There is considerable work to be done. Every intelligent person in the country knows the thing is a joke.

FAG RAG: I don't know. I'm very skeptical. Though I identify with your literary works, I sometimes wonder why you still have this tropism towards belief in the faith. Perhaps they could be manipulated in the right direction. When it comes to personality and style and reason and argument against the 4.4 percent and their money, you're going to lose.

GV: Well, I don't know. I have seen attitudes change a good deal since I began. This magazine of yours would not have existed twenty-five years ago. I think the 4.4 percent changes in its own inscrutable way, but I do not think I believe it will be done by intelligent advocacy. I have said if it is going to change, it is going to be collapse. The system will collapse. It does not work now. The government does not work. And the economic system is not working. Something will crash. Who picks up the pieces? I would want a social democracy as my replacement. I just want to get the goddamn population down by about two-thirds. Then there's plenty of room for everybody and plenty of wealth for everybody.

FAG RAG: The point that continues to plague me is the lack of leadership. I do not see any positive political strategy.

GV: You need a new party. You come back to it again. I made my effort along with these others in '68 and again in '72.

FAG RAG: But what is the base?

GV: If you saw the manifesto I did ["A Dialogue with Myself," *Esquire*, October 1968], you have got to have a party of human survival.

FAG RAG: Regarding the issue of censorship, I'm doing an article on John Horne Burns, particularly the job the critics did on him. Did you know him?

GV: Yes.

FAG RAG: I find in researching him that there are only three pieces still extant since his death: your piece in the *New York Times Book Review*, Brigid Brophy's piece in the Sunday *London Times* magazine, and a piece in *One* magazine, a Los Angeles-based homophile publication.

GV: He was obliterated by the press.

FAG RAG: In rereading him, there is a certain circumspection that comes through.

GV: He's being careful.

FAG RAG: Very careful. The homosexual passion is there, breaking through.

GV: He was careful in the first one, *The Gallery*. *Lucifer with a Book*, however, is when the critics let him have it. I think *The Gallery* is certainly the best of the "war books." It was much applauded, much admired. You see, he did six or seven books before *The Gallery*. He was an awful man. Monster. Envious, bitchy, drunk. Bitter. Which was why *The Gallery* was so marvelous. It was his explosion into humanity at a fairly late date. I think he was in his early thirties, after a half-assed career as an English teacher and writing unprintable novels.

FAG RAG: Have you ever seen any of the manuscripts?

GV: No. But I've been told about them by Freddie Warburg who published him in England who said they were all pretty bad. They must be around somewhere.

FAG RAG: How did he die? I can't find that out. Was he killed?

GV: No, no, no. He was drinking himself to death in Florence. Every day he would go to the Grand Hotel and stand in the bar and drink Italian brandy, which is just about the worst thing in the world. And chew on fruit drops candy. He always said that it would counteract the drunkenness. He was living with a doctor, an Italian veterinarian. They had a rather stormy relationship but nothing sinister about it. One day he was drunk at a bar, wandered out in the hot midday sun and had a stroke. Cerebral hemorrhage.

FAG RAG: At age thirty-seven?

GV: I think he wanted to die. They really wiped him out on *Lucifer with a Book*. We were both, in 1947, the leading writers in the country. The ineffable John W. Aldridge began his career with a piece in *Harper's* magazine, out of which came his book *After the Lost Generation*. He reversed all his judgments later. He began his career as our great admirer. He discovered we were dealing with the horrors of homosexuality. He then exactly reversed himself and began to applaud the Jewish giants who are still with us today. Aldridge is nothing if not a rider of bandwagons. So Burns was absolutely at the top then. We were both admired as War Writers. To be a War Writer was pretty gutsy. You can't knock a War Writer. Then *City and the Pillar*. Then *Lucifer with a Book*. They said: "Oh, my God! What is this we've been admiring?"

FAG RAG: Did the straight critics pick up on the homosexual themes in *Lucifer with a Book* and *The Gallery*?

GV: They got it in *Lucifer with a Book*. He hit you on the head with it.

FAG RAG: One never knows the mentality of reviewers.

GV: We wrote differently in those days, but it was perfectly plain what was going on at that school.

FAG RAG: And was that reason to condemn the book?

GV: Entirely. Any writer suspected of being homosexual. When Norman Mailer met me in 1950, he said: "You know, Gore, I thought you were the Devil." Just terrible but true. The only thing that they respect, that they put up with, is a freak like Capote, who has the mind of a Kansas housewife, likes gossip, and gets all shuddery when she thinks about boys murdering people.

FAG RAG: So Mailer went after you?

GV: They all did. However, Capote never really touched on the subject. He is a Republican housewife from Kansas with all the prejudices. Just as Norman Mailer is a VFW commander in Schenectady.

FAG RAG: It's rather amazing that just as you were accepted, really, for something like *The City and the Pillar*, just as it was becoming acceptable to deal with homosexuality as such, you came out with *Myra Breckinridge* which even among homosexuals is controversial.

GV: I always remember a remark Faulkner made about Hemingway. Faulkner was very guarded in talking about his contemporaries. He once said to me: "You know, Hemingway's problem is that he never takes chances." You have got to keep going as far out as you can, as far as your imagination will take you.

FAG RAG: That is the chasm I see in your life and work. While on the one hand you have a fascination with power, you know more accurately than almost any other writer or politician in America the kind of mediocrities the American electorate coughs up, quashing out any kind of leadership. On the other hand you're such an avant-garde writer, capturing the sensibility so exquisitely at any given time. You should understand that in America there is no true way of jiving them. You can't publish *Myra* without getting the housewife at the supermarket to go: No. Unh-uh. No way. Look at the job they did on Rocky when he married Happy.

GV: Never underestimate their corruption. If you can amuse them, they will forgive you just about anything. And if you are a success, they will crown you.

FAG RAG: What kind of success?

GV: Money.

FAG RAG: Is that why the historical novels?

GV: I'm fascinated with the origins of the United States and Christianity, which were the two subjects I took on.

FAG RAG: Do the historical novels make more money than the earliest ones like *Williwaw* and *In a Yellow Wood*?

GV: Oh yes.

FAG RAG: Why did you publish three mysteries in the Fifties under the pseudonym "Edgar Box"?

GV: I was broke. I needed money. I wrote each of them in a week. Except one of them. I wrote half of it in three days and the house burned down. I had to go back to it, and I had forgotten who was the murderer. So I had to think of a whole new plot halfway through it. Try to figure out which one I had in mind. Ten thousand words a day, seven days.

FAG RAG: Did you have little charts on the wall? Esther here and Warren in the window?

GV: No. When you're young, it is the most amazing thing. You can do formidable things.

FAG RAG: Formula or formidable?

GV: Formidable. Formula takes maturity.

FAG RAG: It seems like the other way around. It seems that someone who's such a craftsman as you would avoid formula.

GV: I think you will find it takes a long time to find your tone of voice. I didn't until *Judgment of Paris*. I published five or six books before I really got it. I wouldn't say got it right, but got it accurate. I was now coming through. For us, it was very difficult to overcome Hemingway and *The New Yorker*. That style was just so oppressive. One hardly knew of anything else. Anything else sounded affected in your own voice.

FAG RAG: Did you know Paul Goodman in the Fifties?

GV: Yes. I'd see him around. I never knew him well.

FAG RAG: How do you measure his impact in terms of the sexual thing?

GV: Well, I haven't read that diary or journals he kept or anything, but he was obviously very daring considering that he made himself the guru of the middle-brow educationalists.

FAG RAG: True. It was not until Sputnik that he almost nurtured his own following.

GV: Yes. I was rather startled that in a way he had that much integrity. I always thought he was a bitter man. Playing up to a constituency. There is nothing worse than playing up to the young, a game I will never get into.

FAG RAG: Of course he was fascinated by the young. Perhaps that explains a part of his sexual fascination.

GV: Yes. You can be sexually fascinated by them and still not flatter them. I think flattery had a lot to do with his sexual techniques. It has nothing to do with mine.

FAG RAG: In *Burr*, you mention a Senator Breckinridge who was Buchanan's vice president. And in the 1940s there was a famous transsexual—

GV: In San Francisco?

FAG RAG: From a very rich family. She was supposedly the biggest queen in the world. And her name was Breckinridge. Is that true?

GV: Well. It is true. Bunny Breckinridge. [*Laughter.*] Now this is the most extraordinary thing. I was reminded years later that I had never met Bunny Breckinridge, but that everybody that I knew had known him and talked to me about him. This was in the Forties. Then it just went right out of my head, and Breckinridge came into my head. I just wanted a very solid-sounding name with lots of syllables. Myra would not be content with just being Smith.

FAG RAG: But the rumor was that she was related to the famous former V.P., Vice President Breckinridge.

GV: Oh well.

FAG RAG: We figured: Vidal's into politics; he'll know that.

GV: No. I didn't know that.

FAG RAG: It's documented, I'm told, in a book called *Queer Street, USA.*

GV: About Bunny Breckinridge?

FAG RAG: Yes. Was she a transsexual or just a big queen?

GV: Just a big queen. Very rich.

FAG RAG: Why did you choose not to go to college?

GV: I was supposed to go to Harvard. It occurred to me. I went into the army at seventeen, got out at twenty. What was the point of going into another institution when I had already written my first novel?

FAG RAG: But did you know that "education" was a fraud then, too? Or just a drag on your career?

GV: No. In those days we thought you could actually go to a place like Harvard and it would be worth doing. But only if you wanted to lead a conventional life and rise in a law firm or something. I had the great pleasure of lecturing at Harvard while all my classmates from Exeter were undergraduates. Greatest moment of my life, I mean I really rubbed it in. It's all been downhill since.

FAG RAG: What about the poetry you wrote while at Exeter? Has it ever been published?

GV: I hope not. There's a book coming out about me. A professor has gone and read it all.

FAG RAG: I suppose literary criticism is one of the penalties for being prolific when you're young. By middle age, you have to start dealing with critical biographies.

GV: Writers younger than I am like Updike and Harold Pinter. There are more books about Harold Pinter than there are about Chekhov. Most extraordinary thing.

FAG RAG: It's Sputnik again. It's all the college-educated *Time* subscribers who buy books now and belong to book clubs.

GV: Nobody reads these books. It is make-work so you can get tenure in universities. Who's not been done from the Forties? Ah, there's Vidal. Willingham. Let's do Willingham.

FAG RAG: I saw a Susskind show recently where he had all the old stable of Philco Playhouse writers.

GV: Oh, really?

FAG RAG: Chayefsky. And who is the Australian who writes novels now?

GV: Sumner Locke Elliot. A great wit. Very charming.

FAG RAG: Were you part of that stable?

GV: Sure. I did *Visit to a Small Planet.*

FAG RAG: Chayefsky said he did *Marty* for $900. He wasn't bitter about it now because he's making lots of money, but the other guests did a little complaining. Now David Susskind and all the critics—

GV: David was their agent.

FAG RAG: My impression is that you did well. *Visit* went on to become a movie and a Broadway play.

GV: Yeah. Chayefsky went on. He made several movies.

FAG RAG: Did you make money out of your television plays?

GV: I never seemed to be able to make more than $7000 a year, year in and year out.

FAG RAG: But you were published before you went and they were not.

GV: Oh yes.

FAG RAG: They were just sort of Kitchen Writers from Brooklyn.

GV: Radio men. Radio joke writers.

FAG RAG: You do a lot of projects. It was mentioned in *Atlantic* that you were doing a screenplay entitled *Plaza.* I looked for this and never saw it.

GV: That was Robert Aldrich. Rather not a bad idea. He blew the financing. It never got made.

FAG RAG: Also, I read in *Life* that you were doing a novel called *Dreams*. Then I never read anything else about this.

GV: I wrote part of it. I never finished it. I think it's mostly going into *Myron*.

FAG RAG: Concerning your relationship with Howard Austen. What is the financial arrangement and/or how will you leave your money?

GV: I have lived twenty-three years with the same person. Presumably because I am older I will die first and just leave it to him. That's all.

FAG RAG: Do you know anything about other "gay" authors who died and left money?

GV: Somerset Maugham left Alan Searle very well provided for.

FAG RAG: Wasn't there a big scandal with the Maugham estate?

GV: Maugham was just so ga-ga. He was making trouble all over the place. He tried to cut his grandson out by saying that his daughter was not really his daughter, and she was—curiously enough.

FAG RAG: Gide was married. Did he have a family?

GV: He had no children. I don't know where Gide's money went. Probably to Marc Allegret, the director.

FAG RAG: Will Capote be very rich when he dies?

GV: Capote has no money.

FAG RAG: Really? Living at UN Plaza?

GV: This is one of the reasons *why* he has no money. He thinks he's Bunny Mellon—to get back to another Bunny. He thinks he's a very rich Society Lady, and spends a great deal of money.

FAG RAG: Where does Auden's money go?

GV: He had no money.

FAG RAG: He leaves an estate, though.

GV: If he left $10,000, I would be very surprised.

FAG RAG: What will Isherwood do?

GV: He would leave it to Don Bachardy, and to anyone he wants to.

FAG RAG: Do you enjoy the historical novel? Or is it a drudge so that you can do something mad in between?

GV: No. I really like them very much.

FAG RAG: Among American fiction writers, who do you read for enjoyment?

GV: Calder Willingham. Southern writer. Very funny.

FAG RAG: I couldn't get through *Providence Island*.

GV: No. That's bad. But *Rambling Rose* is new and rather good. I love *Geraldine Bradshaw*. They're pussy novels, you're right. Just this terrible, relentless quest for pussy. Just full of failure, which is like life, which is what I like about it

FAG RAG: Did you get through *Gravity's Rainbow*?

GV: I don't think I'm going to get to that. I have tried the academic writers. There is a sort of division of literature which I cast a benign eye upon. I'm sure there is a place for it: novels which are written to be used in the classroom. Since I think that's where the novel is going to end up, I think of myself as an anachronism, and *that* is the future. Someone like John Barth to me is just cement. Pynchon. I read *V.*

Some of it is fun, but so heavy-handed. The jokes are so heavy, such awful names. Nabokov remembers him. He was in one of Nabokov's classes at Cornell. Nabokov thinks rather highly of him. Nabokov I usually enjoy, though not as much as he enjoys himself. I like old Saul Bellow. I find him cranky but true.

FAG RAG: Do you mind being exploited? For example, I just read Dotson Rader's new book *Blood Dues*.

GV: A little cunt. A real cunt.

FAG RAG: In *Blood Dues*, if it had not been for you and Tennessee Williams, there would be no book, except for his bloody nose at the end.

GV: I have no intention of reading that book. I read something he wrote in *Esquire* about me and Tennessee; that I had not gone to the church because I was afraid Tennessee would upstage me. Imagine a mind that would conceive that. Tennessee is one of my oldest friends. Vain as I am, that is not the sort of thing that would ever cross my mind.

FAG RAG: The whole Southern mentality is so foreign to me in a way. You had one foot into it. Is it easy to patronize Southern writers?

GV: When I began to write, they were the center of American literature. Much overpraised. Now they're rather underpraised. And the Jewish writers came along, bringing with them their stern patriarchal attitudes.

FAG RAG: What is the prospect for women's liberation, gay liberation and sensuality in America?

GV: I keep coming back to economics. I keep thinking about the collapse of the currency, the shortages in the world.

FAG RAG: It occurred to me a while ago that your whole prophecy of what is going to happen in this country would indicate that American literature as well as politics is gone, going. It has got to be replaced with something.

GV: I don't think it has to be replaced with anything. American literature has always been second-rate. The schools in America, which are also second-rate, could never discuss this because their mandate rests upon pretending that since we were briefly a great world empire, therefore we were a great civilization. When you compare Mark Twain to George Eliot, or compare Dostoevsky to Stephen Crane, or poor Hemingway to Proust, my god! Henry James, a great novelist, became English.

FAG RAG: I think all of your work is in print except *A Season of Comfort*. This is remarkable, and proof that you are saying something. My final question is: Are queens different today in the Seventies then they were in the Forties?

GV: Ahhh, I don't know. That's an interesting thought, though it seems to me that everything is the same always. Certain things are more open now than they were then. But they were pretty open in the sort of ghetto life of the Forties. And New York, Lexington Avenue, was very royal.

FAG RAG: Do you keep a diary?

GV: I kept one in '48. I sealed it and gave it to the University of Wisconsin with my papers.

FAG RAG: To be opened after your death?

GV: After my death or the Second Coming, whichever comes first.

The Gay Sunshine Interview
by Steven Abbott and Thom Willenbecher
1974

GAY SUNSHINE: All the sex magazines have been interested in interviewing you: *Playboy, Viva,* and now *Fanny.*

GORE VIDAL: Well, after all, I'm supposed to be the apostle of bisexuality because I said something in its favor once, and as we all know, I invented homosexuality in 1948 with *The City and the Pillar.* My invention. First there was Orville and Wilbur Wright...

GAY SUNSHINE: ...those two fag siblings.

GV: ...and then there was me. And then...

GAY SUNSHINE: Allen Ginsberg who invented cocksucking in 1956 and, of course, with appreciation, the tandem J. Edgar and Clyde.

GV: I've been asked to do a film about J. Edgar Hoover. It's the first tempting film offer that's come my way. I plan to do it as a beautiful love story.

GAY SUNSHINE: Yeah. *Fag Rag* did a piece entitled "Hoover Goes Under" after his untimely demise. Are there still plans for CBS to do a film on *Burr*?

GV: Yes. CBS has been following me around for three months. They're doing *Sixty Minutes* on my life and times. We've done the Italian part. Now they're shooting me here.

GAY SUNSHINE: Speaking of Italy, advertisements are surfacing for a new book on Italy by Roloff Beny in which you write the epilogue.

GV: A beautiful book, with three kinds of paper. Very lush and decadent. They should put legs on it. It would be a coffee table. I'm afraid the epilogue is a little deflationary. As the world is coming to an end, we won't be able to look upon these beautiful scenes much longer.

GAY SUNSHINE: What's happening with *Sixty Minutes* ?

GV: I'm at their mercy. They're getting old films of me and my grandfather, Senator Gore of Oklahoma. Newsreels and home movies. Mike Wallace, of course, is doing a Hard-Hitting Interview: Wouldn't you say that you were against marriage because your mother and father did not get on? I said: No two-bit Freudianism. Spare the audience that.

GAY SUNSHINE: Did he ask you about "love"?

GV: Yeah. I said to him, "I don't like the word love. It's like patriotism. It's like the flag. It's the last refuge of scoundrels. When people start talking about what wonderful, warm, deep emotions they have and how they love people, I watch out. Somebody is going to steal something. Romantic love as Americans conceive it does not exist. Hence, the enormous divorce rate. When sexual desire cools there's often not much left."

GAY SUNSHINE: What about your quarter-century living situation with Howard Austen?

GV: Haven't I proved my point by living with somebody for twenty-four years? That's obviously not being in love. You don't live with the person you love. At least I've known very few cases of it. You live with a friend which is something quite different from having a grand passion or a love affair.

GAY SUNSHINE: Are they going to allow you to have the final edit?

GV: I suppose not. However, when you do a tape on TV, you can tell them to fuck off, so they have to cut from that point and splice it together again. A series of sharp remarks can bring things to a halt.

GAY SUNSHINE: Expletive deleted. There is definitely a breach of confidence not to allow the person giving the interview to examine and approve the text. The arrangement counts.

GV: Of course it counts, and the person doing the interview must know how to put it together. Everything depends on context. It's not that they mean to be malicious. They are just dumb and out of dumbness they miss things. I could do a much more devastating piece about myself than they could, and I wouldn't mind doing it. At least it would be the right kind of devastation.

GAY SUNSHINE: Have you written your epitaph?

GV: Yes. "When I die, I'm going to take you all with me." I have thoughts about writing my last novel about the end of the world through war, famine, or nuclear contamination. In any case, how are your problems with the governor of New Hampshire and other worthies? [The governor of New Hampshire tried to *Fag Rag* banned. - Ed.]

GAY SUNSHINE: Meldrim Thompson and the *Manchester Union Libel* [*Manchester Union Leader*] live.

GV: A sickening newspaper.

GAY SUNSHINE: The *Libel*'s latest opus was a front-page editorial urging local citizens to view "The Outrage," that *Marcus Welby* show which caused a massive national gay protest.

GV: The fag show about a fourteen-year-old who loses his manhood because he gets seduced ... and he wasn't even buggered, was he? I think he was just drained of his seminal juices.

GAY SUNSHINE: The opening scene featured a boy standing before a mirror, with either hickeys or bruises all over his torso...

GV: Oh, the poor bunny. He was chewed on, then, by this terrible attacker.

GAY SUNSHINE: Raped by his science teacher as the story goes.

GV: Indeed. I suppose the heteros think that the back of his head will now fall off. Or that he will wear eyeliner in the gym.

GAY SUNSHINE: Would you elaborate on a quote from *Two Sisters* that "America's first serious novelist said that the U.S. is fit for many purposes, but not to live in. To which the nation's last serious novelist can only add 'Amen' "?

GV: Did I write that? I think Hawthorne said that around the time he was our consul in Liverpool. Well I suppose one could enjoy living here, but it depends on where. Certainly New York would not be on my list. I could manage New Orleans. I used to have a lot of friends there, but the drink has gotten to them and now most of them are dead, including Clay Shaw. A gentle soul. But I think the heavy drinking would have put me under the sod, as it were, a long time ago. Los Angeles would be intolerable, and so would anywhere between. I think of San Francisco, but the weather is never really right there.

GAY SUNSHINE: People are being advised to stay away from San Francisco and the West Coast if they seriously value their lives.

GV: Why? Because of the pollution?

GAY SUNSHINE: That and the earthquake.

GV: Ah, yes, the earthquake. Americans must always have something to believe in. Do you know how the sodomy laws first got on the books? In the beginning, church laws proscribed all sex but had nothing in particular to say about sodomy. But according to Procopius, the emperor Justinian who was making up the law codes had a great deal of trouble with the archbishop of Constantinople whose particular pleasure was buggering boys. So the emperor outlawed such practices in his code, saying that it was against God's law and quoted scripture as best he could. He also added that, as we all know, sodomy is the principal cause of earthquakes. So I think it highly suitable that the West Coast may some day tumble into the Pacific in the name of the emperor Justinian.

GAY SUNSHINE: From a different historical interpretation, we understand that Justinian's wife, Theodora, who was known as the greatest cocksucker in Asia Minor, coerced her husband into the anti-sodomy measure.

GV: Sexist talk. Anyway, it was a pure political ploy. And, of course, it stayed on the canon law books. No one would stand up to remove it, and from there it got into civil and criminal law.

GAY SUNSHINE: Do you think that our generation will witness the repeal of all sex laws ?

GV: I've been disturbed by the slowness with which legislatures around the country have reacted. They have been slow to act because people have not put the right kind of pressure on them.

GAY SUNSHINE: They feel that by simply declaring all such matters outside the province of the police and courts they are wholeheartedly endorsing mass orgies in the streets.

GV: That's always the simplistic view.

GAY SUNSHINE: Exactly. In Boston, we went three months without any laws against pornograpy, yet we survived.

GV: To the extent that Boston can be said to exist.

GAY SUNSHINE: Now the laws have been restored. *Deep Throat* has continued to play in Boston, even though it gets busted on a regular basis. It's rumored that through the efforts of the "good" Cardinal Medeiros, the people who run the movie houses are going to be brought to court on special criminal charges. They may face imprisonment.

GV: Under the First Amendment, you can't make any laws to ban pornography; it is not possible. But the courts, the legislatures pay no attention to the Constitution. It doesn't interest them much.

GAY SUNSHINE: Do you think that the recent waves of reaction have helped to stimulate the women's and gay movements, just as an upsurge of white racism brought the black movement to its feet?

GV: Well, it happened for blacks. As things started to get better for them economically, their relations with whites grew worse. Newark was set afire after integration there was finally achieved. As things get better, there often develops an enormous irritability, a reaction which leads to a lot of explosions, especially toward the end of the sixties. And it may be as everything got more and more open, and as the hetero dictatorship began to loosen up a bit, the eruption began. The gay and women's movements came to life. So far I don't think the backlash amounts to much. I think it's always true that things begin to liberalize, revolutionize. Once there is an atmosphere for change, change increases exponentially, and reaction only further serves to stimulate more change. Maybe that's what we've been seeing.

GAY SUNSHINE: Do you think these changes or movements, for example, gay liberation, have made a lasting impact on American values?

GV: I don't know. You tell me. I don't think the gay liberation movement is particularly strong. I don't think it's touched 99 percent of the people. You can go into any small town in America and the attitudes of the people there are no different from what they were in 1900.

GAY SUNSHINE: In the heartland of America ...

GV: Where the pulse beat originates. But, you know, only 3 percent of the people read books. So 97 percent never read a book. Only 10 percent read magazines—the circulation of *TV Guide* or *Playboy* . There's still 90 percent who are not reading *Cosmopolitan* on the joys of scraping your Fallopian tubes while talking to house plants. This is still unknown to them.

What has happened since *The City and the Pillar,* which is how I tend to date things, which I remember rather vividly as a book that the *New York Times* would not advertise and everyone was so down on, is now very old-fashioned according to the media. Today the 3 percent who read books and the 10 percent who read magazines are used to these ideas. Not much change for twenty-six years. Eventually the pop culture does begin to trickle down, but it's awfully slowly.

GAY SUNSHINE: Historically, do you see social movements paralleling and reinforcing each other?

GV: The women's movement has been going on since the country started. There has always been a sort of suffragette movement, at some times stronger than others. But the real impetus for that was when the Fourteenth Amendment was passed after the Civil War, giving blacks the vote. The women quite rightly said that if the ignorant black man can vote then so can we brilliant white women. That was the big trigger. It may be that black militancy helped women's liberation, which in turn helped gay liberation by showing that people were no longer satisfied with the status quo, with the prejudices and superstitions of the heterosexual dictatorship. I think some trend is unfolding before our eyes, though I'm not totally optimistic.

GAY SUNSHINE: Has the gay world changed since its seminal beginnings in that riverside cabin twenty-six years ago?

GV: I have noticed a very interesting change in my own lifetime. And that has been the fact that the quality of trade has fallen off. When I was young there was a floating population of hetero males who wanted money or kicks or what have you and would sell their ass for a period of their lives. Later they would marry and end up as construction workers or firemen or in the police department. And that was that. Their phase was over. But these were really all-American types, masculine in the old sense. There has emerged a new physical type who seem feminine to me, and I use the term in its old sexist sense. Very schmoo, soft shoulders, flat muscles, broad hips, high voices. Now I wonder is this your experience around Boston, which has always been a center for Irish Catholic trade? From Scollay Square they used to spread out across the country like an army with banners or shamrocks and foreskins ...

GAY SUNSHINE: Only the Polish and Irish can be said to be intact...

GV: And so perfect to the eye.

GAY SUNSHINE: Does this decline in trade have to do, in part, with the urbanization of society, the society becomes more powerful, the men more cerebral to rationalize—

GV: Yes, but truck drivers becoming cerebral? Or day laborers? Or the average hillbilly boy from Bryant Park to Eighth Avenue? No.

GAY SUNSHINE: Or what are the effects of restraining the body?

GV: I wonder whether the body is changing physically, whether there might be some kind of mutancy taking place, and that nature is instinctively saying that we don't need any more babies. And the men are becoming a bit less masculine and the women a bit less feminine. I don't know. I'm just guessing. Or is it something in the air which makes them play it another way?

GAY SUNSHINE: We'll start with norm control in sex and physical education classes.

GV: It's always true in high schools, as I remember. In my youth, if the handsomest athlete was queer every boy was going to bed with every other boy; but if he wasn't, they'd all imitate him and go to bed with girls. Quite extraordinary how one or two idols would always set the tone. Dr. Kinsey noticed the same thing. He could never understand it; he was very square. There could be two high schools about thirty miles apart in the same region and consisting of students from the same economic class. One would indulge in unrestrained homosexuality, yet at the other there was almost none. He couldn't understand that. So I evolved this theory that most of the students tend to mimic the sexual tastes of the school hero.

GAY SUNSHINE: When was this?

GV: I was about twenty-three at the time and prone to theorizing. Also, I said very vaingloriously that it is possible to make any man. I may not be the person who can do it, but someone can make him. Dr. Kinsey agreed. He said that he had met a young man in Chicago who said the same thing to him. So old Dr. K. took him up on it. Together they went to Division Street where there was a lot of action, and the young man said: now you point out somebody at random. So Kinsey pointed out some guy talking to a girl. He couldn't have been more straight looking. Our hero made the young man. Kinsey said that on three occasions he picked at random and the trick was turned.

GAY SUNSHINE: A wink, touch and stroke of the hand and he's yours.

GV: An erection has no conscience as they used to say in the army many years ago.

GAY SUNSHINE: It's still around as a stiff cock, etc., though one hears such things as a civilian. But you wonder if there has been a change in people's physical construction.

GV: I know at Yale they've been photographing the students naked for something like thirty years now, front and back. I think from that they might be able to come up with something. I know that they say that they are taller than they were, and I would say broader beamed.

GAY SUNSHINE: This probably has something to do with people toasting their toes in front of the tube during their childhood, something which began in the fifties.

GV: It certainly makes for passivity. There's no doubt about that. Boys were once brought up in the back lots, playing baseball and fighting and jumping over walls and all the other things that boys did. That's an interesting thought. It's quite true. They are now brought up from babyhood staring straight ahead at commercials and eating junk food.

GAY SUNSHINE: And educators are making quite a stir over the drop in achievement level, especially with people now going into college.

GV: Well, that of course is Dr. Shockley's theory about whites as well as blacks. Due to incontinent breeding and the fact that we are keeping alive strains that would have died at birth or soon after, a lot of weak strains are being continued. An interesting thought. But obviously a male brought up on television is going to be very different from one who was physically active and doing "manly" things.

GAY SUNSHINE: In other words, they are no longer stalking Division Street or Bryant Park to Eighth Avenue and selling their ass.

GV: No, at best they are lying down somewhere and watching the tube.

GAY SUNSHINE: Or watching *Deep Throat* and reading Alex Comfort in comic book form.

GV: And not having much sex. I don't think they're very sexy. I think that we were far more ... Of course, it was still a great adventure with us. Things were not always as open as they are now. But we all, hereto, homo, or bi, were just obsessed. If you were in town and did not get laid every day, I mean, the spirit died. I can remember when I'd miss two days in a row, and I'd think life was over, that something terrible had happened. And I don't mean just slogging along in some domestic arrangement.

GAY SUNSHINE: Bond pairing with one person. Was there less talk about sex when you were younger or was the talk about the same?

GV: The talk was about the same.

GAY SUNSHINE: Yes, but it wasn't considered a matter to write studies about.

GV: Well, there was less talk in mixed company, as it were; meaning by mixed company, homo and hetero, or even hereto men and women. The talk was more euphemistic than it is now.

GAY SUNSHINE: In your exchange earlier this year in London with Lord Longford, you devastated the poor patriarch with a euphemistic statement: "If you don't love people sexually, you cannot love them at all." This was reprinted in *The Listener*.

GV: I think that's true. If you cannot respond sexually, you cannot be close to another person. That does not mean you have to respond to everybody. To put it differently, if you always inhibit your sexual response, you will have a terrible time dealing with others in other respects. How are the Boston Irish these days now that we're on the subject?

GAY SUNSHINE: A lot of athletes are rumored to be available.

GV: Well, athletes have always been rather more relaxed than anybody else. They are at home in their bodies. And sex, after all, is just one use of the body. They don't feel any commitment to the straight and narrow path because they have already proved their manhood on the field. Everything else they can take as a joke. Whereas the intellectual is the last person you could or would want to get into bed. Or a fag. The uptight queen.

GAY SUNSHINE: They're a parallel to the uptightness in many of the intellectual gay movement types. The cruising scene in Boston is a lot more open than that; there nearly everyone is available at one time or another, indiscriminate promiscuity. Especially the street scene, the Fenway and the Bird Sanctuary, where the perpetual bluebird reigns ...

GV: Like New York's Bird Circuit thirty years ago.

GAY SUNSHINE: Yeah. Outside pursuit somewhat removed from New York's legendary Blue Parrot. The Sanctuary is a forest with low bushes and reeds. People enter, cruise, ball, and split.

GV: And the master of the revels is Al Fresco.

GAY SUNSHINE: Natch! The difficulty of making it with another faggot arises in the bar scene, using booze as a crutch, consistently making the right moves at the appropriate time invariably without acknowledging what's really happening.

GV: Women are actually much more interesting, because you're getting exactly the same psychic charge from a faggot, and it isn't as comfortable. The hetero in the old days was always more fun to go to bed with.

GAY SUNSHINE: I'm not so sure about that now. Why?

GV: There was a kind of kinetic energy about it, it really could get wild. An enormous kinetic intensity, like a lightning storm, is exciting for its own sake, or, to use that word Norman Mailer always misuses, existential.

GAY SUNSHINE: The wildest experiences supposedly may be found in university tearooms, especially the notorious Lamont Library at Harvard. The scene there includes passing notes which outline what one is into, which for most undergrads is mutual masturbation.

GV: Or belly-rubbing. What Wystan Auden called Princeton First Year.

GAY SUNSHINE: *The City and the Pillar* must have done wonders for belly-rubbing.

GV: As *Streetcar* did for nymphomania. All of that came much into fashion.

GAY SUNSHINE: Let's stray over to the fashionable subject of the media. Do you think the decision to televise the House Judiciary Committee's impeachment proceedings played any part in the toppling of Tricksie?

GV: Do you think it had much to do with it?

GAY SUNSHINE: It seems the mail that came in as soon as the proceedings got under way went from opposition to impeachment at the beginning to ten to one in favor of impeachment at the end.

GV: Because of the Committee?

GAY SUNSHINE: Yes, and soon a number of congressional people began to reverse or reconsider their decisions when the tally was being counted up. But this prostitution was not exactly creative democracy at work.

GV: I think something changed in the weather. I think the people always knew instinctively that he was a criminal. After all, we are nation of shoplifters as Napoleon said the British were a nation of shopkeepers. Americans know a crook when they see one, as they have had a lot of experience with crooks. So it was highly suitable that a nation of shoplifters should elect a criminal as their president. Only you do not get caught shoplifting. And as president, you mustn't get caught stealing money for your houses, or buying earrings for your pretty wife with money that has not been declared to the IRS. I don't think that anyone was really surprised to find out that he was a criminal. Only that he got caught.

GAY SUNSHINE: True, though one in five still supports the exiled emperor. When the press discerned that his fall was imminent, they got themselves busy dolling up another hero. Tweedle-Dum and Tweedle-Dee magazines had Kissinger on the cover. What would Myra say about Kissinger?

GV: Well, Myra would probably find that in a sense he continued the tradition of S. Z. Sakall, known as "Cuddles," who appears as a minor actor in many films, with his heavy accent and seriously pendant jowls. So there probably isn't a need for a Kissinger figure at the moment.

GAY SUNSHINE: How do you see Kissinger?

GV: The thing I love about Kissinger is that he has made his career out of comparing himself to Metternich. Metternich was an Austrian diplomat, an international figure, master of the Congress of Vienna. But Kissinger has never told us how Metternich's career ended. After about thirty years, the Congress of Vienna, with its balances and interdependences and linkage, was overthrown in 1848, in a spontaneous popular uprising all over Europe in which a number of crowned heads were swept away. Will Kissinger like Metternich bring on a world revolution?

GAY SUNSHINE: Kissinger will not last that long. He's a good liar but he doesn't have Metternich's attention for detail. Any idea what sort of hero might rush in to fill the breach, as it were?

GV: It will evolve. Americans are simple and their heroes easy to design. I mean, you can invent them overnight. Look at Ford. Ford did himself in with the pardon, but before the pardon he was well on his way to being Jack Armstrong, all-American boy. The people loved him. He cooked his own breakfast and had a nice smile and a twinkle in his eye. He wasn't especially bright, but that only meant that the electorate could identify with him much more readily than with, say, the towering intellect that Kissinger has been made out to be. So through his upright stupidity he was on the way to enjoying a perfect symbiotic relationship with his electorate.

GAY SUNSHINE: The comparison to Ford as the man in the horror movie: the first man who sees the monster and comes rushing in to report that there's something terrible and green in the meadow, is unparalleled. A remake of *The Last Will of Dr. Mabuse*. He may have seen the monster while he was being taught by Johnson to chew gum.

GV: With his foot in his mouth. But he looked all right for a couple of minutes. Had he not granted the pardon, he would have become the Leader by this point. They're all interchangeable. It is the system, not the personality, which determines the state of affairs. I was on the box with Arthur Schlesinger yesterday. Arthur said, "Well, Watergate would never have happened if we had a conventional politician in there, such as Humphrey or Muskie." And I let that go, but I'm not so sure that it would not have happened. It was due to happen. The system was so corrupt. So much money is gathered and used illegally. Something was bound to surface. It's just that Nixon was so incompetent. He did too many bad things. You see, Nixon wanted to be caught. You must remember that. From the moment he became president he had to contrive his own ruin. His character demanded this. No matter what situation he was in, no matter what peak he attained, he would contrive to get his back to the wall.

GAY SUNSHINE: The American public does not want to deal with the godhead as vulnerable or impotent. Witness the tepid reception to your play *An Evening with Richard Nixon*. What do you see as the most memorable character trait of Nixon?

GV: He did the most extraordinary thing. It's documented on the tapes. Right after he won the great election victory, he was talking with an aide about someone in a federal bureau: "Is so-and-so a friend?" Nixon said, "Let's face it [expletive deleted] we have no friends." Now, a man who has just been elected with all those votes says "we have no friends." This means that he doesn't like the people who elected him and he knows that through trickery, through the media, through big money, through smearing his enemies, through underground dirty tricks he got the job. That to me was the tragic moment when you saw the real Nixon saying "I am not worthy, I'm a sort of Iago, I'm a Richard III. I have taken this place which is not rightfully mine." And there was a sense of not only evil, but self-perception.

GAY SUNSHINE: You have often said that a military dictatorship is in the offing, in the form of 100 percent Americanism, a democracy which will give people what they want, for a time.

GV: Yes, I think it's possible.

GAY SUNSHINE: Has Watergate affected the possibility?

GV: Oh, no. Watergate will not affect the chances of it coming about.

GAY SUNSHINE: How do you envision the next superhero?

GV: Whoever becomes our next dictator will be like Arthur Godfrey—folksy and very democratic in appearance, very warm and talkative and will say a lot about how much he loves the people. He will seem all right. He will also have the full support of the Pentagon and of the big industries intertwined with the Pentagon, members of Congress who support the Pentagon. But first things will have to get unstuck.

GAY SUNSHINE: Due to the economy?

GV: Well, people were very docile in the Depression of the 1930s. There was 20 percent unemployment, which was fantastic compared with today's figures, and there was no talk of revolution. The worst thing that happened, as I remember, is when the jobless veterans marched on Washington. That did scare the shit out of everybody. I remember riding down to the Senate in my grandfather's car with its senatorial plate, and they stoned the car on the Capitol grounds. It was my first experience with a mob. Then Douglas MacArthur dispersed them. People were very docile then, but not now. They all have Saturday night specials, and they all watch TV which has shown them all the pretty things they cannot afford, junky pretty things that they think they ought to have yet can't buy. So I think that when unemployment reaches ten or fifteen percent, they are going to go down to the grocery store with their guns and they are going to take what they want. And they are going to refuse to pay their bills. This is happening in Italy now: they refuse to pay the light bill. And it may well be that the power companies are going to have to shut down because they cannot afford to pay for fuel. With a setting like that people will not be as docile as they were in 1929. They will be militant, and therefore the military will act. But they won't act through a general. As dumb as they are, they won't be that crude. They'll use somebody like Henry Jackson to shut the door to our cage.

GAY SUNSHINE: Will they make use of a scapegoat? Will the industrialists come out and blame the liberals as they did in Italy in the 1920s, leading to the ascent of Mussolini?

GV: Certainly they will always blame the liberals, the people who wanted to waste money on niggers and schools and things like that instead of defending the country against the international menace of communism, wherever it may show its head in any part of the world. They'll do that automatically. The blacks will probably get it too. Nobody likes them. It's fascinating to watch my Jewish intellectual friends become anti-black.

GAY SUNSHINE: Oh, is social acceptance still *the* issue? The Bernsteins had blacks in.

GV: They have not had them in for a long time. That was 1960s chic. This year's radical chic is to light a fiery cross in Harlem.

GAY SUNSHINE: In the *Playboy* interview you said that you would feel "secure though uninspired" about Rockefeller as president or vice president. How do you feel now?

GV: Did I really say that? I'd be inspired to real insecurity nowadays. I did not know then what I know now. I certainly knew he was bad news in New York State. I knew quite a bit about his operations in Albany. I daresay that I had said so many negative things about politicians that I should, I thought, demur on those two, Rockefeller and

Muskie. Tactful, I think, is the word for it.

GAY SUNSHINE: Could Rockefeller be the new hero?

GV: He's very much the man on horseback. I would say that of any politician who is now on the scene, he is the potential dictator. Certainly he has an authoritarian mind, loves the Pentagon, loved the Vietnam war, would double the military budget. He would never cut it, neither would Ford. If you cut it, the whole country's going bankrupt, because that is where the corporations have sunk most of their investments.

I have a theory that John D. Rockefeller, because he was suckled on mother's milk in his seventies, eighties, and nineties, attributing his long life to that, never died; that John D. Rockefeller II and John D. Rockefeller III are the same. It's the original. He is still alive at this very moment running the United States. Nelson is just one of his clones. Somewhere out there is an old man suckled on mother's milk guiding our affairs to total disaster.

GAY SUNSHINE: But could one individual—even the original John D.—make all that much difference?

GV: Well, we're beyond leadership now. Other tides are running. Individuals are not going to make that much difference with what's about to happen. They're all interchangeable. Whoever he is, the dictator will arise by accident. History requires great change and individuals do not make that change. At least not in a period of disaster. The French Revolution just happened, you know. Nobody started it, and nobody controlled it. Then when it had run its course, Bonaparte picked up the pieces. After that an individual does have a great effect.

GAY SUNSHINE: How do you see sports heroes and the role of American adulation?

GV: I just read somewhere, the *Miami Herald*, I think it was, that there's a book coming out on homosexuality and the baseball world. Needless to say I cannot wait for these revelations. I do remember a very funny (and it wasn't meant to be funny) interview with Joe DiMaggio talking about the young baseball players today, and the fags among them. He said: "I mean, it wasn't like in the old days. They are so ... open. I mean they hold hands right in front of you." What used to be done in a quiet corner of the shower room is now out in the open in the biggest dressing room of all. A shocking interview. Joe was scarlet. But I look forward to that. I can't imagine anyone who was not largely homosexual wanting to be a baseball or a football player, having to live with other boys so much of the time.

GAY SUNSHINE: Not to mention the men who are mesmerized watching athletes on television.

GV: I've always maintained that this is the greatest sign of effeminacy in the male, wanting to watch other men play games.

GAY SUNSHINE: It's interesting that so many faggots are turned off by sports on the box.

GV: It's actually fascinating. The faggots who in theory ought to like watching handsome young men playing body contact games do not like it and the heteros are just out of their minds. I guess it's the only time when the heteros may openly enjoy what they secretly dream of.

GAY SUNSHINE: There's obviously some sort of sublimated orgasm going on, not to bring in old Freud. But it's not like Athens where homosexuality and sports went, figuratively speaking, hand in hand.

GV: No, in Athens and all those societies, people did play games until they were very old. You kept yourself up. But the American male at twenty-five weighs 250 pounds, is soft and paunchy and out of shape, and so identifies with the professional athletes who have to keep themselves in shape. So they are his male surrogates as well as his male lovers, in a psychic sense.

GAY SUNSHINE: Your essay "Pederasty, Plato and Mr. Barrett" has been sealed by the Madison Historical Society. Would you like to talk about your response to Mr. Barrett's essay "New Innocents Abroad"?

GV: As I remember, it was sealed for one year. My answer was irritable. I said nothing in it that I haven't said ten million times since and much better. Barrett was stupid. And inaccurate. André Gide said, *"Je ne suis pas tapette, monsieur, je suis pédéraste,"* which was said about Capote, and not about me.

GAY SUNSHINE: The Catholic Church has once again begun to flex its political muscle in some states. It has managed to push through laws which completely fly in the face of the Supreme Court decision on abortion. Catholic organizations are now sponsoring a proposed constitutional amendment which would completely abolish this hard-won right. And where their efforts have proven unsuccessful, or, in the case of New York City, failed a bit, they have turned against pending gay rights legislation. Do you think that if Mother Pope succeeds in revoking the right to voluntary childbirth, that the fags will be next on the scaffold?

GV: Why not? If I were dictator or president or otherwise in control of a well-run country, the first thing I would do is to forbid the Catholic Church from educating anyone. I would not allow them to have any schools as I regard their education to be inimical to the best interests of the Republic. Where the Catholic Church has dominated there has never been a democratic society. This even goes for France which is largely secular and atheistic. But nevertheless, it is sufficiently Catholic to prevent it from governing itself except as a kind of confused oligarchy. Democracy, as we know it, the modern Republic, is an essentially Protestant phenomenon. Whatever the Protestant fails at doing, the Protestant at least protests. But I would not allow any religious group to have schools. And without schools, there would be no Catholic Church in two generations because their doctrines are so insane that nobody in his right mind would accept them. Then I would tax all churches heavily. That would reduce their influence by 90 percent.

GAY SUNSHINE: Do you think the Church bears much of the

responsibility for the current overpopulation and food crisis?

GV: Yes.

GAY SUNSHINE: Historically, how do you see the power base of the Roman Church in America?

GV: I think the Roman Catholic arrivals here have not been—how shall I put this tactfully—a great addition to our Republic and its ways and customs. They bring with them a love of authority, an inability to make decisions on their own and an essential bigotry, directed specifically toward Jews and also toward the lesser breeds. It is no accident that the great support that Richard Nixon and George Wallace have is in the ethnic suburbs of the North, the Irish Catholic and Polish Catholic suburbs, just as they have the fundamentalist WASPs and other illiterates in the rural South.

GAY SUNSHINE: Have we not been making whipping boys out of the Irish Catholics of Boston? Are you familiar with the school situation in Boston and the opportunism of Louise Day Hicks?

GV: I know about Louise Day. On the other hand, the people from Southie have a very good point aside from their native bigotry and so forth. They feel impotent and screwed by an impersonal government which won't let them send their children to the schools they want them to go to.

GAY SUNSHINE: And people are being bused from bad schools in black neighborhoods to bad schools in white neighborhoods.

GV: Yes, as if the American public school system is any good anywhere. Wherever you go, you get a lousy education. What difference does it make if it takes an extra hour to get there?

GAY SUNSHINE: Additionally, in the upper-middle-class South End of Boston special experimental schools, which blacks for some reason avoid, have been set up.

GV: Experimental schools. They get the blacks and then spend no money.

GAY SUNSHINE: Though in America all races have an equal right to illiteracy. The usual practice is to shove people through schools, willy-nilly, people who are not being educated. Those who manage to achieve their grade level are shoved into college.

GV: Without ever realizing what a verb was.

GAY SUNSHINE: Is there a positive way of looking at that? In a vein of humor, are people perhaps concentrating more on the substance and less on the grammar? Are they discovering one another and not concentrating on mere academic aspects ?

GV: Oh, no. Words are words and gropes are gropes. And it's nice to be able to render a grope into words.

GAY SUNSHINE: Witness the recent, innumerable acts of linguistic genocide committed by the House Judiciary Committee, beginning with Rodino's "the gentle lady from New York" and leading us to the overwhelming question, "Will the president continue to offense the Constitution?"

GV: "Offense the Constitution?" Oh, no. I wish I'd heard that. I didn't witness any of the hearings, I was abroad. That's very nice. That's what I call Near English. Have the immigrants done that, the schools?

GAY SUNSHINE: Perhaps it's the television media with pablum programming and *Time* magazine.

GV: Well, *Time* magazine is more into neologisms. You know: Portly, well-educated, balding ...

GAY SUNSHINE: And empty of content. While we're on the subject of verbiage, do you know that one of your nemeses, Truman Capote, says that he's doing a column every three weeks for the *New York Times* ?

GV: Oh, no. That's pure Truman. He invented it as he invents most of his conversations. The *New York Times* printed a rebuttal which went out over all the wire services, and it was very embarrassing. Poor Truman. It wouldn't be a bad idea to let him be Suzy for a while. In *Pictures from an Institution*, Randall Jarrell said about Mary McCarthy, calling her Gertrude, I believe: Gertrude may not be much of a novelist, but she's a wonderful liar. That would be poor Truman.

GAY SUNSHINE: How do you feel your novel *Myron* is being received? *Time*, in a scatological review, uses the word "evil" thrice, and *New York* magazine claims that you do not have the courage of Myra's convictions.

GV: Oh, yes. I read that. Fremont-Smith referred to *Myra* as a classic. He forgot that he used to be the daily reviewer for the *New York Times*. Originally he was horrified by *Myra B*. Obviously he's changed. Philip Roth has done a marvelous job on the *Times'* book reviewers. It started with a piece in *The New York Review of Books*, in which he went after Christopher Lehman-Haupt who then made the mistake of writing a long letter to *The New York Review*. And then Philip answered it. It was very funny. Those people are simply not competent and ought not to be doing this kind of thing. We do not want what they laughingly refer to as their thoughts on any subject. Just try and describe a book, which is difficult to do.

GAY SUNSHINE: We were talking about Heller's latest opus and generalizing. We couldn't understand how a reviewer could pick up a book, glance at it, write a review and then compare it to a book written in a different decade.

GV: Well, you write that sort of review in advance. There are two reviews you could give it: One, that it is not as good as *Catch-22*. That's the usual one. We all know that sequels are not s good as their originals. We all know that *Huck Finn* was much worse than *Tom Sawyer*, naturally, a great failure. So you can write that review very safely. Or two, you just zero in and say that it has to be a very good novel because it's very long, and the author is middle-aged, Jewish, and heterosexual. These are the three most important things that you can be, the sine qua non. So how could you knock such a triad?

GAY SUNSHINE: We hear Mick Jagger visited you in Italy and that you cooked Irish stew for him.

GV: He stayed with me three days, but I forget what I gave him. We had a cook. And he had a diamond in his tooth, which is the first thing I noticed. I said I thought he had caught something between his teeth. He said, "Yeh, it's me diamond." I said, "Isn't it uncomfortable?"

GAY SUNSHINE: We would venture to say that *Myron* is your most self-indulgent, though your best, book. And only you could have written it which isn't quite true of the historical novels.

GV: Well, I think that. And I would say that some of the response here and there around the country, Richard Poirier and so on, is that it has to be read line by line. And, you know, readers nowadays, particularly the academics, read by the page. They figure there is not going to be much on a page anyway, so the eye zigzags down: cock, cunt, Marilyn Monroe...E. M. Forster. Turn the page, and so on. I work line by line, and if you miss a couple of lines you miss the point. I make little puzzles, like Agatha Christie. You know, I keep planting my clues.

GAY SUNSHINE: Sherman cigarette butts in Peter Sargent's ashtray.

GV: Yes, remember that later, because it may be a key point.

GAY SUNSHINE: It looks as though *Myron* will not reach a large audience. How does that strike you?

GV: Well, you do feel that you have failed when you realize people are not getting you at all. But it's ignorance which most irritates me. I've been doing interviews, eight a day, and the square ones ... and I finally told one yesterday, who was rather bright but extremely rectilinear, that I always have to remind myself that I'm in America, and that I'm the author of a bad, dirty book like Jacqueline Susann or Harold Robbins. In Europe *Myra's* regarded rather seriously. So I take it for granted that interviewers want to discuss it seriously. Then I suddenly remember that they don't know what it is. So I have to start all over again. Explain about literature.

GAY SUNSHINE: Last year you talked of a way around censorship and the *Smith* v. *California* decision with *Myron*, but your lips were sealed on the subject. You've taken measures to ensure that *Myron* is not banned as pornography. You've cleaned up some of the tart language.

GV: Yes, I've cleaned up *Myron*, I've removed the dirty words and replaced them with clean words.

GAY SUNSHINE: What words?

GV: Well, I thought and thought for a long time: what are the cleanest words I can find? And I discovered that I could not come up with any cleaner words than the names of the five Supreme Court justices and two other good citizens who have taken on the task of cleansing this country of pornography. I inserted the words in place of the dirty words. For example, a cock becomes a rehnquist. And a cunt becomes a whizzer white—

GAY SUNSHINE: After Byron White, the football hero who cracked the kamikaze code in World War II.

GV: To fuck becomes to burger, and an ass becomes a blackmun and so on.

GAY SUNSHINE: Interesting in view of the fact that psychologists and psychiatrists from Freud to Malinowski have indicated that one can always tell what a given culture worships by determining what words are taboo. The ancient Hebrews could not take the name of the Lord in vain; for the medievals sodomy was not to be spoken of; and for us, the American pantheon consists of such deities as cock, cunt, ass and fuck. In any case, do you think *Myron* is sufficiently sanitary to get by in Drake, North Dakota?

GV: In Drake, I wonder. I think they'll be upset. People will get upset as Susskind told me last night. I guess he was trying to get some conservatives on the show to debate me, and he tried to get Rehnquist.

GAY SUNSHINE: Our wise justice or—

GV: No, the cock. And Rehnquist said no; that he never appeared on television, which is true. So that was that. Then David rang up the solicitor general, Mr. Bork, and said, "Will you appear on television with Vidal?" And he said, "I will not." And David said, "Why not?" And he said, "I do not think the solicitor general of the United States should ever become hysterical on television." And David said, "Oh, have you seen the book?" And he snapped, "I've heard about it." And David, being the *yenta* that he is, said, "What do the justices think?" And Bork said, "I wouldn't dare to mention such filth to them!" It's nice to know that in Washington there's a ticking bomb. There will come the day when someone hands Warren Burger a copy of the book as he goes into court.

GAY SUNSHINE: I am surprised that you or Random House have not sent the justices review copies for their judicious approval.

GV: Actually I want them to change their names to what I substituted their names for.

GAY SUNSHINE: Do you think *Myron* will set America back on the road to rectitude?

GV: Rectitude is an exquisitely chosen word.

GAY SUNSHINE: We have a fantasy about *Myra* and *Myron*, namely, that there will be a third book, one of those dystopic science-fiction things about overpopulation, entitled "Normy," an anagram for Myron, about this misanthropic McDonald's chef who makes his way to power and attempts to destroy the human race through indiscriminate breeding. Myra, of course, steps in to thwart his plans, depowelling him as he emerges from the VFW headquarters in Schenectady. Is Myra still in wait?

GV: Well, I don't know if there is any sign that Myra will strike again. I can't see it from here. But you can never tell. Somewhere she's rapping away. Inexorable!

GAY SUNSHINE: Recalling our discussion of the Everard Baths last year [*Fag Rag 7/8*], a recent issue of *Straight to Hell*, a journal on cocksucking and current affairs, documents the rumor that Truman Capote plays the part of the voyeur on his regular visits to Sauna here in New York.

GV: I can't say, as I don't visit the Sauna. But I've read *STH*. Quite an imaginative little paper, as imaginative as Truman when it comes to telling stories about people. Yet I hoped that the Bob Hope story was true.

GAY SUNSHINE: Do you still have the tape of that evening with Mailer, Ginsberg, etc., which you described in *Two Sisters* ?

GV: Paul Bowles taped Ginsberg, Orlovsky, Norman and me. Mailer got drunk and finally just lay down on the floor. It was a hot summer night and he had his shirt off and his belly stuck out. Allen rested his bare feet on Norman fat stomach, and said: "Of course, you know he's crazy." And then we had this long discussion about Mailer as he lay there comatose on the floor. Afterwards, I asked Paul what the tape was like. He said it made no sense at all. Every now and then you heard a screech from Orlovsky. Paul thought he was going to have memorable piece of tape.

Also, while we're on the subject, I got a letter from Kerouac's latest biographer. He wrote me saying you'll be interested to know that I've come across a letter from William Burroughs to Jack Kerouac saying that Burroughs was coming around and would like to meet me, because he thought I was a nice-lookin' cat. And could Kerouac be so kind as to set this up? I didn't realize. Kerouac rang up and asked if I'd like to go to dinner with him and a friend. Burroughs was unknown then. He'd just shot his wife and I think he'd published *Junkie* under another name. So we all met down at the old San Remo in the Village. Burroughs was kind of stunned-stoned. Kerouac was stunned with drink. Strange summer night. We then went to Tony Pasteur's, a big dyke hangout. I don't know what possessed us to go there. Jack and I always sort of contemplated going to bed together, but we never got around to it. And I guess Jack did it to head off Burroughs. So he got rid of Bill at one point. By then I was well out of the idea because he was too drunk. But Jack insisted, so off to the Chelsea we went. Somebody should get a copy of the hotel register, because I think we signed our right names.

This was in the late Fifties. I guess around the summer of '56. I know I was already doing television plays, because a couple of nights later Kerouac was down in the San Remo and was sitting in a corner shouting, "I blew Gore Vidal!" This was overhead by a guy named Jack Barefield who worked for the advertising agency that put the money up for CBS's *Studio One* series. I was doing a *Studio One*. And Barefield, a very nervous Southern type, said, "I just don't think this is very good publicity for you. That crazy man down there saying such things." I said, "Well, that's just Jack."

GAY SUNSHINE: Burroughs was in Boston recently for a poetry reading.

GV: He's never said an intelligent thing in my presence. He's a bit like Andy Warhol—

GAY SUNSHINE: With scissors. Have you had any contact with Warhol?

GV: I don't run with that crowd. The media have made him out to be a sort of a menace, and like Norman, very obligingly, he plays the part.

GAY SUNSHINE: I love his so-called theory of film.

GV: I asked him what was the most difficult thing about movie-making and he said, getting the film into the camera.

GAY SUNSHINE: Will you direct a film?

GV: I've written several movies in the past.

GAY SUNSHINE: *Ben Hur, Suddenly Last Summer, The Best Man, Is Paris Burning?* with Francis Ford Coppola, *Ad infinitum...*

GV: *Ad Infinitum* opened in Brooklyn, RKO Albee. As for directing, I think my moment has passed. I considered it seriously a few years ago. But I think I'm too old now. You have to do it when you're full of energy. Not that directing itself takes that much energy, but dealing with the money people takes an awful lot out of you. I think I'm too old and spoiled to cope with any of that.

GAY SUNSHINE: Have you thought about filming *Myra* or *Myron*?

GV: I never saw the first film of *Myra*. Judging from the reviews, I was fortunate. They never used my script.

GAY SUNSHINE: Unfortunately. I read the script last month in Madison when I was reviewing your papers. The memorable episodes involved Myra as various stars: Bogart, Julie Andrews (*The Sound of Music*), James Mason (*The Seventh Veil*), Bergman (*Joan of Arc*), Garbo (*Camille*), culminating with Myra as Queen/King Kong to Rusty's Fay Wray. Would you like to see a film of *Myron*?

GV: Yeah, but it would be kind of tricky; it would probably include a lot of literary foreplay, all that stuff about a film within a film and never getting to the point. Things of which the French are so fond. But I would fancy a film of *Myron*, possibly starring Woody Allen. Or Tricia Nixon.

GAY SUNSHINE: In *Myron* there is the view that Hollywood has definitely altered our concept of ourselves. It seems to say that if Myra could go back in history and change several aspects of *Siren of Babylon* and thereby manage to save Hollywood, that history itself would be altered. Going back to the past to change the future which is now the present. Surely this is all jest. But do you see more hope of changing society through the film than through the printed word? And, secondly, do you think that to be the goal of any conscientious filmmaker?

GV: No. I don't think that any film nowadays can have the slightest influence in the way those films had when everybody went to the movies. The equivalent today would be the TV commercials.

GAY SUNSHINE: An industry where some of our most creative people master the art of subliminal seduction.

GV: Yeah. A television series, maybe. I'm sure that *All in the Family* and *Mary Tyler Moore* have had more impact on American mores. But you won't see the impact for ten to twenty years, the same way as you did not see the influence of Hollywood in my generation.

GAY SUNSHINE: What about your fascination with George Arliss?

GV: Everything I've ever wanted to be, he's played: The Green Goddess, Disraeli, Cardinal Richelieu, oh my God, did I love that. He only had one expression which I always admired. You know I hate actors who have lots of expressions. He had just one. The eyebrows would lift, and he would look with absolute disbelief at what was going on around him whether the scene called for it or not. You could see plainly he did not know what was going on. Oh, he was great.

GAY SUNSHINE: How was your generation influenced?

GV: Mailer, for example, is still playing John Garfield. I mean he'll never really play anyone else. That's in his head, though he sometimes attempts Bogart and tries to shift around. We all have these mythical figures in our heads. That was the first thing that really compelled our imaginations. But it is no longer film, nor will it ever be, because the film speaks only to specialized audiences. I can't imagine a nation changed by Ingmar Bergman. So few people go to see him.

GAY SUNSHINE: Our generation appears to be influenced by Mick Jagger, David Bowie, Elton John's androgyny or bisexuality.

GV: Well, when Jagger came to stay with me I got the impression that he was a rather shrewd, very intelligent, rather donnish businessman who really is mostly hetero and square. And then from somewhere inside himself he throws this switch and suddenly goes into this bisexual number. I said, "I think you are getting away with murder with this bisexual number." He giggled.

GAY SUNSHINE: We have been working on a piece involved with the nexus between Jagger and the gay sensibility. We concluded that Jagger is basically hetero, but his appeal to homo vis-à-vis hetero, is dissimilar.

GV: This travesty number has been going on forever.

GAY SUNSHINE: You said to *Playboy* that you wrote first to create a work of art and secondly to change society.

GV: Yes, and not necessarily simultaneously.

GAY SUNSHINE: You told *Fag Rag* last year that as an artist you do not have a political function. Has your feeling changed? What are your latest feelings now that you have published *Myron*?

GV: Well, I don't think it does, overtly, no. But I've always said over and over again that the one immutable law of physics is that there is no action without a reaction. So therefore anything you set into motion will lead to some response, though you cannot calculate what it will be. It could be political, social or what have you. Obviously there will be something. Some waves will be made by what one throws into this vast sea.

GAY SUNSHINE: Critics expect writers to improve with each work. This is certainly good reason to live abroad. How do you see your work? Do you feel your best work lies ahead?

GV: Oh, God, I don't know. I would doubt it only because you cannot do good work without a future sense of time. And I have no sense of future time. I don't think Western Civilization as I've understood it and cared for it will continue. I don't really in my mind's eye see the human race in existence for another hundred years, right or wrong. When you feel like this, it makes it very difficult to create a work of art because I think the principal impulse to create is the will to make something permanent, even though you know that from the standpoint of eternity, nothing is permanent. But certainly in terms of the generations of man, as the Bible would put it, you do have a sense of continuing and addressing future generations. And so you will not become entirely extinct because of what you have wrought. Well, if you don't have that sense or if you are fairly convinced that there is going to be no future either for the written word as you practice it or for the human race as such, well, this sort of takes the moxie out of you. And I don't think that I'm the only one to feel this. I think that the deterioration in all the arts that we see now is a sign of this.

GAY SUNSHINE: You wrote, "You have nothing to say, only to add." [*Two Sisters*]

GV: I said it to Dwight Macdonald.

GAY SUNSHINE: About the decline in the condition of the arts?

GV: They are being destroyed from the inside by the practitioners. Music which is made up of silences, pictures which are at random and are made to fall apart, sculpture that sings to you, writing that is intercut with words found at hazard. This is the general direction in all the arts.

GAY SUNSHINE: How do you see the continuing demise of the novel and the status of literature in academia?

GV: It seems to me there are only two survivors: the type of novel that is written by a Harold Robbins or an Erica Jong for a general public, books with lots of violence, not too many big words, books for those who are bored with television, extolling the virtues of citizenship and virility. The others are written within and for the universities, dull books written to be taught in class as examples of experimental technique, to keep people busy deciphering the allusions. Barth and Pynchon, those people. I would say that apart from TV, the universities have been the worst thing for literature. But Literature with a capital L has gone the way of Andy Hardy and Louis B. Mayer.

GAY SUNSHINE: The former junk dealer turned mogul. In 1968 you said to a *Boston Globe* reporter that your life was your business.

GV: I'm personal in an impersonal way.

GAY SUNSHINE: Now that several scholarly reviews of your work have come out, how does it feel to be officially regarded as part of the literary tradition?

GV: A prize for endurance. Not to be taken seriously.

GAY SUNSHINE: Perhaps Modern Library or someone will come out with paperback editions of your works for undergraduate courses, with a few changes to accommodate the new generation.

GV: Such as printing ironies in red, major points in boldface type and figures of speech in brackets.

GAY SUNSHINE: It's been nearly thirty years since you published your first novel. You've been saddled with a number of alliterative labels: Bernard Dick's Apostate Angel, the Permissive Puritan, and soon, presumably, the Pontifical Pederast and Clairvoyant Catamite. How do you respond to the media image in capital letters of GORE VIDAL?

GV: There is no such person. One becomes a fictional character in other people's work. Actually, I have been for some years, secretly, of course, Lon McCallister, star of *Home in Indiana* (1944).

The Sadness of Gore Vidal

by Larry Kramer
September 1992

He sits across from me at a comfortable, quiet table in the *Edwardian Room* at the Plaza Hotel. The staff knows him and is attentive. The woman at the next table leans over to inquire what he thinks of the upcoming Presidential election. He is very fat. His face is lined. His hair, all of which he still has, looks like it's at the end stages of a coloring job. He says he has to worry about his health, but he orders a steak.

He is one of my heroes and, like me, he's obviously very tired. Of fighting and seeing so little progress. Of raising a voice no one hears with any sufficiency. His voice rises almost automatically to sound angry—to sound the anger that he knows we expect from him. His list of wrongs that provoke this anger because they are wrong is by now too familiar to him. He goes on automatic anger. His conversation is sprinkled with the buzzwords of a lifetime; they no longer seem to convince even him. I identify with him completely. Who has listened to him? What has his wrath made right? The world is further away than ever from his dream.

He *calls* me the romantic.
I protest. He is as romantic as I am.
He denies it.
I tell him that anyone as angry as he is must be a romantic

because otherwise life would be unbearable.

He has fought and created and never stopped trying for as long as we have known him. At the end of our meal, which was excellent, and our conversation, which was great fun, and my being with him, which was, for me, exceedingly moving, he pulls his huge self up and lumbers out of the room and into the lobby and into the street. He has many people to speak to while he is still in our city. He is still trying. He may be exhausted and despondent and cynical (no, the romantic never becomes cynical), but he is still trying.

Oh, that I can go on, still trying.

LARRY KRAMER: I should like to start by saying that you are one of my all-time heroes and role models, for more years than either of us wants to count. I pulled out my copy of *The City and the Pillar* and I looked at it in terror to see what year I read it—I was thirteen years old. Can I tell you that it is probably one of the seminal books of my development? Good heavens, and you were twenty-one when you wrote it, which was extraordinary.

GORE VIDAL: 1948, yes, I was twenty-two.

LK: Twenty-two. Well, I guess what I want to talk about today mostly is homosexuality.

GV: *Startling* subject to bring up.

LK: At the Edwardian Room of the Plaza. Well, it was enormously courageous of you to write this book in 1948 but you've said that afterwards you didn't write anymore about homosexuality because you thought you would hurt your career in a literary way.

GV: Oh, no. I never take back anything. It certainly did me great damage, yes. And you know the story which I repeatedly tell: Orville Prescott of the *New York Times* said he would never read, much less review, a book of mine again, and didn't for five books, a couple of which were among my better efforts. *Time* and *Newsweek* also refused to review me. I was so dead-broke I went into television, movies, theater, politics. And in ten years I made enough money so I didn't have to bother about doing work I didn't want to do. I came back to novel-writing with *Julian*, and I've never let go of the subject when I felt I had something to say about it. I'm sometimes put out at how little that I've written on the subject is known. Nobody seems to know my essays at all in all these quote gay unquote—"gay" is a word that I hate—periodicals. I mean there is so much that they can mine from what I've written about sex as politics. I've done a lot of work in that field, trying to analyze the situation, rationalize...

LK: Maybe some of it has got to do with the feeling—whether it's only perceived or accurate, I don't know—that for many years you didn't announce your homosexuality or that you maintained that you were bisexual and that sort of put you on the outs with a certain political correctness.

GV: Yeah, well, that's bad luck for them because I have a lot to say on the subject. I don't categorize—that's the first position I take. There is no such thing as a homosexual person. There are homosexual *acts*—

LK: Well, let's talk about that.

GV: We all know about *heterosexual* acts. Is anybody 100 percent one thing or the other? I rather doubt it. Is anybody fifty-fifty? I rather doubt that too. I haven't seen many examples.

LK: But isn't that just a safe kind of definition? *(A waiter interrupts.)* No, no, I'm interviewing Mr. Vidal, and he's more important than the chicken soup.

GV: Look, what I'm preaching is: don't be ghettoized, don't be categorized. Every state tries to categorize its citizens in order to assert control of them.

LK: But you're living in a time when many of us *want* to be ghettoized and categorized.

GV: Well, I disapprove.

LK: Because there's safety in numbers and perhaps we feel that's a way of exerting—

GV: Well, I'm on a double-track. It never occurred to anybody before St. Augustine that there even *was* such a category. I've never applied [these labels] to myself nor have I applied them to anybody else, even when they have invited me to. Simultaneously, the other track: If the categorization is going on in a vicious way, as it does on the part of our monotheistic, near-totalitarian state, then one *does* organize, and one does fight back. I have two things in my mind. One, that there is no such category, and two, that if the category is invented by the powers that be—largely Christianity, although the Jews are not much better on the subject—then, indeed, it must be fought. I'm all for organization, politicization. I'm even for violence.

LK: Oh, we must talk about *that!* So you approve of ACT UP?

GV: I approve of ACT UP very much—but I approve of successful violence, not unsuccessful. You have to pick the way to do it. You *have* to have a strategy.

LK: Well, we've tried many strategies, all unsuccessful, I'm afraid.

GV: I'm completely in agreement with the spirit of it, that the only thing Americans really respect is a kick in the teeth. And if the police need it or the courts or the Congress or the President needs it, let the kick in the teeth come. It's intolerable to allow this situation to go on. AIDS has been a "Spaniard in the works," as John Lennon would say. It's helped the demonization all over again of the category that *I* say does not exist, but *they* say *does* exist and therefore I would certainly protect those who have been stigmatized.

LK: You've not spoken too much about AIDS.

GV: I'm not a virologist.

LK: No, but surely you must have lost a lot of friends or people that you've known or whatever. And, certainly, aside from everything else, it's a phenomenon.

GV: Well it's an ever-present phenomenon, certainly. I'm not a hand-wringer. If I don't have anything useful to say, what am I to say? It's a terrible thing. Of course it is. AIDS hasn't come to me closely except in my own family. I have a twenty-nine-year-old nephew—my sister's son—who is, of his generation of my family, the only talented member. Hugh Steers, you probably know his paintings. He paints about people with AIDS.

LK: Oh, indeed, yes.

GV: Becoming quite famous.

LK: I didn't know he was your nephew.

GV: Yes. I think he's been diagnosed for eight years and he's twenty-nine, and that obviously brought it home dramatically to me.

LK: Is this not cause for you to write an essay of great strength and anger about what this country has not done to save this young man's life?

GV: Well, yes. But don't you think it's better that I attack the national security state which has given us a kind of police state? Isn't it better I attack the Supreme Court that takes away our rights? And isn't it better I attack Jesus Christ and Moses who have brought on the mentality that has done this? I'm radical—which means I go to the root of it.

LK: Let me say no in answer to all those questions because you have *done* all of this and we know how you feel on all these issues but we *don't* know how you feel on this new one, which is perhaps closer to home and much more personal.

GV: That is wrong in my view. Why get upset only when it touches you personally?

LK: Oh my goodness!

GV: Shouldn't you be, in the abstract, for *justice?*

LK: Now you're getting too existential for me.

GV: I really believe—

LK: I never became political *until* it touched me personally.

GV: I've been political my entire life and politics need not ever have touched me.

LK: Well, I don't know if that's an answer.

GV: Isn't there something in you that makes you feel an obligation to see that justice is done?

LK: Indeed, but—

GV: I believe in going deeper and deeper into the roots of *why* it exists.

LK: But back to this "categorization" business. I wonder if it isn't more of a generational thing than a philosophical thing. What I find, and I'm certainly closer in age to you than I am to the "Young Turks" of today, but I think that, for some time, there's been a very strong desire to be categorized as homosexual, to he proud of being gay and to almost *resent* the notion that people consider gay people bisexual. I think most gay people today don't *want* to be bisexual whether it's in their purview or their skills to be so.

GV: You know, I haven't been *plugging* bisexuality. All I say to interviewers who bring up the subject of my private life—which I was brought up not to discuss, and I *don't* discuss—I just say, "Everyone is bisexual," and I quote Freud, his standard textbook definition. The next thing, I read "Gore Vidal Proudly Claims to Be Bisexual." Well, I never *said* it. I always give the same answer the same way. So that goes, as you know, into the computer, and every time they press that button, they come up with "Gore Vidal Proudly Claims to Be Bisexual."

LK: I don't think I've ever seen "Gore Vidal Says He's Homosexual."

GV: Because I don't believe in it.

LK: But, Gore, you *are* gay. You've lived with a man for forty years or something, and everyone who knows you personally knows you're gay. And I think *you* think of yourself as gay.

GV: I promise you I don't think of myself in these categories. It's like saying, "I'm a carnivore." Well, yes, I *am* a carnivore, but I'm very fond of the movie *Airplane.*

LK: Which is very carnivorous.

GV: I regard it as more vegetarian.

LK: As someone who made a film for Ross Hunter, I can assure you it's carnivorous.

GV: You poor thing! I didn't realize that.

LK: It's nothing I brag about. But I made more money than I made on anything in my life...I guess we desperately want to claim you.

GV: Well, *everybody* has. I don't mind that.

LK: Again, this is something that AIDS has brought about—this desperate need for role models, for people we can call our own...We want to somehow tip you over the edge so we can have, I don't know, *The City and the Pillar*—the Nineties. So you can write about your life as it applies to our lives now, in a personal way.

GV: You have to take into account our temperaments. You're a subjective and romantic writer. I'm an objective and classical writer. The two are totally at odds. I've had the same conversation with Norman Mailer. He is in your situation and I am in mine. We see the world entirely differently.

LK: But I bet there is a big romantic streak in you. Perhaps that's why you're so angry. It takes a romantic to be so angry.

GV: Well, perhaps when Bette Davis in *Dark Victory* is planting her plants. That is universal! No, that is Warner Brothers!

LK: My brother would not know who Bette Davis was in *Dark Victory*. It takes a romantic to be as caring and as angry and as put-out and...

GV: Raging!

LK: Raging—as you are. So, don't give me, "I am not a romantic."

GV: I was brought up with a very over-developed sense of justice—and not only about myself. I have a general view that this is *my* country. My family helped start it, and we've been in political life of one kind or another since the 1690s, and I have a very possessive sense about this country, an ecumenical sense. I don't divide people into men and women, blue eyes and brown eyes. Obviously I do on some levels—we are all filled with wild prejudices and madnesses that strike from time to time. But it's this sense of justice that keeps me going and fuels my rage. It isn't just that I feel upset that I've been discriminated against, as indeed I was. I was blacked-out as a novelist. I was practically destroyed. My friend John Horne Burns *was* destroyed.

LK: But what difference does it make what fuels the rage?

GV: The difference is in the tactics you use.

LK: I use the same tactics as you use.

GV: Except a lady stopped by here before and wanted to know what I thought about the election this year and the Constitution—

LK: Well, we can walk down the street and someone will stop and ask me a question.

GV: But it won't be about the Constitution.

LK: Because I don't think my constituency believes the Constitution is worth shit. Your nephew is not going to live because the Constitution has not extended the necessary rights to him that would force the NIH and the FDA and Congress to see that his disease is researched.

GV: Those things don't have anything to do with the Constitution, although there are many things wrong with the Constitution. It has to do with Congress.

LK: *Fuck* the Constitution, Gore.

GV: It has to do with the Congress. It has to do with the rulers. The *rulers* are the people you have to lean on.

LK: *Lean on?* We've done everything short of kidnapping them and if I knew how to do that, maybe we would have tried that too.

GV: Why don't you fuck Bush and give him AIDS? And say, "This will happen to the next President and the next President and the next."

LK: Don't think we haven't thought....Bush has a nephew who's at the University of Pennsylvania. We talked around a few ideas of that nature. But, basically, the trouble with gay warriors is that, when it comes right down to it, it's very hard to rouse the anger past a certain pitch and we're a very small percentage of the gay community unfortunately. As is always the case.

GV: Well, my experience is with the left in America, but it's all the same. You get into a lot of divisiveness, theatricality, thwarted self-love. It's monstrous. I was co-chairman of the People's Party with Dr. Spock. I tried to get Spock interested in politics. He didn't have any—he was just against the war. We had the makings of a real party of the left. All the kids wanted was to avoid Vietnam. And I quite agreed with that. That's why I was helping out. But to try and interest them in any kind of real politics which might affect their lives—sexual politics, economic, racial—you couldn't turn 'em on. I don't know what it is. Something is done in the public educational system that just undoes their reception. They just can't pick up on it.

LK: Has there ever been a radical movement that's been well-organized and continuing?

GV: I suppose Lenin would say that *he* pulled it off, at least for his generation.

LK: What destroys, in the end, is the divisiveness. ACT UP has lasted longer than most.

GV: It has more reason for being than most.

LK: It's also on its last legs.

GV: And Queer Nation?

LK: Queer Nation is all but gone.

GV: I'm a great admirer of Jonathan Ned Katz. I love him on American history.

LK: Jonathan has not really been a part of either movement, ACT UP or Queer Nation. He's much more of an academic. Marty Duberman also hasn't been a part of either. Marty has sort of, in his own way, moved on to that quiet place that academics go when they reach a certain age.

GV: Called tenure.

LK: I don't know how to say this politely, but we miss him!

GV: Did you read his memoir? It was one of the funniest books I've read. I don't know that he would like my taking it that way.

LK: I don't think so.

GV: But going through all of that agony, to find Miss Right and then to find Mr. Right. Imagine going to somebody else for advice on these matters! I've never understood psychiatry. I mean there's no one's advice I want on anything to do with my life. And he took it so seriously—that white-picket-fence dream he has.

LK: Now, now, you're touching very close to home here. You're looking at another white picket fence...

GV: All right, it's a white picket fence with an *absolutely* straight boy inside.

LK: Well, I don't know about *that*. But you have all of that and you've had it all your adult life. You have a white picket fence in Ravello, and you have one in Rome, you have one in...

GV: In L.A.

LK: You have a very nice man who's been with you and loved you and looked after you tenderly and efficiently, for many years. I mean, that's everybody's dream. And you've managed to support yourself doing what you want to do.

GV: I don't deny the luck. But don't deny me the amount of shit that I've had to put up with.

LK: But surely you and I have welcomed the shit in some sort of perverse way because it fuels the engines.

GV: But I must say, it was rather startling a few years ago, to see a kind of great textbook come—five hundred novelists since the Second World War—and my name was never mentioned. Now I'm afraid it's all going the other way—altogether too many pieces about me in academe. It's all gone into reverse. But, um...

LK: Gore, so *what?* Who gives a shit what those people do with their fucking stupid idiotic lists? You do what you want to do and you're getting your rocks off every time you sit down at a typewriter, and screw them.

GV: Well, you have to have it in close-up so you *can* screw them.

LK: You're *too* slippery. As someone who's taken a lot of shit over the last ten years, after a while you just say, "Oh, fuck it." No matter *what* you say, X number are going to approve and X number are not going to approve, so you might as well say what you want to say.

GV: I'm really interested now in trying to destroy monotheism in the United States. That is the source of all the problems.

LK: A worthy cause. But I'd rather have you fighting for your heart— exploring what it means to be a gay man at age sixty-five in the world today—

GV: Sixty-seven.

LK: Sixty-seven in the world today and looking back...I've just written a play, which is basically an exploration of a journey.

GV: You're talking to your younger self—yeah, I remember reading about that.

LK: And, uh, the journey of my homosexuality. As you know, I started out in an entirely different way and certainly did not expect to be such a political animal.

GV: I never thought it was a big deal. Maybe that's the difference in the way we were brought up. [Homosexuality] was practiced quite widely in my adolescence. In schools, in camps, in the army. Some stayed with it and some didn't.

LK: But why is it so important for you—this notion that we are all bisexual? I keep coming back to this—it bothers me because I admire you so. I don't even think Freud went beyond the idea that all men had it in ourselves to, you know, fuck a woman or whatever, and that there was a scale, a Kinsey scale from one to ten. I think what we have now is millions and millions of people who just glory in being in love with, or drawn to, someone of the same sex....We just want you, whole-heartedly and full-blown—if you'll pardon the pun—on *our* team.

GV: I *am* on your team. After all, I have been there all along. They have very good dessert here.

LK: What are you going to have?

GV: I'm not going to have any. I have to watch my weight.

LK: Do you read any gay literature or gay authors that you've liked?

GV: Jeanette Winterson is wonderful.

LK: Yes.

GV: I feel she's a discovery of mine. I read her first book and drew as much attention to it as I could. And I like Edmund White, particularly *Nocturnes for the King of Naples*—a lovely book. You know, Tennessee was asked these same questions: Why he didn't make his characters queer. And he responded very simply, "Why should I diminish my audience even more than it is?"

LK: Well, I think we're finding now that we have our own audience.

GV: You have to make the case for ghettoization. Maybe I'll agree with you. And maybe I won't.

LK: The ghetto is now so big that it's hardly a ghetto.

GV: But it's not the world and it's got a hostile government.

LK: But do you write for an audience or do you write for yourself?

GV: It's the same.

LK: I don't know if it is. I never think of going out to increase an audience or to decrease it. I write what I want to write.

GV: Playwrights do. And you're a playwright.

LK: I'm a novelist, too.

GV: Yeah, but when I'm talking about a playwright I'm speaking specifically of Tennessee, who wanted people to see his plays, and who didn't want to limit his audience any more than his romantic, subjective nature already did.

LK: You see, that's why I think it's a generational thing. I think that, if Tennessee were a young playwright today, he would write gay characters—just as I think that, if *you* were a novelist today, you would have carried on from *The City and the Pillar* and not have been diverted.

GV: Oh, no. I'm interested in so many other things.

LK: But that doesn't limit you from writing the other things.

GV: Well, I've written about those things, but it's not the center of my life.

LK: Well, I feel now this *is* the center of our lives and the center of *most* gay writers. That's how the world has changed. Because we found there were more of us or because AIDS made us learn that we have to fight for survival.

GV: Well, on solidarity, I am as one with you—in the matter of AIDS and in the matter of this very bad political system.

LK: Let me give you an example—you are an eminent biographer of Lincoln—it was Jonathan Katz who first presented it to me. There has been talk in gay historical circles that maybe Lincoln had some sort of gay relationship.

GV: I'm fairly convinced of it, yeah.

LK: Well, isn't it important that this be written about?

GV: Yeah, but you see, I wasn't covering that period of his life.

LK: He had an alleged affair with a man, Joshua Speed, and the letters that they exchanged were very...

GV: Very odd.

LK: Very romantic. And then when they got married, they each wrote to the other that they...

GV: Found it hard going, yeah.

LK: But, who better to tell the world than you?

GV: If I'd been writing about the young Lincoln I would have done it, but I'm writing about the Presidency during the Civil War.

LK: But I want you to write about the young Lincoln! Who better to tell the world than Gore Vidal? It would be ten times more useful than attacking the Constitution, to tell this fucking country that its most beloved President was gay, or had a gay period in his life—it would do so much to shake the notion of sexual freedom and rights.

GV: It's tempting. But, I've just written a book in which St. Paul is in love with Timothy, who is straight, to use that word, and puts out only to get on the road with him.

LK: I'm not going to in any way disparage that endeavor, I'm just going to choose your next one. I think it's important that we claim our historical characters. It took us so long, for instance, to get Walt

Whitman acknowledged as a gay writer.

GV: And that only happened because the academics finally were shamed into it by the Europeans who said, "What is this nonsense? You exclude your greatest poet!" So they invented homoerotic.

LK: Don't you loathe that word?

GV: I do. Yes, Whitman had daydreams, but, of course, he wouldn't do anything. And, all you have to do is read the poems or the letters or look at some of the photographs of Walt with his young friends and it's very, very clear.

LK: Did you read the Ellmann biography of Oscar Wilde—the part when [Wilde] met with Walt Whitman?

GV: Yes.

LK: Wouldn't you have loved to have been there? Are there other gay historical figures that you know to have been gay that we don't?

GV: President Buchanan is generally agreed to be. And President Pierce is certainly an interesting case. I can't write about young, romantic love.

LK: Oh, I doubt that

GV: Well, I can't, not now. It's a matter of age....

LK: That's exactly when one can write about it. You're too hard on yourself.

GV: I leave that to you. Anyway....

LK: I'm fifty-seven, you're sixty-seven.

GV: So there was Franklin Pierce and Nathaniel Hawthorne, who was the most beautiful writer of his day. And Pierce was one of the most beautiful Presidents.

LK: You think Hawthorne was gay?

GV: Oh, yes! And I think Melville was in love with him.

LK: Oh, *that* I've thought.

GV: I don't think anything happened, because Melville was...

LK: There's a wretched piece by John Updike in *The New Yorker* this week about Nathanial Hawthorne and his "terrible secret." Not once is mentioned the possibility that he was gay.

GV: Oh, he would never do *that*. It wouldn't be Updikian. For him everybody's a cunt-hound.

LK: Gore Vidal has called John Updike a *cunt-hound.*

GV: No, I've called him an admirer of the cunt-hound in his novels. I know nothing of his private life.

LK: You know, that's almost too complimentary a term for John Updike.

GV: I can't read him...

LK: He's so boring....

GV: He writes very well and he manages never to interest me. Which is *quite* a trick. A good writer can generally interest me.

LK: So Franklin Pierce, James Buchanan, Nathaniel Hawthorne, Lincoln and Joshua Speed...

GV: Well, there's also a great case to be made for George Washington and Alexander Hamilton.

LK: Really! Talk about that for a minute.

GV: I practically said it straight out in *Burr*. But if you don't have the evidence...

LK: But they don't have the evidence for Jesus!

GV: I can do anything I want to *him*. But I take Alexander Hamilton and Jefferson much more seriously than I do these Middle-Eastern freaks. Hamilton was an extremely randy fellow, very handsome. A cunt-hound and demonstrably so. Caught often, but with enormous talent. He was brought up by an older man in the West Indies. The older man was about twenty-eight, he was about fourteen. He was a mathematical genius trained by a Sephardic Jew. There was a whole bunch of them for some reason on this island. At fourteen, he was a first-rate accountant, working for this man—a bachelor of twenty-eight or twenty-nine from New York, who liked him so much he sent him to college. Hamilton made his way by making older men fall in love with him. A lot of guys do this. The sex isn't that great, but the emotion is just the same. And specifically in the case of George Washington, it's very clear that Washington was very much in love with him. Whether anything happened I rather doubt. First of all, there was a great deal of speculation about Washington's potency...er, activity. He might not have been able to do *anything*. But he certainly was in love with Hamilton, who treated him so rudely when he was his Commander-in-Chief and then when he was Secretary of the Treasury. In effect, Hamilton was prime minister for eight years. Washington was king. Hamilton treated him like a beautiful boy would treat a sugar daddy: standing him up, being rude to him. There was this whole pattern there. For a young writer coming along it's a lovely theme, the love affair between Washington and Hamilton— which invented the United States.

LK: But Gore, why not you?

GV: Because I'm out of historical novels. I'm done with it. But I'm throwing out some nice themes here. The ironies—which are the best fun: The United States is then formed, mainly to protect Washington's investment out on the Ohio River. Then they're separated. Hamilton's practicing law down in Mt. Vernon. Washington writes him a hysterical letter: "We've got to start a Republic, a strong federal government. We're about to lose our property. Because the guys who fought in the revolution got nothing out of it, and are being taxed and are angry." So Hamilton said, "All right, I'll give you a Republic." Now throw in the fact that it was a kind of love affair between these two men that started the whole country on this foundation—a more perfect union!

LK: That's what you should call it! "A More Perfect Union." You should do it as a play. You were a very successful and amusing playwright. It sounds like this would lend itself well to a play. Your return to the stage.

GV: "Where is my wig, Alex?" That will be the first line....

LK: "Where are your teeth, George?"

GV: "I thought I had them in!"

LK: "They're still down around my crotch!" Did you not have *any* notion to write another play? I think if you wrote a play about a love affair between George Washington and Alexander Hamilton, we would find a way to get it on.

GV: But could you get the folks to come?

LK: I think. But you can't worry about that. Just do it. What are your next writing projects?

GV: I'm doing a movie with Scorsese. On Theodora and Justinian.

LK: I always find [Scorsese] to be an enormously homophobic man. Am I wrong?

GV: I wouldn't use *that* adjective....A boy trained by Jesuits who is uptight about *a lot* of things. He's much more that, I think.

LK: There are few directors who are as gifted visually. I'm just getting a little tired of all his continued macho violence.

GV: So is he. More than "homophobic," you might say he's somewhat of a misogynist. He cannot deal with women in a serious way.

LK: And after the movie?

GV: I'm supposed to do a final summing up of the six American historical novels. It will be the final one, in which I'll be the narrator. I'll look back over my own life, bringing in some of the fictional characters and some of the real characters I've known. It will center a lot on the foundation of the national security state in 1950 by Harry Truman, which made us a garrison state. Which made us what we are today—broke and unloved and with our military out of control.

LK: Does David McCullough say all this in his book?

GV: He says it, but he doesn't know what he's saying. He doesn't understand at all the politics of Harry Truman's life. He's a charming writer, McCullough, but it's part of the constant falsification of American life and American history. He's unrelenting. After that I'll let drop the feather.

LK: No! I think if anything you're getting sharper and wiser. Certainly no less angry.

GV: I'll say.

LK: And you must never stop.

QW Magazine

Index

A

Acheson, Dean, 80
Adams, Stephen, 116
Albee, Edward, 121
Aldiss, Brian W., 54
Aldrich, Robert, 214
Aldridge, John W., Jr., 208
Allegret, Marc, 215
Allen, Woody, 121, 247
Ambler, Eric, 162
Amis, Kingsley, 29
Andrews, Julie, 247
Apuleius, 39
Archilochus, 39
Arliss, George, 248
Arnold, Matthew, 168-69
Auchincloss, Hugh D., Jr., 199
Auden, W. H., 85-86, 90-92, 94, 216, 230
Augustine, Saint, 25, 255
Austen, Howard, 215, 220

Austen, Jane, 177
Austen, Roger, 116

B

Bachardy, Don, 216
Baldwin, Faith, 200
Balzac, Honoré de, 74, 153
Barr, Candy, 20
Barth, John, 216, 251
Barthes, Roland, 116, 130
Bauer, Gary, 186-87
Beardsley, Aubrey, 33
Beaverbrook, William Maxwell Aitken, Lord, 165
Beckett, Samuel, 32, 34, 147-48
Beerbohm, Max 150
Bellow, Saul, 47, 217
Bergler, Edmund, 40, 51
Bergman, Ingmar, 248
Bergman, Ingrid, 164, 247
Bernhardt, Sarah, 152-53

Blackmun, Harry A., 243
Blumenthal, Ralph 125
Bogart, Humphrey, 247-48
Bork, Robert, 244
Boswell, James, 140
Boswell, John, 115, 124
Bowie, David, 204, 249
Bowles, Paul, 87-88, 245
Boy George, 145
Brando, Marlon, 137, 145
Breckinridge, Bunny, 211-12
Breckinridge, John C., 211-12
Brooks, John Ellingham, 161
Brophy, Brigid, 207
Browne, Thomas, 34
Bryant, Anita, 102, 104-5
Buchanan, James, 267-69
Bulwer-Lytton, Edward 167
Burger, Warren, 243-44
Burns, John Horne, 206-8, 259
Burroughs, William, 34, 245-46
Bush, Barbara, 183-85
Bush, George, 183, 260
Bussy, Dorothy, 74
Byron, George Gordon, Lord, 140,
    148, 154, 161

C

Caesar, Julius, 16, 88
Cain, James M., 175
Calder, Robert, 155-77
Callas, Maria, 121
Calvin, John, 21
Camus, Renaud, 116, 129-32
Capote, Truman, 131, 136, 200,
    209, 215, 240-41, 245
Carlyle, Thomas, 71

Castro, Fidel, 101
Cato the Censor, 21, 58
Cavett, Dick, 201, 203
Chambers, Haddon, 170-71
Channon, Chips, 171
Chaplin, Charlie, 36
Charlemagne, 148
Chayefsky, Paddy, 213-14
Chekhov, Anton, 142, 158, 170,
    213
Christie, Agatha, 242
Churchill, Winston, 165
Clinton, William, 186, 192
Cockburn, Emma, 65
Cohn, Roy, 200
Connolly, Cyril, 31, 93-96
Conrad, Joseph, 156
Cook, Nancy, 79
Copland, Aaron, 88
Coppola, Francis Ford, 247
Coward, Noël, 161
Crane, Hart, 133
Crane, Stephen, 218
Cromwell, Oliver, 14-17
Cronkite, Walter, 203
Cukor, George, 164
Cyrus II, King of Persia, 107

D

Dakin, Reverend, 137-38
Darwin, Charles, 63
Davis, Bette, 52, 163, 259
Decter, Midge, 118-32
de Gaulle, Charles, 31-32
Devlin, Lord, 15-16
Dickens, Charles, 158-59, 167
Dickerman, Marion, 79

DiMaggio, Joe, 236-37
Donleavy, J. P., 32, 34
Dostoevsky, Fyodor, 218
Dows, Tracy, 81
Drabble, Margaret, 163
Dreiser, Theodore, 27, 163
Duberman, Martin, 261-62
Duncan, Robert, 196
Durrell, Lawrence, 23, 28, 31, 171

E

Eastwood, Clint, 132
Eddy, Mary Baker, 123
Eliot, George, 152, 170, 218
Elliot, Sumner Locke, 214
Ellis, Havelock, 28
Ellmann, Richard, 147-54, 267
Epstein, Joseph, 111, 118, 126-27
Erikson, Erik H., 64
Evans, Oliver, 144

F

Farouk, King of Egypt, 46
Faulkner, William, 84, 209
Ferenczi, Sandor, 126
Fields, W. C., 59
Figes, Eva, 57-69
Fitzgerald, F. Scott, 134
Flaubert, Gustave, 75, 159, 170
Fleming, Ian, 162
Fliess, Wilhelm, 139
Folsom, Joseph, 67
Ford, Charles Henri, 34
Ford, Gerald R., 232-33, 236
Forster, E. M., 242
France, Anatole, 174
Frederick II (the Great), King of

Prussia, 16, 39, 124
Freud, Sigmund, 42, 50, 58-59, 64,
  105, 119, 123, 125-26, 128,
  181, 243, 257, 264
Friedan, Betty, 62

G

Garbo, Greta, 84, 247
Garfield, John, 248
Genet, Jean, 25, 33-35
Geringer, Jim, 187
Gide, André, 151, 215, 238
Gingrich, Newt, 187
Ginsberg, Allen, 219, 245
Girodias, Maurice, 31-36
Godfrey, Arthur, 234
Goldman, Albert, 155
Goldwater, Barry, 114
Goncourt, Edmond de, 152
Goodman, Paul, 54, 211
Gore, Thomas Pryor, 76-77, 152,
  220
Grant, Ulysses S., 152
Graves, Robert, 61
Gray, David, 81
Greer, Germaine, 58

H

Hamilton, Alexander, 269-70
Hand, Learned, 20
Hardy, Thomas, 166, 170, 176
Harriman, Daisy, 76
Harris, Frank, 25
Hart, H. L. A., 13-14, 21
Hatch, Orrin, 114
Hawthorne, Nathaniel, 267-269
Haxton, Gerald, 162-164

Hayden, Tom, 203
Hazlitt, William, 176, 179
Heller, Joseph, 241
Hemingway, Ernest, 60, 93, 141,
    159, 165-66, 171-72, 179, 197,
    209, 211, 218
Hemingway, Mary, 141
Herodotus, 108
Hickock, Lorena, 192
Hicks, Louise Day, 239
Himes, Chester, 34
Hitler, Adolf, 48, 64, 81, 93, 113,
    118, 123, 126
Hoffenberg, Mason, 32
Hoffman, Abbie, 203-4
Hoover, J. Edgar, 52, 195, 204, 219
Hope, Bob, 245
Horace, 74
Hoving, Walter, 100
Howard, Richard, 116
Howe, Irving, 65-67
Humphrey, Hubert, 233
Hunter, Ross, 258
Huxley, Aldous, 84
Huysmans, Joris-Karl, 152

I

Ibsen, Henrik, 158
Inouye, Daniel K., 203
Isherwood, Christopher, 84-96,
    118, 166, 216

J

Jackson, Andrew, 75
Jagger, Mick, 242, 249
James, Henry, 62, 153, 160, 172,
    218

Jarrell, Randall, 241
Jefferson, Thomas, 187, 269
Jesus, 17, 48, 100, 105-7, 157, 256,
    269
John, Elton, 249
John Paul II, Pope, 130
Johnson, Lyndon B., 52, 125, 144,
    195, 204
Jong, Erica, 251
Joyce, James, 147-48, 154
Justinian I (the Great), Byzantine
    Emperor, 16, 21, 223, 271

K

Kahane, Jack, 31
Katz, Jonathan Ned, 261, 265
Kauffmann, Stanley, 39
Kazin, Alfred, 110, 118
Keller, Helen, 46
Kennedy, Caroline, 79
Kennedy, Jacqueline, 140
Kennedy, John F., 76, 140-41, 192
Kennedy, Joseph P., 81-82
Kerensky, Alexander, 162
Kerouac, Jack, 192, 198, 245-46
Kinsey, Alfred C., 28, 30, 53, 149,
    183, 192-93, 227
Kissinger, Henry, 232
Klein, Calvin, 145
Klein, Milton, 126
Koch, Ilse, 36
Kopkind, Andrew, 103
Kramer, Hilton, 112, 118
Kubie, Lawrence, 139, 144

L

Lash, Joseph, 70-83

Lawford, Patricia Kennedy, 136, 140

Lawrence, D. H., 28, 30, 44, 65, 160

Lawrence, Gertrude, 161

le Carré, John, 162

Le Hand, Missy, 78-79

Lehman-Haupt, Christopher, 241

Lehmann, John, 87, 92

Lennon, John, 155, 255

Leslie, Warren, 20

Lévi-Strauss, Claude, 60

Lincoln, Abraham, 82, 266, 269

Logue, Christopher, 32

Longworth, Alice, 75-76

Lott, Trent, 187

Lovecraft, H. P., 27, 65

Luce, Henry, 139, 145

Luther, Martin, 93

M

McAllister, Ward, 74

MacArthur, Douglas, 234

McCarthy, Joseph, 112-13, 124, 200-1

McCarthy, Mary, 47, 241

McCullough, David, 271

Macdonald, Dwight, 196, 250

McLaughlin, John, 201

McLuhan, Marshall, 202

Mailer, Norman, 58-59, 65-66, 208-9, 230, 245-46, 248, 259

Malamud, Bernard, 54

Mallarmé, Stéphane, 151-52

Malraux, André, 32

Malthus, Thomas, 99

Mann, Thomas, 171

Mansfield, William Murray, Lord, 14

Marcus, Steven, 21

Marlowe, Christopher, 91

Marx, Karl, 59

Mason, George, 111

Mason, James, 247

Mather, Cotton, 111

Maugham, Lord, 21

Maugham, Robin, 157, 161, 164

Maugham, W. Somerset, 134, 155-79, 215

Maupassant, Guy de, 158, 170

May, Elaine, 10

May, Henry de Courcey, 171

Mayer, Louis B., 251

Mead, Margaret, 63

Melville, Herman, 115, 268

Menninger, Karl, 126

Mercer, Lucy, 77

Mill, John Stuart, 13, 59

Miller, Earl R., 78

Miller, Henry, 23-28, 31, 34, 58, 65, 140

Millett, Kate, 58, 62, 64-67

Monroe, Marilyn, 242

Montaigne, Michel Eyquem de, 179

Montgomery, Robert, 94

Moran, James, 55

Morgan, Ted, 155-56

Morrison, Arthur, 158

Moses, 43, 50, 59, 61, 105, 107, 123, 128, 256

Muskie, Edmund, 233, 235

Mussolini, Benito, 235

N

Nabokov, Vladimir, 32-33, 47, 217
Naumann, Max, 132
Newman, John Henry Cardinal, 154
Nichols, Beverley, 161
Nicolson, Harold, 197-98
Nietzsche, Friedrich Wilhelm, 64
Nin, Anaïs, 28, 31
Nixon, Richard M., 58, 78, 100, 103, 201, 204-5, 231, 233, 239
Nureyev, Rudolph, 205

O

O'Neill, Eugene, 145-46
Orlovsky, Peter, 245
Orwell, George, 28, 117
Oursler, Fulton, 79

P

Paine, Thomas, 202
Pangborn, Franklin, 124
Parker, John J., 19-20
Paul, Saint, 17, 48, 61, 106-7, 111, 128, 266
Pepys, Samuel, 140
Peter, Saint, 38
Philip, Prince of Hesse, 123
Phillips, Howard, 113
Pierce, Franklin, 267-69
Pinter, Harold, 213
Pius XII, Pope, 165
Plato, 111
Plutarch, 71
Podhoretz, Norman, 112-13, 118-19, 132
Poirier, Richard, 134, 242

Pomeroy, W.B., 30
Prescott, Orville, 253
Presley, Elvis, 155
Procopius, 223
Proust, Marcel, 9, 83, 152, 218
Pynchon, Thomas, 216-17, 251

Q

Queneau, Raymond, 33-34
Quennell, Peter, 92-93

R

Rader, Dotson, 217
Rahv, Philip, 122
Raphael, Frederic, 163
Raye, Martha, 36
Reagan, Nancy, 136
Reagan, Ronald, 132
Rehnquist, Wiiliam, 243-44
Renard, Jules, 168
Reuben, David, 42-56
Rimbaud, Arthur, 134
Robbins, Harold, 243
Roberts, Oral 49
Rockefeller, John D., 236
Rockefeller, Nelson, 235-36
Roehm, Ernst, 48
Roethke, Theodore, 134
Roosevelt, Eleanor, 70-83, 124, 192
Roosevelt, Elliott, 72-73
Roosevelt, Franklin D., 70-83, 194
Roosevelt, Sara Delano, 72, 75
Roosevelt, Theodore, 72, 74-76, 112
Ross, Jean, 88
Ross, Robert, 148
Roth, Philip, 9, 241

Rousseau, Jean Jacques, 63
Roussel, Raymond, 131
Rushdie, Salman, 184
Ruskin, John, 152
Russell, Bertrand, 125

S

Sackville-West, Vita, 197-98
Sade, Marquis de, 33, 35-36
Santayana, George, 173-74
Sarotte, Georges-Michel, 115-16
Schafly, Phyllis, 58, 113-14
Schine, David, 200
Schlesinger, Arthur M., Jr., 233
Schopenhauer, Arthur, 63
Scorsese, Martin, 270-71
Searle, Alan, 161, 164-65, 215
Shakespeare, William, 162, 165
Shaw, George Bernard, 30, 159,
    167
Shays, Daniel, 202
Shepard, Matthew, 187
Solomon, Andrew, 191
Sontag, Susan, 121
Southern, Terry, 32
Speed, Joshua, 266, 269
Spellman, Francis J. Cardinal, 112
Spender, Stephen, 85-88, 90
Spock, Benjamin, 204-5, 260-61
Spoto, Donald, 136, 140-41
Stapleton, Ruth Carter, 136
Steers, Hugh, 256
Stein, Gertrude, 110
Stephen, J. G., 16
Stevenson, Adlai E., 195
Stopes, Marie C., 28
Strachey, Lytton, 71, 74

Suetonius, 39
Susann, Jacqueline, 243
Susskind, David, 213-14, 244
Sutton, Grady, 59
Swinburne, Algernon Charles, 152

T

Taft, William Howard, 46
Taylor, Jeremy, 168
Thatcher, Margaret, 149
Thomson, Virgil, 194
Toklas, Alice B., 110
Tolson, Clyde, 195, 219
Tolstoi, Leo, 44
Tracy, Spencer, 164
Travolta, John, 120
Tribich, David, 126
Trocchi, Alex, 32
Truman, Harry S., 76, 271
Turner, Lana, 84
Twain, Mark, 142, 159, 218
Tyler, Parker, 34

U

Updike, John, 213, 268

V

Vaccaro, Marion Black, 144
Victoria, Queen of England, 106
Viertel, Berthold, 94
Viguerie, Richard, 113-14, 186

W

Wallace, George, 239
Wallace, Mike, 139, 220
Walpole, Hugh, 176
Walsh, David Ignatius, 32, 194-95

Warhol, Andy, 246-47

Washington, George, 268-70

Waugh, Evelyn, 94, 178

Weininger, Otto, 61

Wellcome, Syrie Barnardo, 162

Welles, Orson, 46

Wells, H. G., 159, 170

Wescott, Glenway, 161

Wharton, Edith, 160

White, Byron, 243

White, Edmund, 264

Whitman, Walt, 266-67

Wilde, Jane, 150

Wilde, Oscar, 147-54, 157-58,
    161-62, 167, 267

Wilde, William, 150

Wilder, Thornton, 146

Wilhelmina, Queen of Netherlands,
    80

Williams, Cornelius, 137-38

Williams, Edwina, 137-38

Williams, Rose, 137-39

Williams, Tennessee, 9-10, 92, 121,
    133-46, 174-75, 217, 265

Williams, Thomas Lanier see
    Williams, Tennessee,

Willingham, Calder, 213, 216

Wills, Garry, 112

Wilson, Edmund, 166-67

Wilson, Woodrow, 76, 194

Winterson, Jeanette, 264

Woolf, Leonard, 87

Woolf, Virginia, 87, 166

Wray, Fay, 247

Wright, Orville, 219

Wright, Wilbur, 219

Y

Yeats, William Butler, 147-48, 151,
    154

About the Author

Gore Vidal was born in 1925 at the United States Military Academy, West Point. He is the best-selling author of twenty-three novels, including *Williwaw* (1946), *The City and the Pillar* (1948), *Julian* (1964), *Washington, D.C.* (1967), *Myra Breckinridge* (1968), *Burr* (1973), *1876* (1976), *Lincoln* (1984), *Empire* (1987), and *The Smithsonian Institution* (1998) among others. Vidal's essays have been collected in ten volumes, most notably *United States*, (1993), winner of the National Book Award. The London *Sunday Times* has called his memoir, *Palimpsest* (1995), "one of the best first-person accounts of this century we are likely to get." Selections from the author's fiction, essays, and plays appear in *The Essential Gore Vidal* (1999).

About the Type

This book is set in Sabon, a typeface designed in 1960 by German-born graphic designer Jan Tschichold (1902-1974).